Masterpieces

from the musée du quai Branly collections

*musée du quai Branly

ISBN 2-915133-22-0
Dépôt légal juin 2006

Masterpieces

from the musée du quai Branly collections

musée du quai Branly

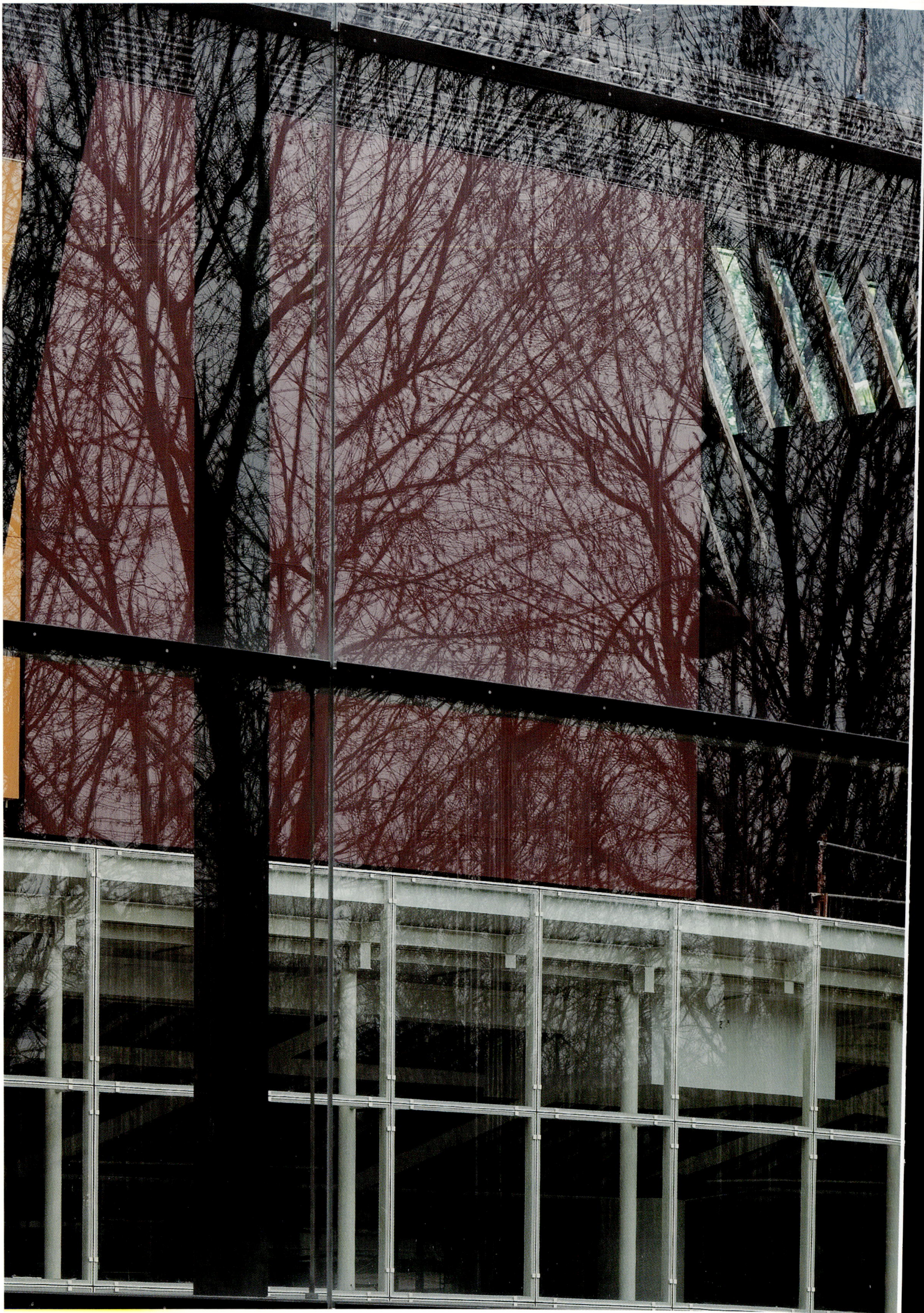

Preface

The term "masterpiece" is generally used to refer to icons of Western art, but applies equally well to sculptures from Africa, Asia, Oceania and the Americas. In publishing this album of 80 of the greatest masterpieces in its collections, the musée du quai Branly wished to pay tribute to the approach adopted by Jacques Kerchache in designing the pavillon des Sessions. Once again, we are seeking to present the public with the key items in the museum collections, grouped by geographical area.

The idea is to examine the art not from an "encyclopaedic" point of view, but to focus instead upon the unique identity of each work, and what it tells us of the artist's inventive genius. With this as guiding principle, the choice of items is incontestable in terms of art. The present selection is made up of objects diverse in form and which defy comparison however evocative and illuminating, and finds consistency in its emphasis on quality.

Each work is presented in its own light, by the aura that surrounds it, or the material in which it is made. The aim is to introduce readers to the pleasures of contemplation and instil in them a fascination for these works: their aesthetic perfection, their beauty, and often, their complexity. Many were created not for their aesthetic appeal, but to meet other needs, or to fulfil other functions altogether: to ensure fertility, to win favour with the spirits, or to honour ancestors. It is therefore equally important to highlight their social, historical, sociological and sometimes even psychoanalytical diversity, in order to come to a better understanding of the cross-fertilizing influences that so often inspired their creation.

It is no easy matter, however, to make manifest the beauty of these works and the genius of the artists who created them through text and images. Interpretation of motifs, or of the artist's objectives or intentions, is sometimes impossible, and what it is that catches the eye is also often mysterious. All the skills of the authors of this album have been called upon in order to make this album a fitting anthology of the museum's emblematic works. In my view, they have achieved their goal: to reveal the genius of these civilisations, so fully expressed in the diversity of the works presented here. It is hoped that the album will also inspire readers to view things from a new perspective, as the museum inspires its visitors, to reassess their ideas on the genius of other peoples, and to sharpen their sensibility to the expression of other forms of art.

Stéphane Martin
President of the musée du quai Branly

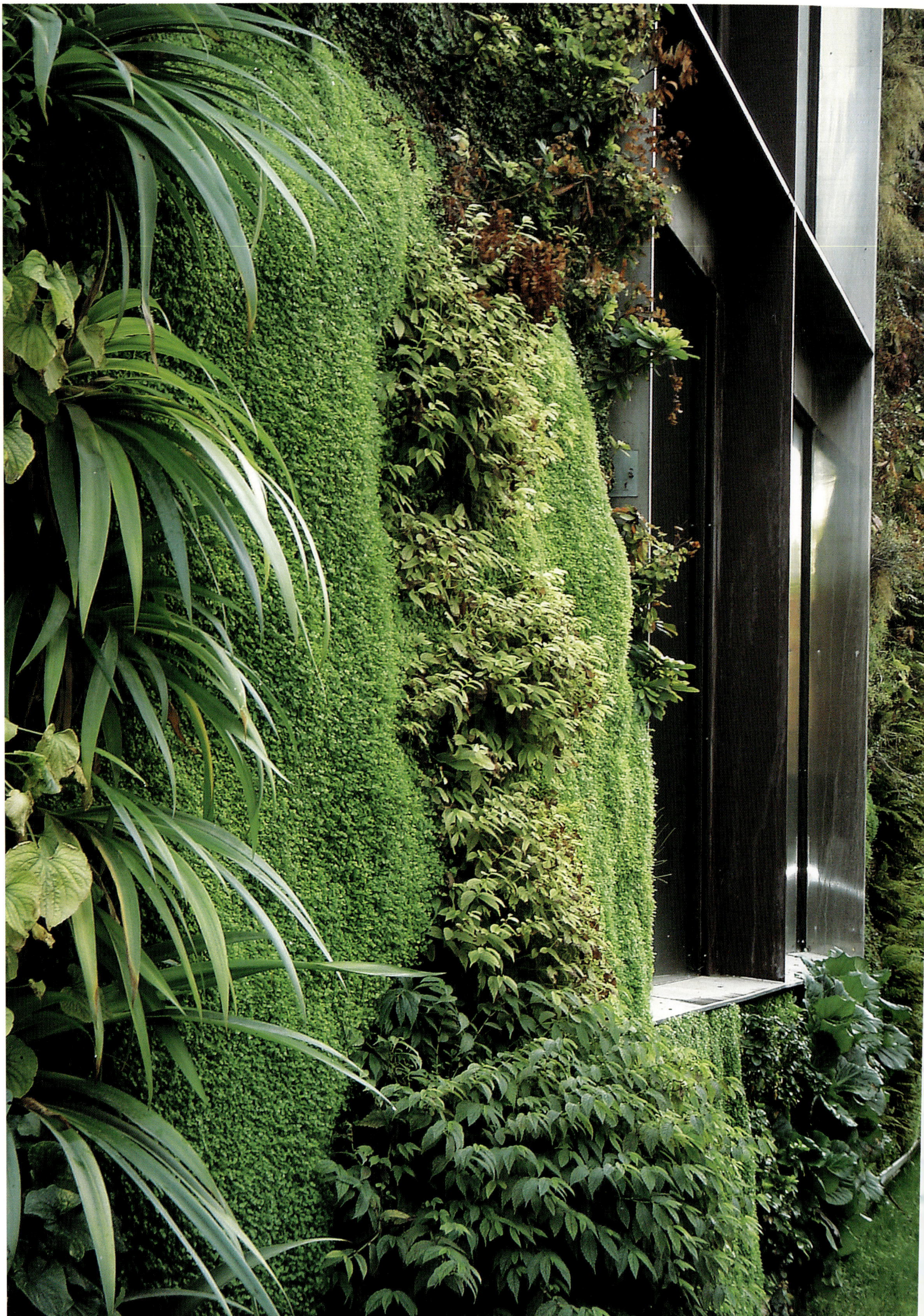

Foreword

This is a museum whose aim is to be different, while doing what it is expected to do: exhibiting the objects it is called upon to preserve, sharing information, and enhancing knowledge and understanding. The cultures represented here are distant both in time and space; termed "traditional", they are often part of animist societies without writing which already have disappeared or are threatened with extinction. Yet they still enthral, are influential in their relationship to the modern world and very much present in our own societies, through those who one day will wish to claim this heritage as their own.

This album cannot possibly provide a full picture of the museum; the works presented have been selected for their craftsmanship and unique qualities, as well as for their ability to recall the different encounters and many surprises of a first visit. Each visitor might well have chosen differently, opting for pieces that he or she found particularly impressive or captivating; however the anthology will surely open up new avenues of discovery.

We are well aware that a museum is a tool for preserving and transmitting knowledge, bringing together scattered fragments brought down to us by the twists and turns of fate. A museum gives these fragments meaning through the permanent or temporary exhibitions that it organizes, and serves as an intermediary between the public and the objects offered for study and contemplation.

Museology, the art of making these fragments available to the visiting public, must form part of an overall approach that leads visitors from the outside world into the very heart of the collections, acquainting them with the history of the cultural heritages presented, their meanings, and the prospects that they open up for the future. It is the result of a long collaborative process. The initial programming work enabled us to determine the practical requirements and the functional relationships between the different responsibilities of an institution in the process of becoming a reality; it helped to accurately target the areas needed to give the public access to the full range of the new museum's resources.

Jean Nouvel's project, which now houses these collections, was selected by the international architecture competition jury not only for its architectural inventiveness, but also because it met each and every one of the programme's requirements. It also made the museum an integral part of Paris, blending its different buildings into the city's urban fabric, while distancing it by means of the exterior glass wall, the planting of tall trees, and the landscaping of the garden. These surroundings include numerous features that reflect the artistic aspect of the approach from the outside, including Patrick Blanc's plant-adorned facade and Yann Kersalé's lake of lights, both suggested by Jean Nouvel, as well as ancient artefacts (the *mwai* head and other stone sculptures) and contemporary works, such as photographs by Maori artists from New Zealand and paintings by Australian Aboriginal artists. The upward slope of the grounds continues in the building reception area, then in the access ramp leading to the museum's collections areas. As they enter, visitors face the glass tower containing the musical instruments reserves, a structure mirroring the visual and auditory nature of the treasures it houses, and the massive Kaiget totem pole from British Columbia. Along the ramp, the filmmaker Trinh T. Minh Ha has provided a subtle mental exercise designed to adapt the Western mindset to other ways of thinking. The architecture itself immediately puts visitors in the right frame of mind for their visit, reinforcing the museological requirements established by the programme.

The architect was asked to design the museum's interior furnishings, and to create itineraries corresponding to its proposed contents. His original design already emphasized the importance of allowing visitors the opportunity to wander at will and explore separate areas within a single open space, in harmony with the exterior: an undulating architectural landscape rich in possibilities, and encouraging unrestricted but subtly orientated journeys of discovery.

Deciding how best to approach the works, both physically and intellectually, was of course essential to the project. The display cases, whose structural presence the architect has sought to minimise, place full focus on to their contents. They are large in size, designed for frontal viewing of major works, or placed side-by-side at eye-level for the examination of smaller-sized objects such as adornments. Other display cases rise like steles, containing single items of statuary. A set of large display shelves presents a suite of Asian costumes.

At the very start of the project, Jean Nouvel came up with a system of "boxes" that corresponded to our idea of providing a "sanctuary" for artefacts containing human remains and endowed with strong spiritual significance. Emblematic of the fragmented architectural style that highlights the complexities and richness of the cultures presented in the museum, the boxes on its northern façade each exhibit a specific geographical and cultural ensemble.

Coming from the ramp and into the heart of the museum, visitors immediately find themselves face-to-face with two exceptionally impressive works – one, the 10th century Djennenke-style statue, because of its age, the other, the great painted facade from Papua New Guinea, because of its size. They may then follow an itinerary that leads them from Oceania to Asia, from Asia to Africa, and from there to the Americas, or may wander at leisure from one part to another of the collections area. The itinerary has been designed to instil a sense of wonder in the visitors, and a desire to deepen their knowledge. Their wanderings are punctuated by thematic sequences in which objects illustrating a given subject throw

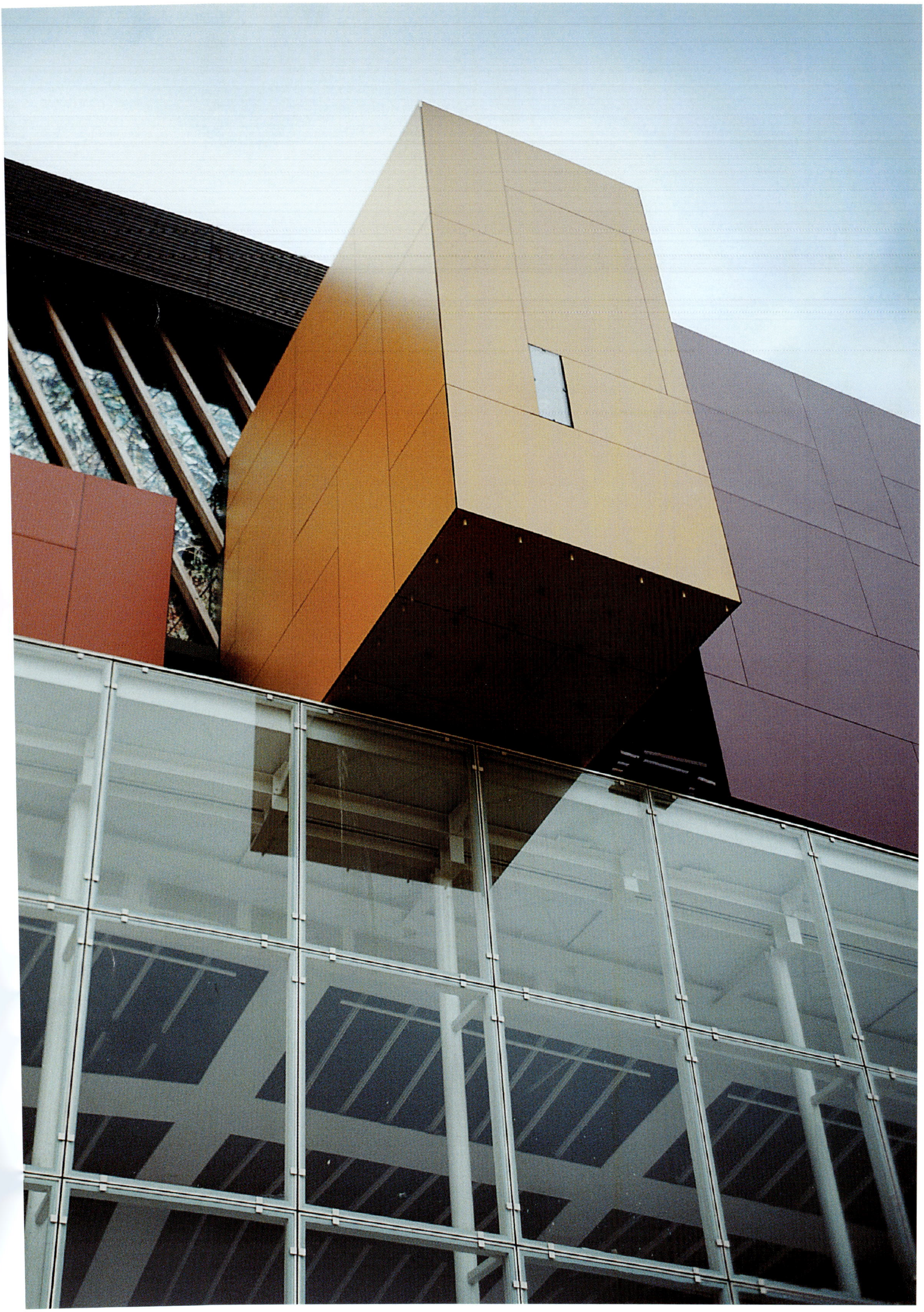

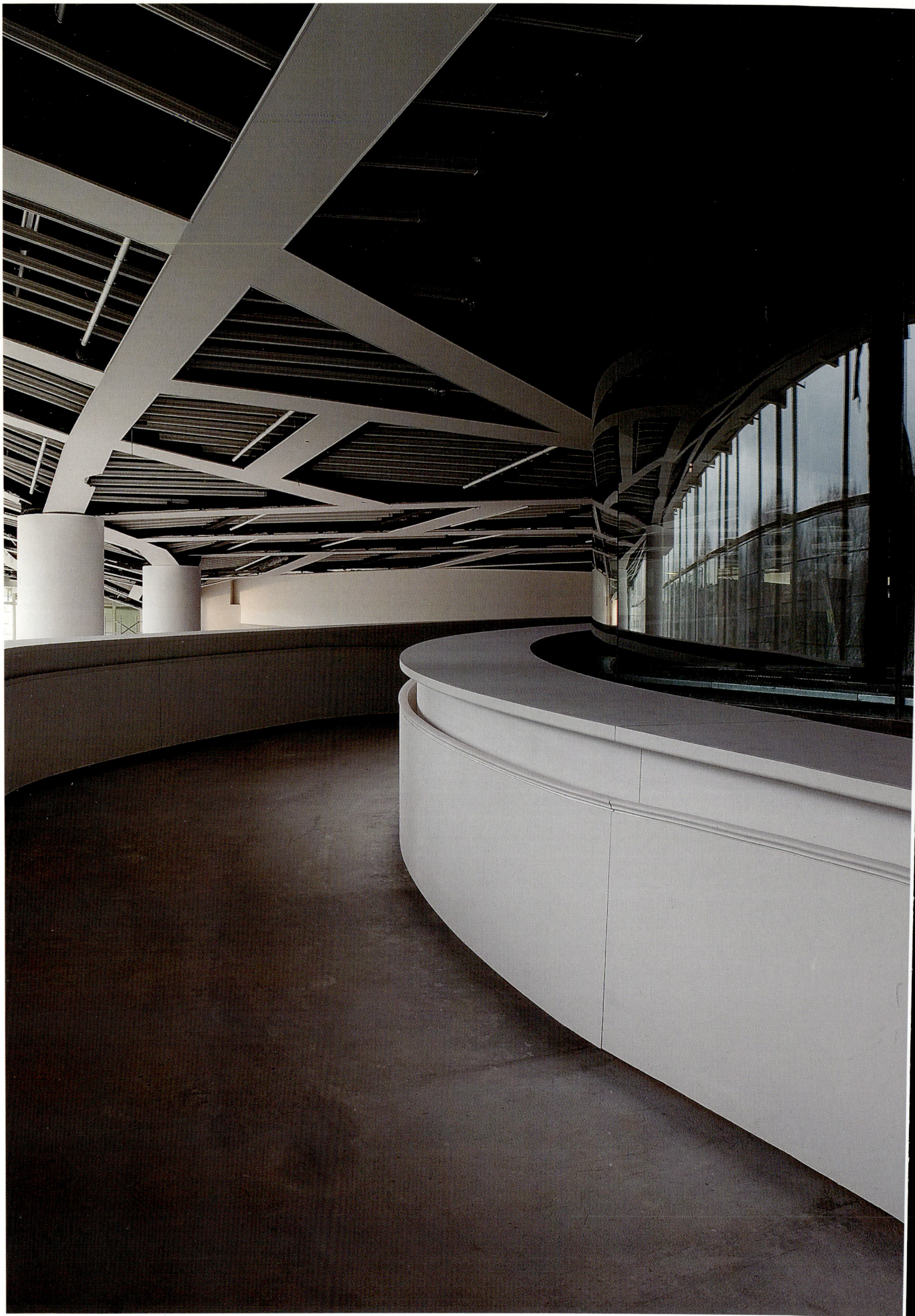

further light upon the cultures that produced them. The presentation as a whole is crossed by transversal sequences highlighting cultural relationships and influences present in worlds more interdependent upon one another than might be imagined.
This way of exploring the collections underscores the plastic qualities of the works exhibited, but also provides information on them, as discreetly presented as it is plentiful, increasing in detail from exhibit labels, often annotated with short texts, to tri-lingual commentaries on display-case sides, with maps showing the works' exact places of origin and small screens putting them in a visual context. Interactive information is provided through systems integrated into the central leather-covered structure, baptised the "Serpent" (Snake) by Jean Nouvel, which runs alongside the "Rivière" (River) on its lengthy journey across the centre of the collections area. The "Rivière" also offers a sensorial itinerary for the visually-impaired. The central mezzanine overlooks the collections area, its interactive data bases providing references on anthropology, music, languages, and the entirety of the museum collections.
This album is a composite of memories of the permanent collections, however two other areas in the museum itself have been set aside to accommodate temporary exhibitions to be held for varying periods of time. At the west end, around the tower housing the musical instruments reserve, a thematic area, produced in collaboration with major private collections and other European museums, puts objects in the anthropological spotlight, posing such questions as the "Qu'est-ce qu'un corps?" (What is a body?) asked by the anthropologist, writer and filmmaker Stéphane Breton in his exhibition of the same name. At the east end, special theme exhibitions explore museum resources from a range of different viewpoints. Thus, the museum is an ever-changing forum for discussion, while permanently displaying the very best of its collections. This emphasis on debate is, of course, part of the institution's general cultural action policy, the ongoing programming of its theatre and cinema events, and its all-out action *vis-à-vis* the public at large. It is also essential to its research and teaching tasks, enriching the links that should be developed between the various networks that animate modern-day intellectual and artistic life. This is the challenge facing of museums today, as we confront the upheavals and changes in the fabric underpinning the modern world. Artefacts are becoming more than ever observers who accompany us on our way, and who question us as we go.

Germain Viatte
Scientific Consultant

The Arts and Civilizations of Africa, Asia, Oceania and the Americas

Oceania and Insulindia are linked by a history of Austronesian settlement dating back to 4000 years BC, and by continuing exchange routes across the Pacific Ocean. Brought together under the same cultural heritage grouping, the collections are founded on those assembled by such late 18th century art collectors as the Marquis de Sérent and Dominique Vivant Denon, and on those of French seafarers such as Jules Dumont d'Urville and of the 19th century missionaries. They were much enriched in the 20th century by scientific expeditions undertaken on behalf of the musée de l'Homme and the musée national des Arts d'Afrique et d'Océanie, as well as by recent acquisitions made by the musée du quai Branly.
This selection of major works, chosen on the basis of their aesthetic appeal, manufacturing techniques, and function – ritual for the most part – testify to remarkable inventiveness. The use of widely differing materials – shells, jade, and beaten bark, for example – and the often spectacular combination of the above, are features specific to Oceanian and Insulindian arts. The sophistication of adornments expresses social status and the individual's concern for self-protection. Whether ephemeral or handed down from generation to generation, these artefacts indicate the relationships of power and exchanges between men, as well as those between men and their ancestors in Melanesia and Insulindia, and between men and their gods in Polynesia. Their forms, whether figurative, abstract, or a hybrid mix of human and animal, illustrate the remarkable richness of artistic expression.
Paintings by Australian Aboriginal artists reveal the existence of a contemporary art that has successfully interpreted traditional forms through new media and in new contexts.

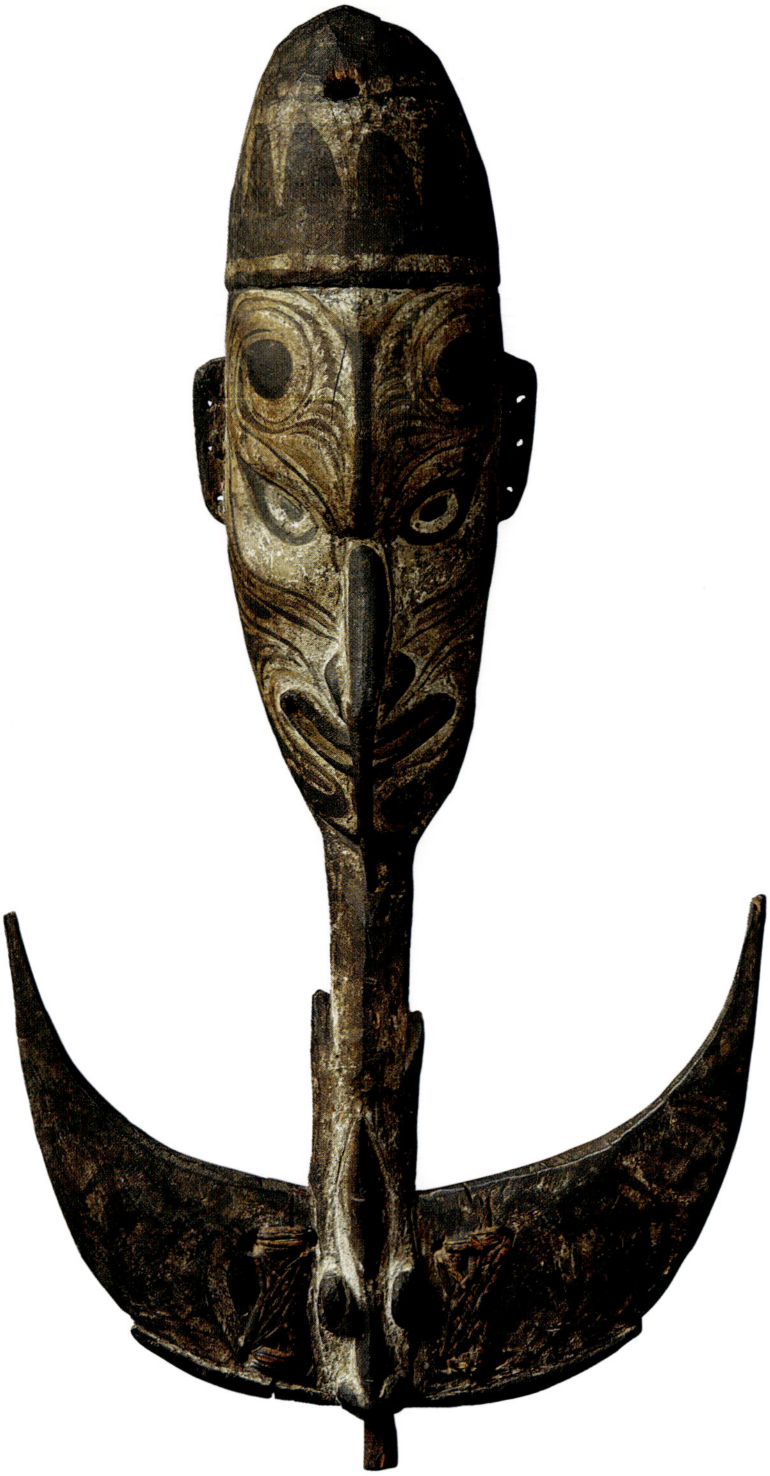

Magical hook for warfare

Iatmul

Papua New Guinea, Middle Sepik, village of Chambri
Mid 20th century
Wood, natural pigments
66 x 32.5 x 9 cm
Françoise Girard Mission, 1955
Inv. 71.1955.76.197

In Oceania, some hooks were used for keeping food out of the reach of rodents while others, of a sacred nature, were kept in ceremonial houses. It is particularly in the Sepik region that suspension hooks bearing the head of Janus* were carved.
This piece features curved motifs unique to the Iatmul people. The figure, with its stylised face, half-man, half-bird, represents a clan ancestor or mythical hero with a protective role, its spirit meant to protect its owner in time of war.
It is likely that two bunches of areca nuts* were hung from this hook in a symmetrical fashion, one on the left to bring about the defeat of enemies, and the other on the right to bring a warrior luck. In the centre, a magical stone was placed in a fibrous bag, a *bilum*, symbolising the division of the cosmos and the balance of the complementary forces (male and female, the living and the dead). MD

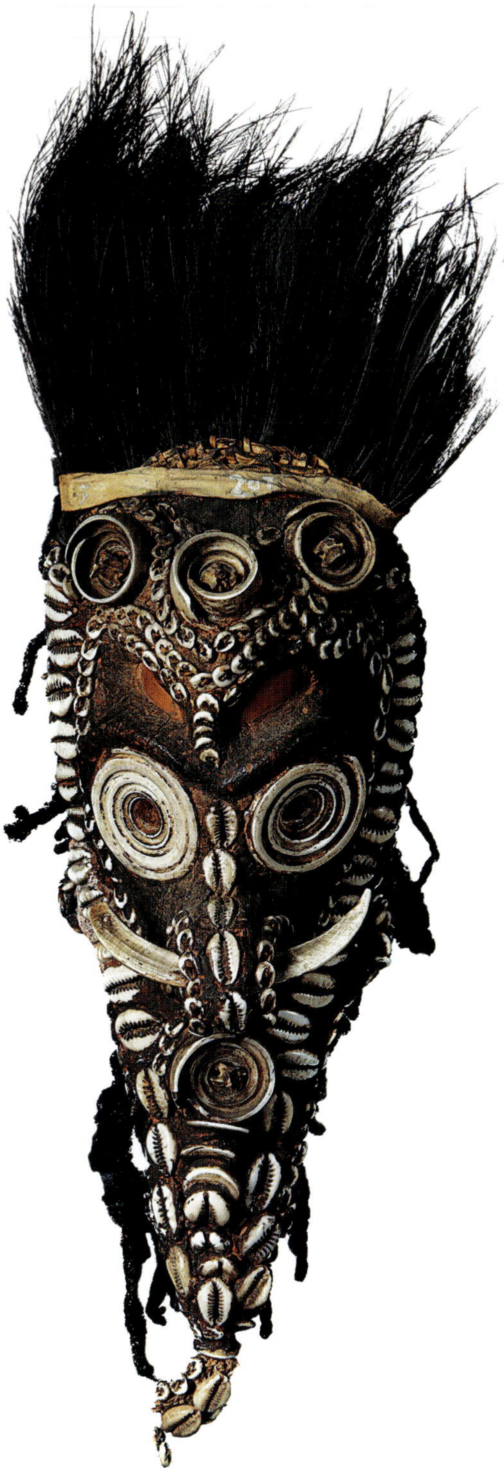

Flute mask

Tin dama

Papua New Guinea,
Lower Sepik,
Keram Valley,
village of Kambot
19th century
Coating, bone, shells, cassowary feathers, human hair, pig's tooth, fabric
47.5 x 12.7 x 13 cm
Former collections
Walter Bondy,
Félix Fénéon,
Dr Girardin
Inv. 72.1983.1.1

Collected around 1909, this exhibit was presented at the Renaissance gallery in 1930, in the first exhibition of Oceanian art in Paris. It has been in the possession of a number of famous collectors, including the art critic and merchant Félix Fénéon who, in 1920, conducted a survey on so-called "primitive" arts, in which he asked many celebrities of the period the question: "Will they be accepted in the Louvre?"
In any case, it is certain that this ceremonial mask, made from a diversity of materials, held great appeal at a time when the search for "poetic objects" was all the rage. The framework is of bone, probably from a cassowary*, covered with wickerwork and a plant mastic coating in which shells were inlaid to increase the strange character of the face.
This accumulation of materials adds to the symbolic effectiveness of this effigy of a bamboo flute, a sacred instrument played by men only in the Sepik valley, and whose melody revealed the voice of ancestors. This undoubtedly depicts a bird ancestor who, out of the sight of women, sang of its warrior feats. MD

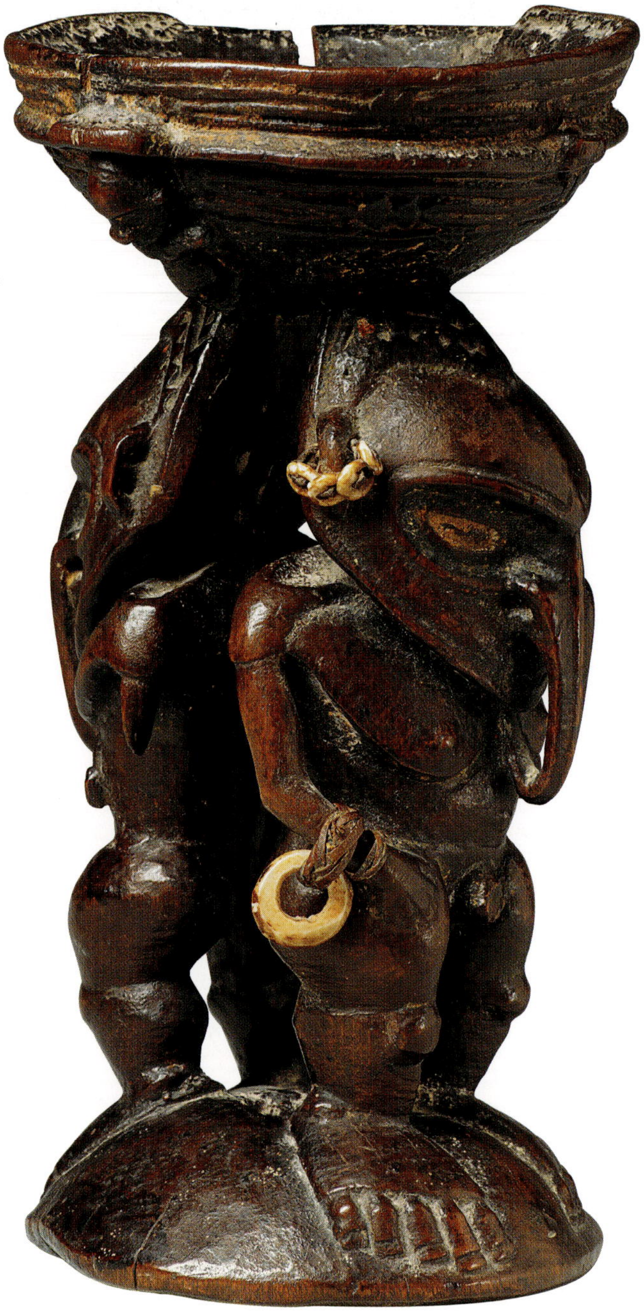

Betel mortar

Papua New Guinea, Lower Sepik, Angoram
Probably late 19th century
Wood, shells, woven plant fibres
23.5 x 8.6 x 12.5 cm
Jean Guiart Mission, 1965
Inv. 72.1965.11.3

Betel quid is made from areca nut* and plant leaves, lime and aromatic seeds or bark. Its slightly intoxicating effect when chewed helps men to speak their minds, and is in widespread use throughout Asia, Insulindia and several Melanesian islands.

The mortars are used by the elderly, above all on the north coast of New Guinea and in part of the Sepik basin, as their worn-down teeth prevent them from masticating the betel quid. They are also insignia of social prestige, associated with the history of origins and of clans. This is the case for this symmetrically composed piece showing two figures back to back, mythical, enemy brothers, the first founders of the men's house*. The presence of a female between the feet of one of them evokes the adultery that was at the heart of their quarrel. This type of artefact takes on magical powers at fertility rites. MD

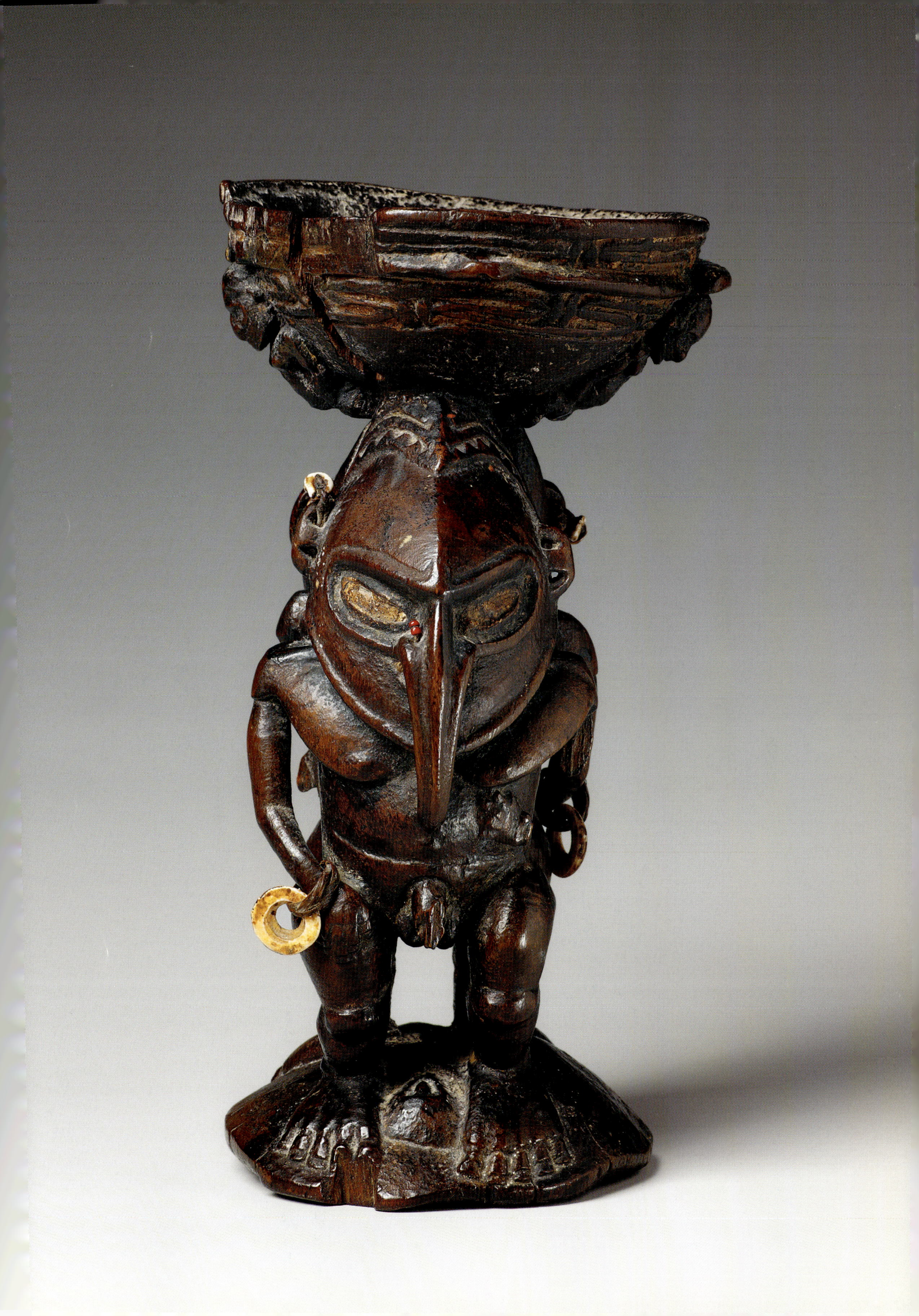

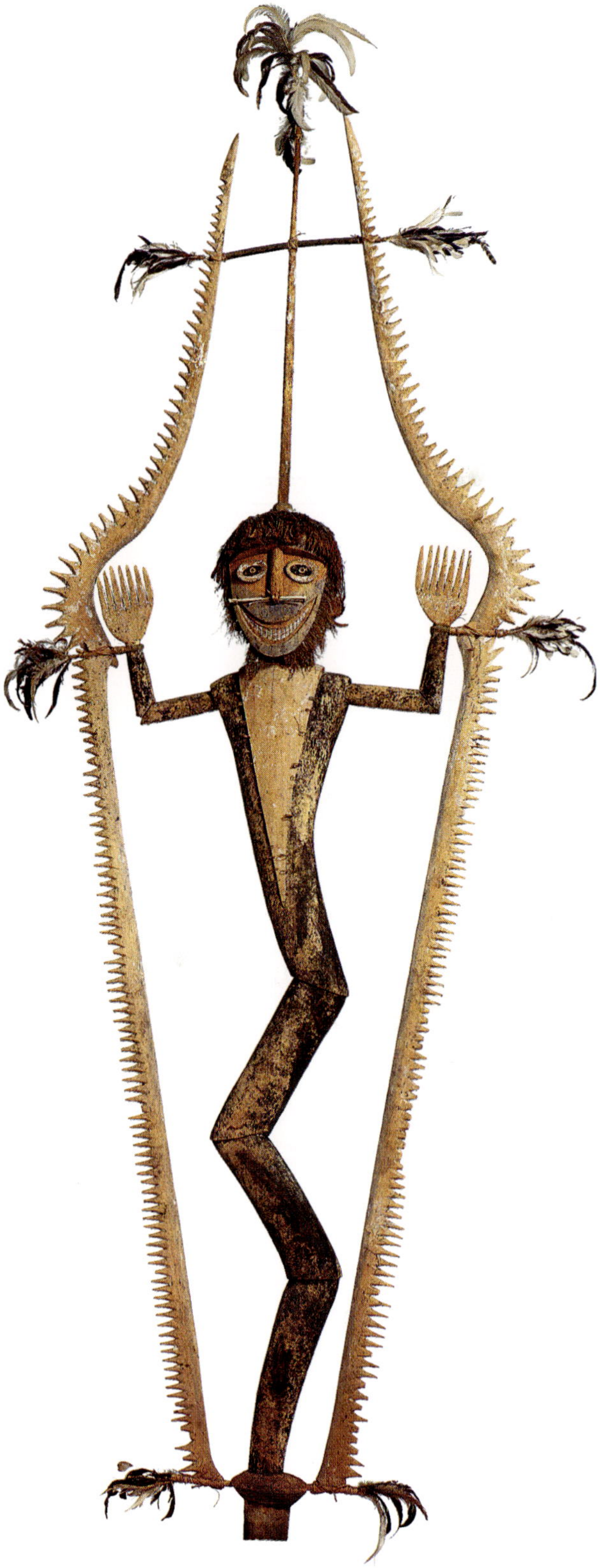

Iniet sculpture

Tolai

Bismarck Archipelago, New Britain Island, Gazelle Peninsula
19th century
Assembled wood, fibres, feathers, scales, bone, pigments
380 x 126 cm
Inv. 72.1987.4.1

Living in the northwest of the Gazelle Peninsula and Duke of York islands, the Tolai created the *dukduk* and *iniet* secret societies. The latter and most ancient was a male association empowered to exert justice. Its members had to pass singing, dancing and sculpting tests before being allowed full admission. It was also responsible for the initiation of young boys.

Iniet dance sticks depict ancestral figures. Secretly fashioned out of a particular type of wood and kept in a sacred enclosure, they were used during dance ceremonies called *pokopoko*, reputed for impressing onlookers. According to tradition, they were linked to spirits who took on the form of snakes when in contact with men.

This large sculpture was made in one sitting, a technical *tour de force* that certainly required remarkable skill on the part of the artist, who reserved all rights of reproduction for himself.

MD

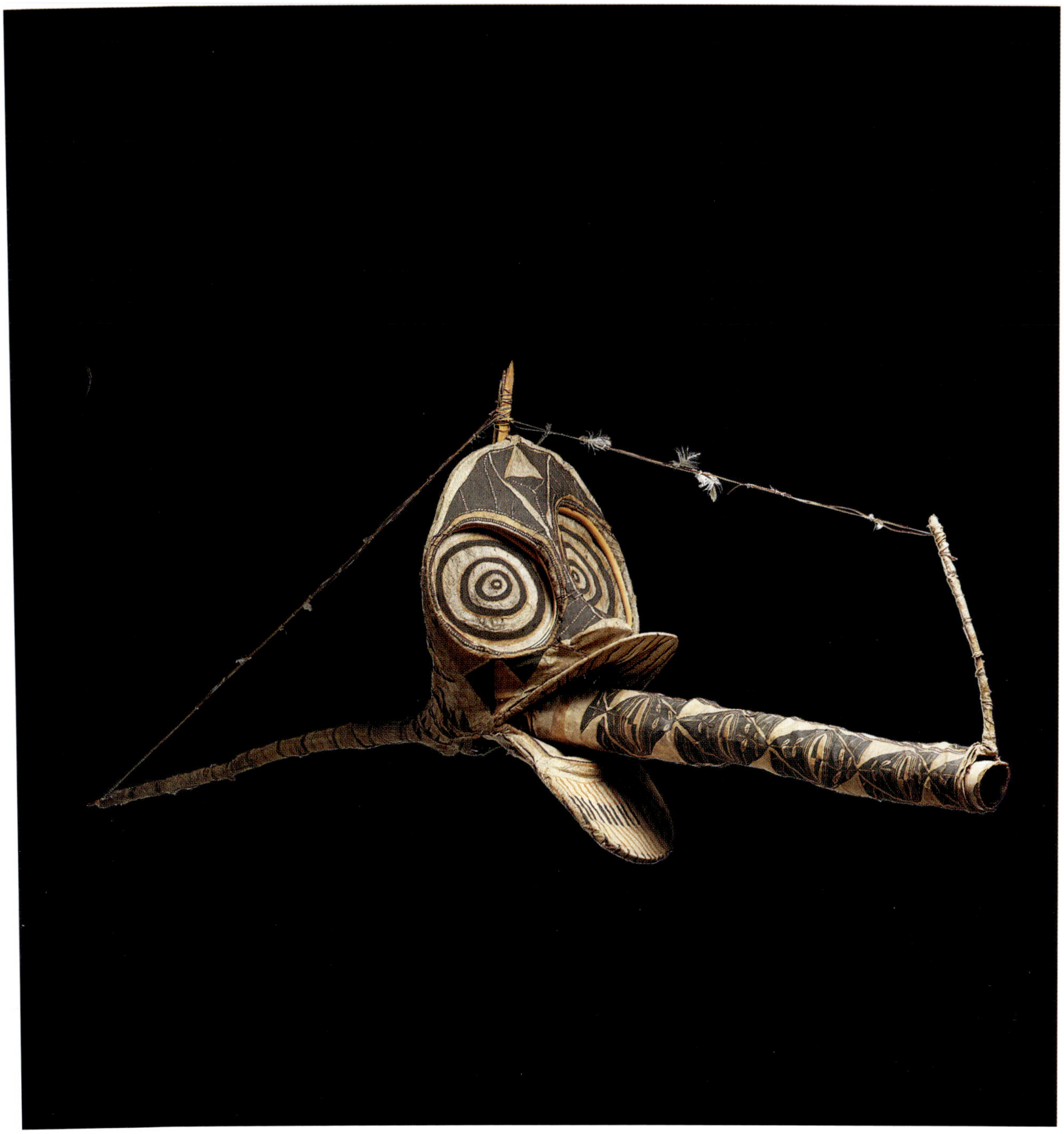

Vungvung mask

Kairak Baining

Bismarck Archipelago, New Britain Island, Gazelle Peninsula, Warangoi River Valley
Early 20th century
(or late 19th century)
Beaten bark (*tapa*), bamboo, natural pigments
92 x 290 x 70 cm
Former collections
Museum für Volkerkunde, Leipzig; Barbier-Mueller Museum, Geneva
Inv. 70.2001.9.2

This work was collected by Phoebe Parkinson, the wife of Sidney Parkinson, a planter in New Britain at the turn of the 20th century and author of a noted ethnographical work: *Thirty Years in the South Seas*.

The spectacular *tapa* masks made by the Baining of eastern New Britain swiftly caught the eye of Westerners. They were made well out of the sight of women and the uninitiated and were frequently destroyed after use. The most simple were called *kavat*. Fixed on a rattan frame, they were coated with a dye obtained from chewing plants and coal.

This type of *vungvung* mask featured a bamboo stem used as a resonator, with which it announced its presence when emerging from the bush. It was brought out during night-time ceremonies on the occasion of initiation rites for young boys as part of their integration into the world of adults. MD

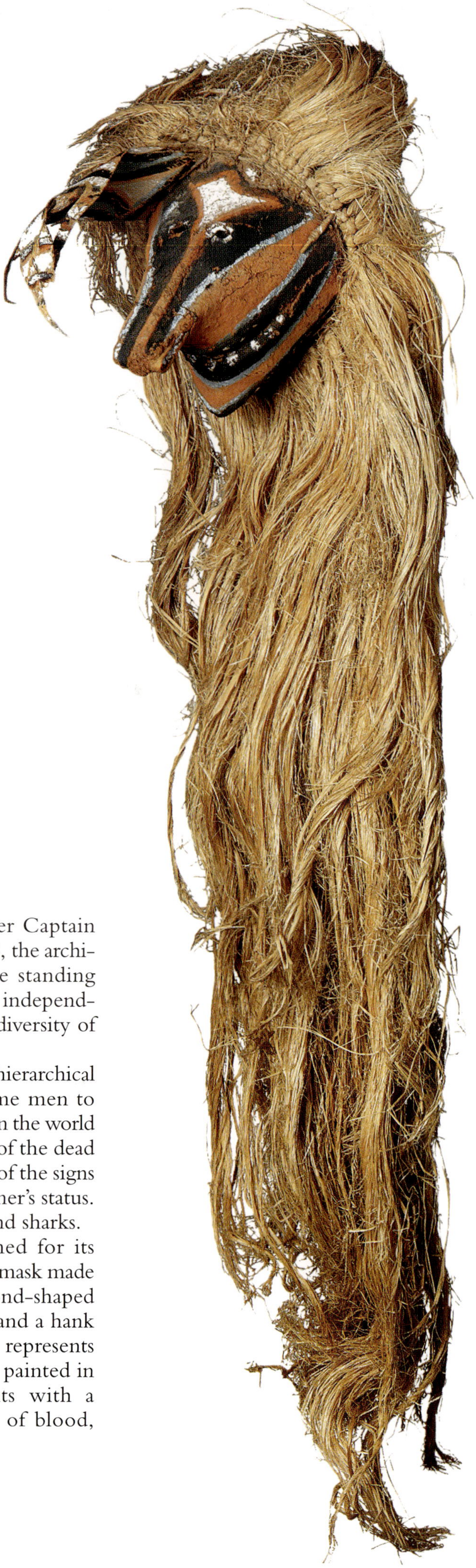

Mask

Melanesia, Vanuatu, Ambae Island
Mid 19th century
Plant fibres, wood, bark, natural pigments
88 x 22 cm
Donated by Dr Jollet
Inv. 71.1894.9.6

Baptised the "New Hebrides" after Captain James Cook* passed through in 1774, the archipelago was renamed Vanuatu, "the standing country", in 1980, when it gained independence. It is characterised by a wide diversity of cultures and languages.
It is also distinctive for its extremely hierarchical grading system, which enables some men to access power, riches and knowledge in the world of the living as well as in the world of the dead and ancestral beings. Masks are one of the signs of prestige which indicate their owner's status. Used in dances, they depict birds and sharks.
Coming from Ambae Island, famed for its production of woven fibre mats, this mask made of vegetable materials has a diamond-shaped face. The long nose evokes a beak and a hank of coco fibres attached to a string represents hair. The projecting side is crudely painted in white, black and green pigments with a predominance of red, the colour of blood, symbolising the life force. MD

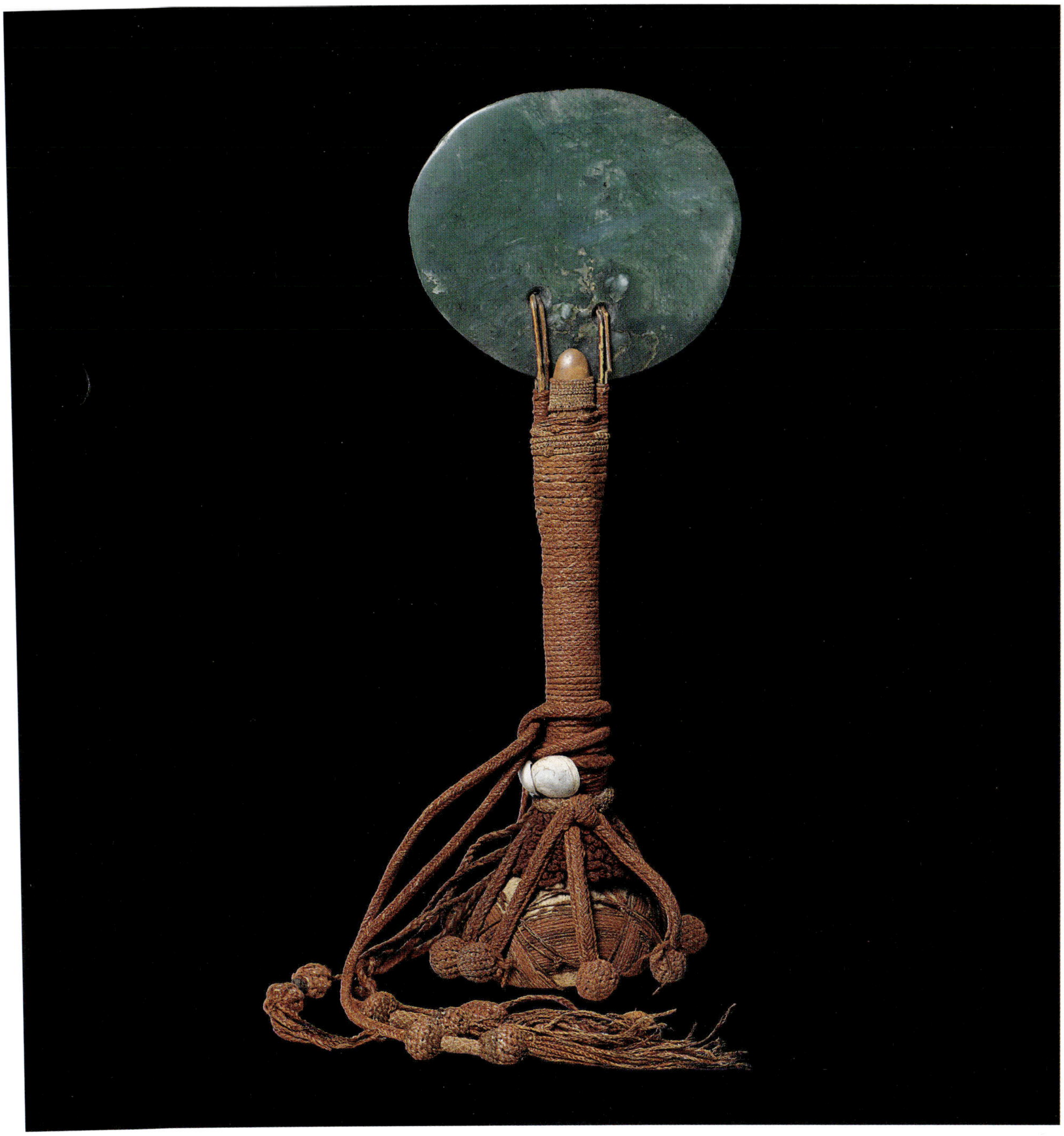

Monstrance axe

Kanak

New Caledonia
Wood, stone, esparto*
flying fox fur, shells,
rattan
57.3 x 21.7 x 16 cm
Inv. 71.1946.0.51 X

This ceremonial axe gets its name "monstrance axe" from the officers of admiral and explorer Bruni d'Entrecasteaux (1737-1793). In New Caledonia, however, it is known as a "green club". The disk, in exquisitely worked polished jade stone, is thinned along the whole of its circumference and its beauty highlighted by the sun, which makes the edges translucent. It is set on a wooden handle covered with either a *tapa* or woven wickerwork. A coconut filled with magical, symbolic shells forms the base. Shell beads enhance the value of such axes, which form part of a vast ceremonial and monetary exchange system. They are also used as bells when chiefs brandish these prestigious artefacts as a staff of authority, a symbol of power while making a speech.
Monstrance axes may also be used by rain-makers to ritually strike at the sun. MD

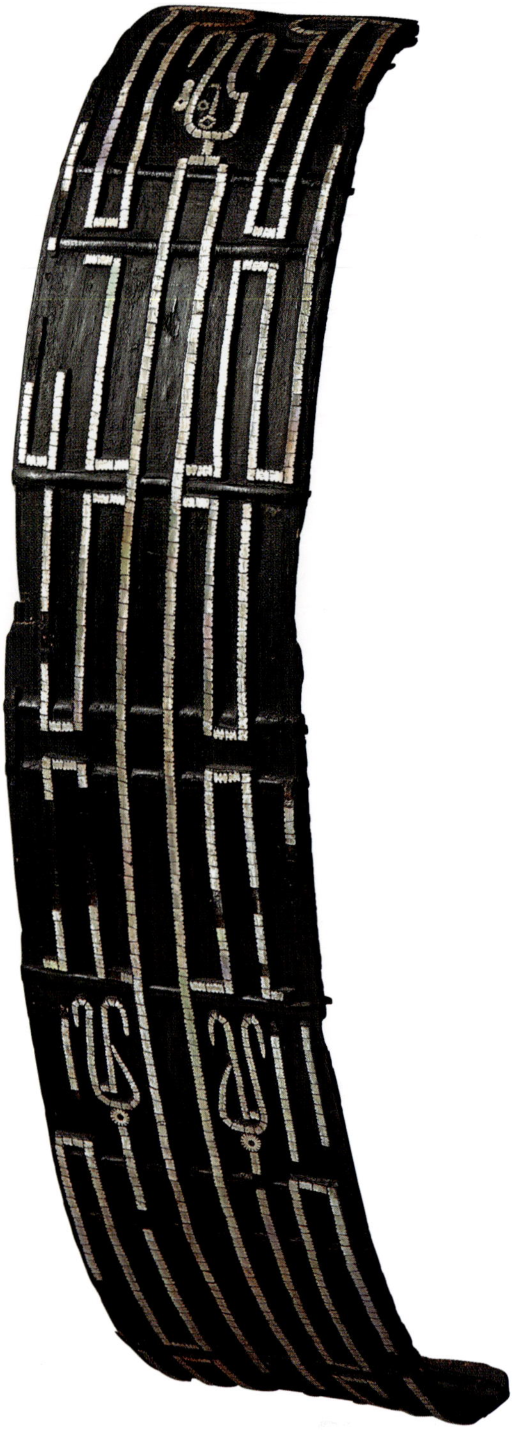

Shield

Solomon Islands, Santa Isabel Island
Early 19th century
Bark, pearl, vegetable resin, rattan
87.5 x 23 x 23 cm
Former collection Hunter
Inv. 70.2003.4.1

Exhibited in the 1850s at Hafton House*, this shield came from a collection assembled at the turn of the 19th century in Scotland by the Hunters, a family of ship owners.
The numerous tessera tiles* of pearl nautilus* fixed on the bark with parinarium nut* paste break down into a particularly refined ensemble of geometric lines.
At one end of the shield, an extraordinary motif in the shape of a stylised half-face can be observed, prolonged by two long parallel strips. On the sides appear two equally stylised figures, frigate birds, symbolically linked to fishing and headhunting*.

This is probably a parade shield, not so much used in warfare as in ceremonies simulating combats relating particularly to headhunting, a widespread ritual practice in Melanesia until the end of the 19th century. These ceremonial weapons were a key component of the power and prestige of the chief who owned them. MD

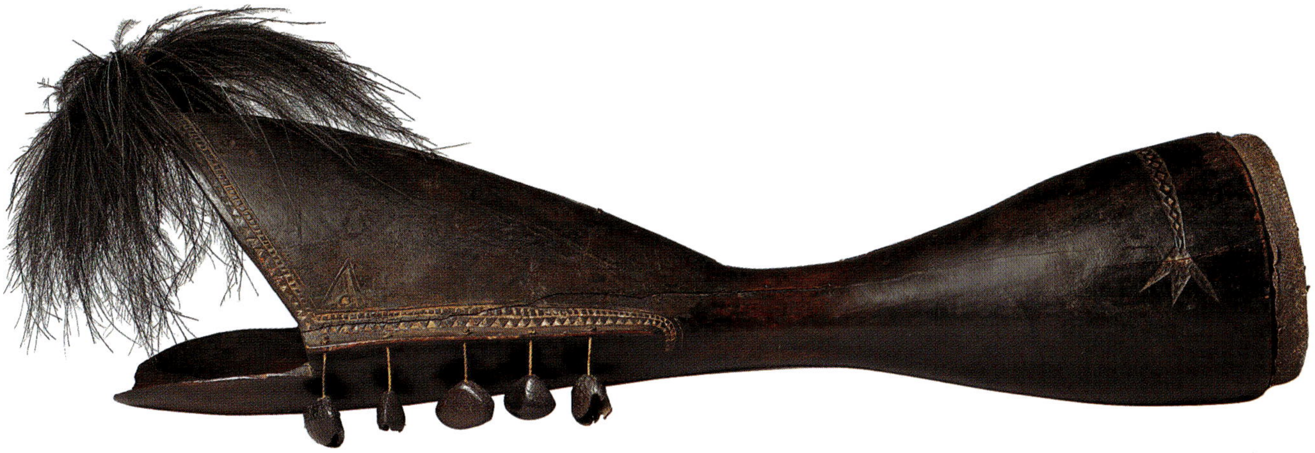

Warup skin tambourine

Australia, south of the Torres Strait
Carved wood, cassowary feathers, seeds
40 x 111 x 31.5 cm
Inv. 72.1977.1.1

At the northernmost tip of Australia, the Torres Strait separates New Guinea from the York Peninsula. Up until the turn of the 20th century, this archipelago was where funerary ceremonies and rituals took place, often in secret, celebrating mythological heroes. Large wooden or tortoiseshell masks were associated with these cultural events. The *warup* skin tambourine accompanied the songs of the *warup-le*, "tambourine men", during initiation dances marking the passage of young men from adolescence into manhood. As throughout southern New Guinea, it is shaped like an hourglass. One of the two sections, in a triangular shape with incised decoration, seems to represent the open mouth of a shark or crocodile. It is quite possible that this type of instrument was made in New Guinea and exported to the Torres Strait Islands.
This tambourine is handleless and was carried on a woven fibre belt. It is characterised by its large size and high aesthetic quality, all the more apparent as it still has its adornments of cassowary* feathers and nuts, used as bells. MD

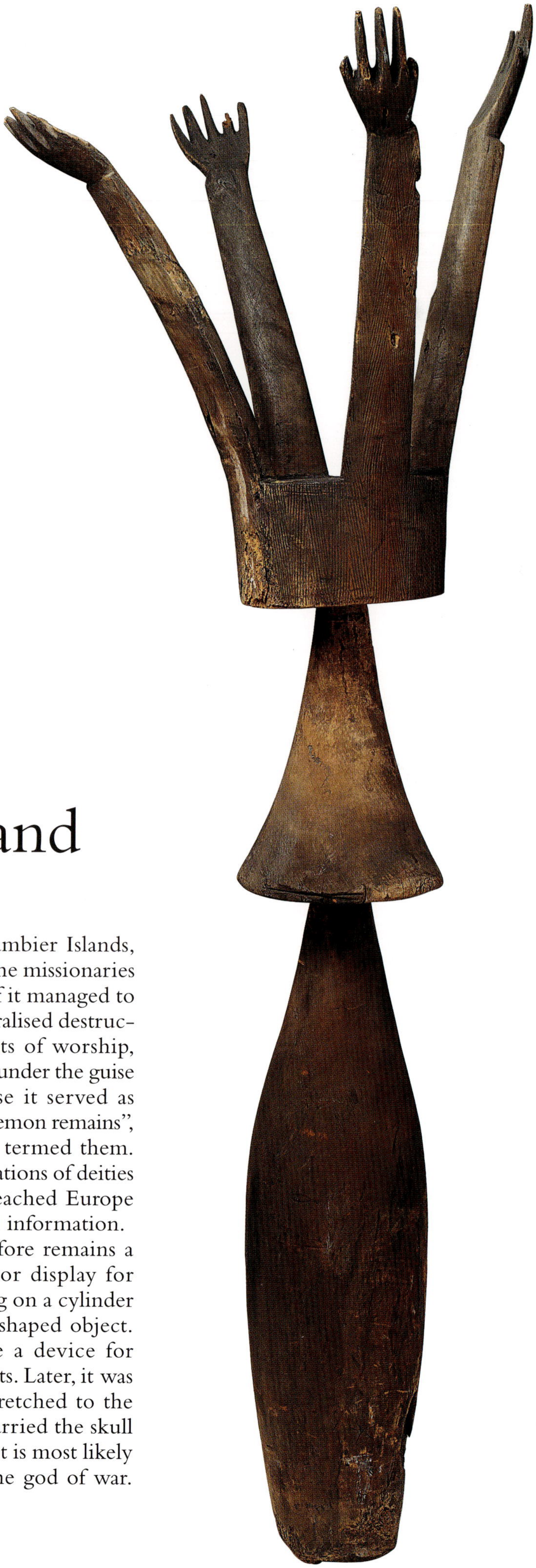

Patoko offerings stand

Gambier Archipelago, Mangareva Island
Late 19th century
Wood
180 x 68 x 60 cm
Donated by
Dr Louis Capitan
Inv. 71.1929.14.921

Found in a temple on the Gambier Islands, this object was confiscated by the missionaries of the Picpus Congregation*. If it managed to resist the auto-da-fé* and generalised destruction of sanctuaries and objects of worship, perpetrated in the 19th century under the guise of evangelisation, it is because it served as evidence, as did all "idols" or "demon remains", as the missionaries themselves termed them. Thus preserved, these representations of deities or venerated ancestors have reached Europe with almost no ethnographical information.
The use of this artefact therefore remains a mystery. It could be a stand or display for offerings with four arms resting on a cylinder that in turn stands on a cone-shaped object. It was long considered to be a device for keeping food away from rodents. Later, it was thought that each hand, outstretched to the sky, might have symbolically carried the skull of an enemy killed in combat. It is most likely that it was dedicated to Tu*, the god of war.
MD

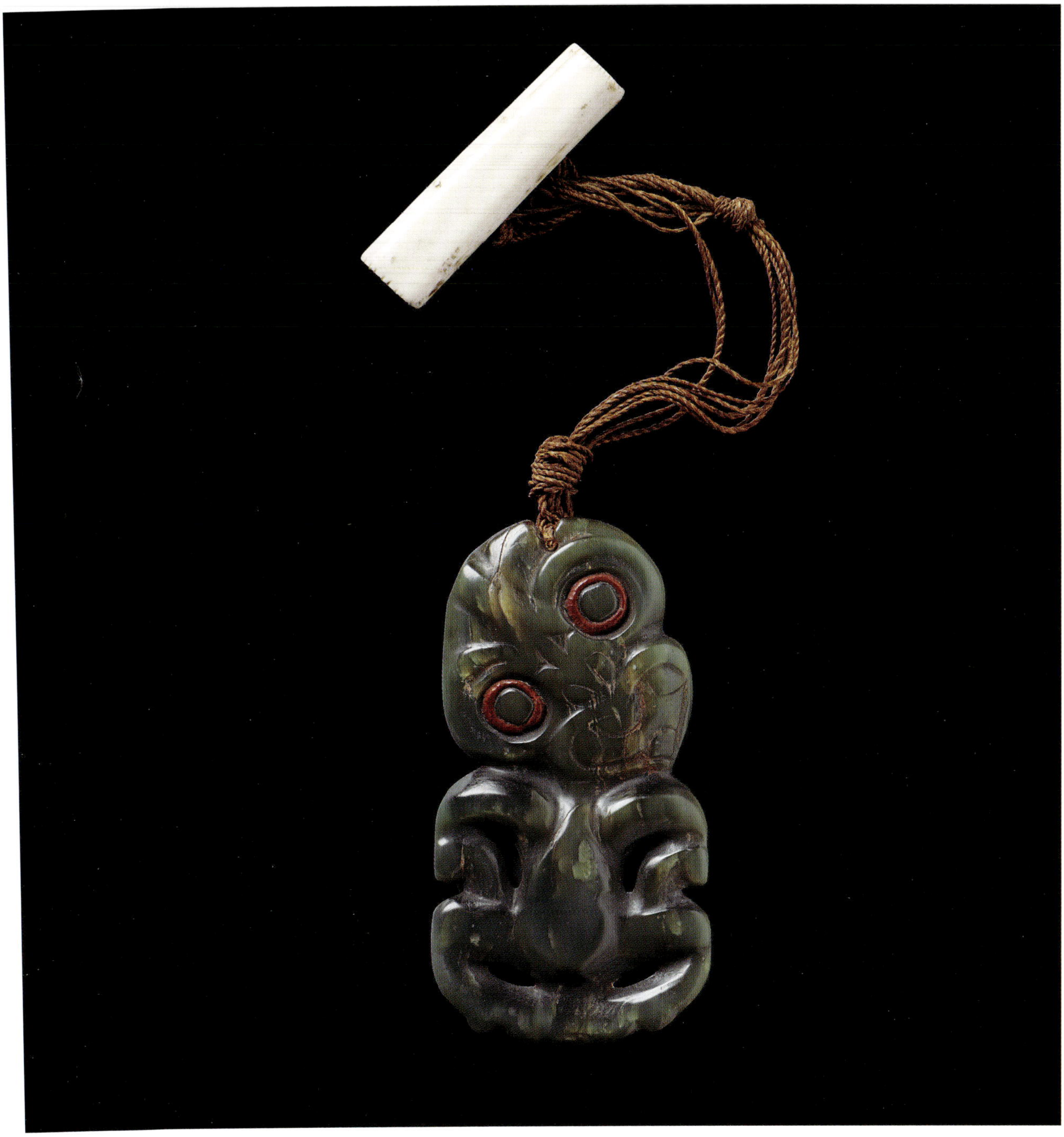

Hei tiki pendant

Maori

New Zealand
Early 19th century
Jade, vegetable fibres, bone, wax
15.5 x 9.8 x 1.3 cm
Former collection of King Charles X
Inv. SG 84.225

The Maori of New Zealand fashioned artefacts out of extremely delicate nephrite* or jadeite. Jade, *pounamou*, was only found on the southernmost island, in places that were difficult to access. Its colours range from light grey to dark green.

Worn as a pendant by men and women, this type of *hei tiki* (*hei* means "pendant" and *tiki* refers to any form of human representation) was attached to a fibre string with a bone clasp. It was a symbol of fertility with supposed magical or talismanic power, and was handed down from generation to generation, increasing in value along the way. It was often given a proper name.

After three visits by James Cook* to New Zealand in the late 18th century, *hei tiki*, and Maori sculptures in general, swiftly became highly prized objects of exchange or trade for Westerners, who, in admiration of the beautiful stone and exotic workmanship, also recognised their decorative and ornamental qualities. MD

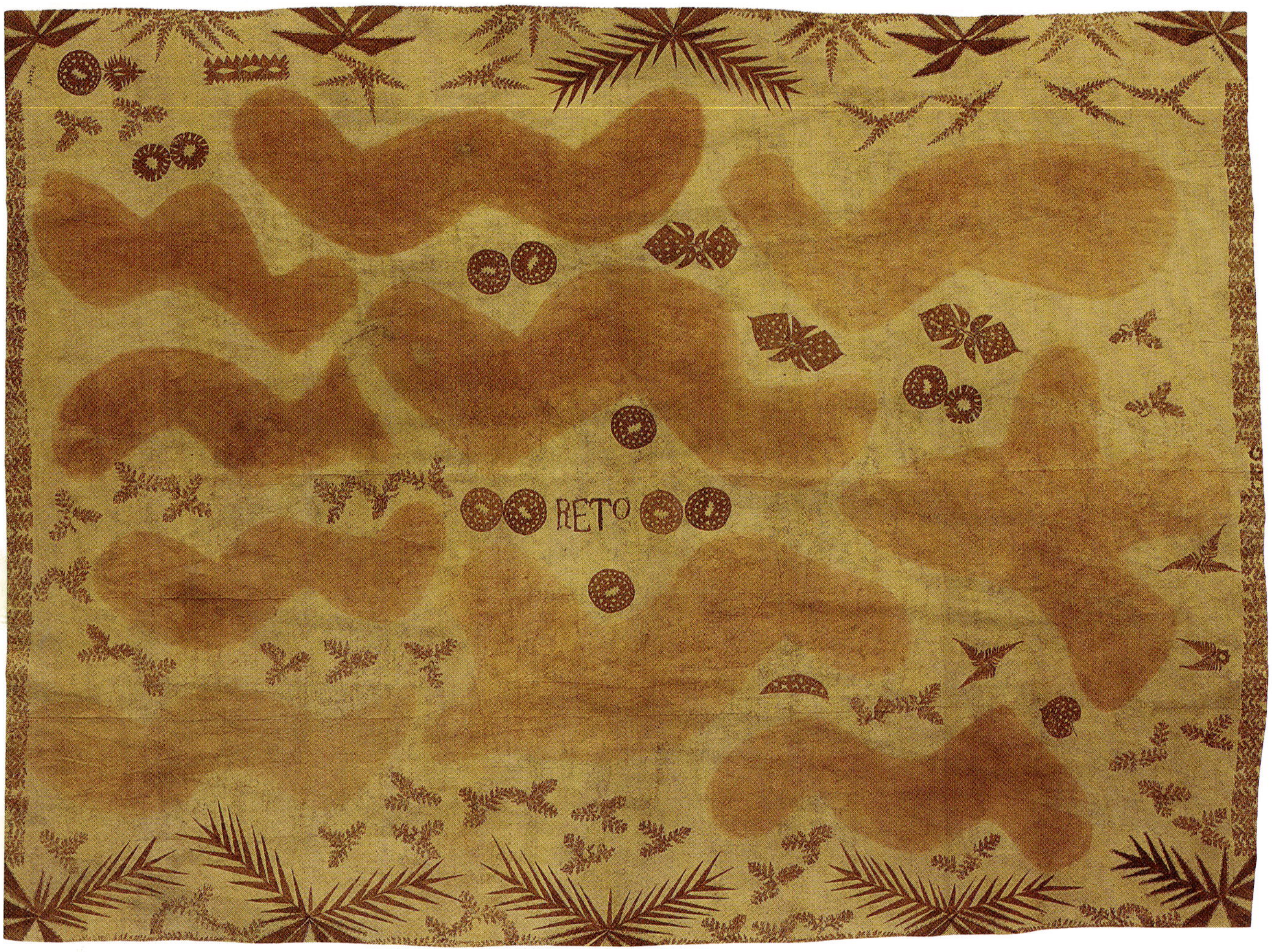

Tapa

Society Archipelago, Tahiti
19th century
Beaten bark,
natural pigments
183 x 243 x 0.5 cm
Collected by
Dr René-Primevère
Lesson
Inv. 71.1894.24.1

Beaten bark fabric has reached a high degree of refinement in Polynesia, in Tahiti in particular. *Tapa* is made from the phloem (inner bark) of paper mulberry or breadfruit trees*. Preparing the phloem is women's work, and involves soaking it for two or three days in water. The strips of bark are then beaten using a beater before being joined together. Motifs are applied by printing from plants and fern leaves usually dyed in red, black, brown or yellow ochre. Traditionally, they might be used simply as decoration or read as symbolic signs. Used both in the home and at funerals, these objects could also play a ceremonial role, as is the case for this exhibit, with its exquisite motifs and colours, which was worn as ceremonial attire.

Used as objects of exchange and prestige by Oceanians, *tapa* were highly rated and much collected by travellers as "exotic curios". MD

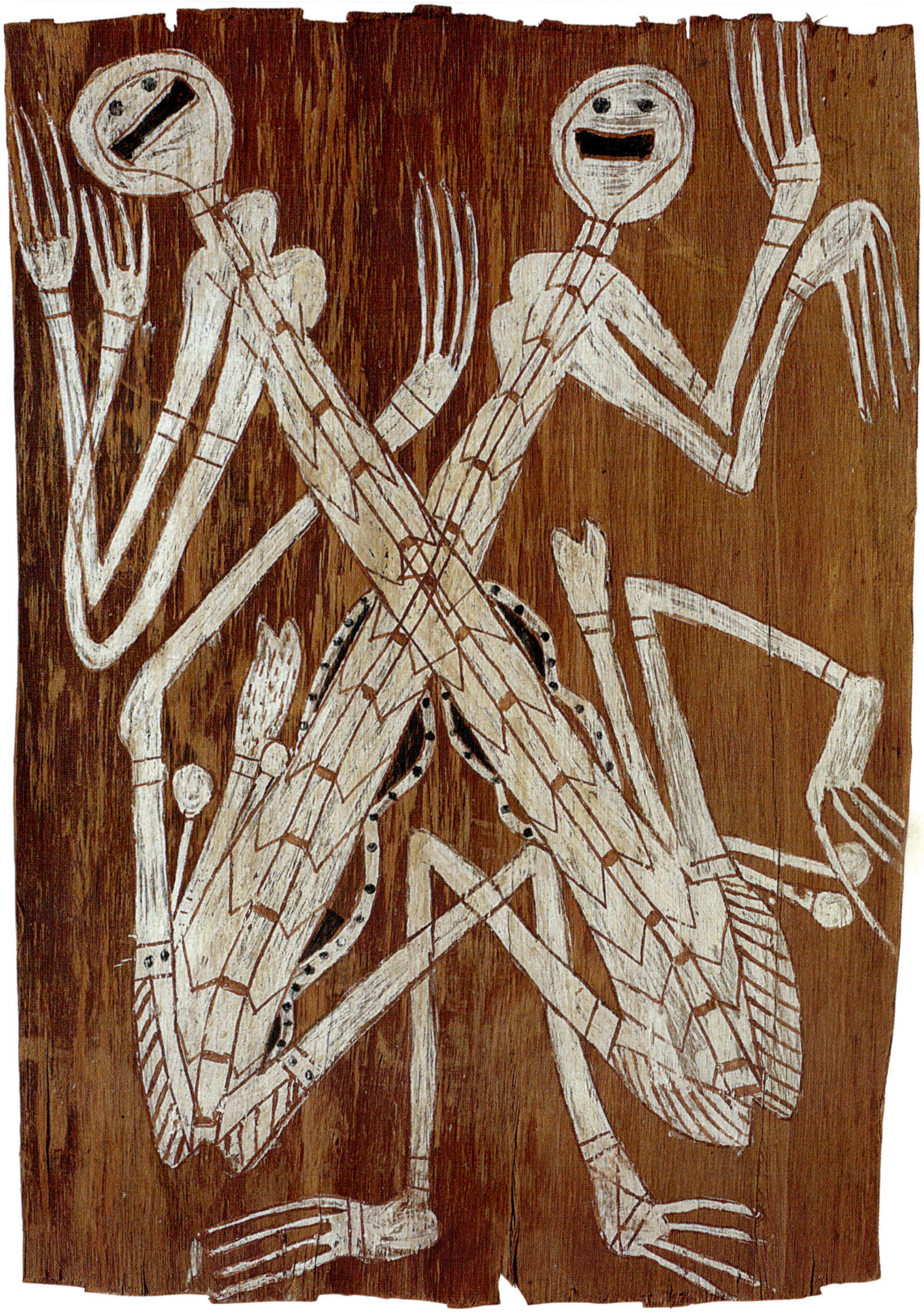

Two *mimi* men

Billy Yirawala,
Gunwiggu group
Australia,
western Arnhem Land,
Croker Island
Mid 20th century
Eucalyptus bark,
natural pigments
63 x 42 cm
Karel Kupka Mission,
1963
Inv. 72.1964.9.79

Paintings on eucalyptus bark traditionally accompanied recitals of myths during rituals. These myths refer to a fundamental notion, "Dreamtime", which relates the origins of the world and geography of the Australian continent. Aboriginal art is inspired by the mythical spirits of this vast imaginary creation, as much a product of the past as of the present. In West Arnhem Land, spirits included *maam* and *mimi*. The latter, fragile, slight, almost bodiless and residing hidden away in rocks, lead a life in parallel to humans, who they taught to hunt, cook, dance and paint. Their histories, a teaching aid for children, are reproduced on rock faces.

This work was collected by the Czech artist Karel Kupka who brought back over a thousand artefacts in the 1950s and early 1960s, around 250 of which became part of the collection of the musée national des arts d'Afrique et d'Océanie in Paris. His research is published in two major volumes, notably *Un art à l'état brut*, with a preface by André Breton. MD

Dream of Tjunginpa to Tjunginpa, northwest of Kintore

Mick Namerari Tjapaltjarri
Australia, Central Desert, Papunya
1996
Acrylic on canvas
153 x 122 cm
Inv. 72.1998.1.3

The painting, apparently nothing more than a mass of yellow dots against a black background, seems to challenge the viewer. However, in exploring the surface, he will begin to perceive infinite variations in colour and density. A landscape, or rather an aerial view of a place, takes form. The place, known as Tjunginpa, is in the Australian Central Desert, northwest of the Kintore community. In the eyes of all Aborigines, the desert is a living thing. Topographical features – springs, rock piles, faults and valleys – are not simply locations, but are evidence of the activities of mythical ancestral beings. Each site was the scene of a drama whose power remains to this day. By painting the hills of Tjuginpa, Mick Namerari Tjapaltjarri is evoking a moment in the creation of the world. He does so by using signs that can be interpreted either as tracks left by mice, or as *kampurarrpa* (one of their preferred foods), or as a carpet of flowers. But above all, the artist is seeking to show us the energy that flows from the place and in doing so, to experience the process of its creation.
PP

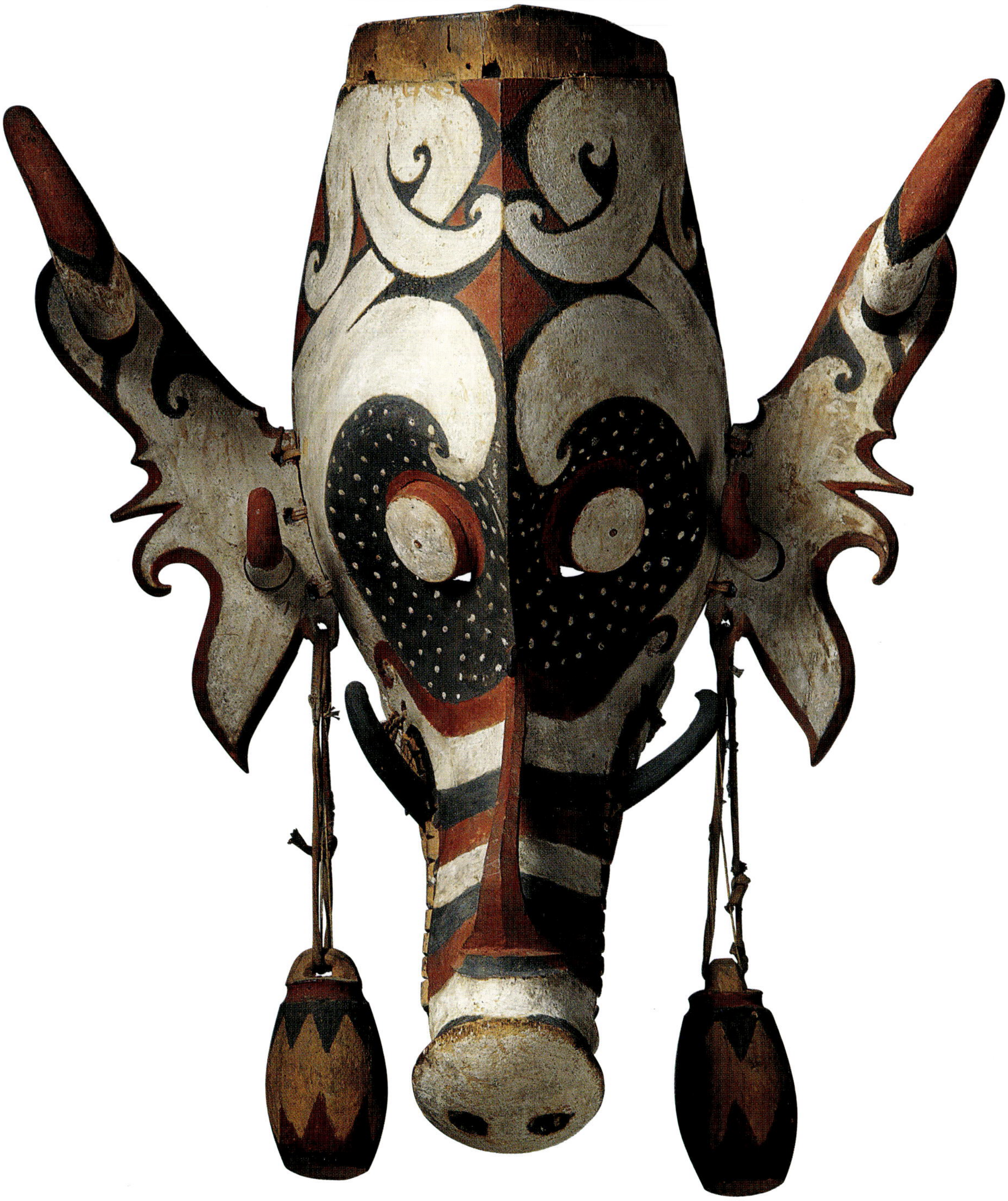

Hudoq mask

Kenyah Kayan

Indonesia,
Borneo Island,
East Kalimantan,
Mahakam basin
Early 20th century
Wood, pigments, rattan
58 x 53 x 31.5 cm
Former collections
Alain Schoffel;
Barbier-Mueller
Museum, Geneva
Inv. 70.2001.27.234

Exuberantly designed with pronounced jaws, pointed teeth, prominent groin and ears, painted motifs and an abundance of spirals, *hudoq* masks are made in the forests from pieces of carved wood by the men who wear them. They are worn during ritual dances, performed by village communities at all stages of rice cultivation – in April for example, during the harvest festival.

These ceremonies are accompanied by the rustling of the leaves on the dancers' attire, the almost supernatural sound of their laughter, the striking of gongs and the beating of drums. A chick is sacrificed to herald the parade of housewives, who supply themselves with rice seeds that they distribute to the various members of the community.

Although they represent stylised wild animals such as a boar or panther, *hudoq* masks are associated with "good spirits", protectors of the earth, who ensure fertility and prosperity for the village. MD

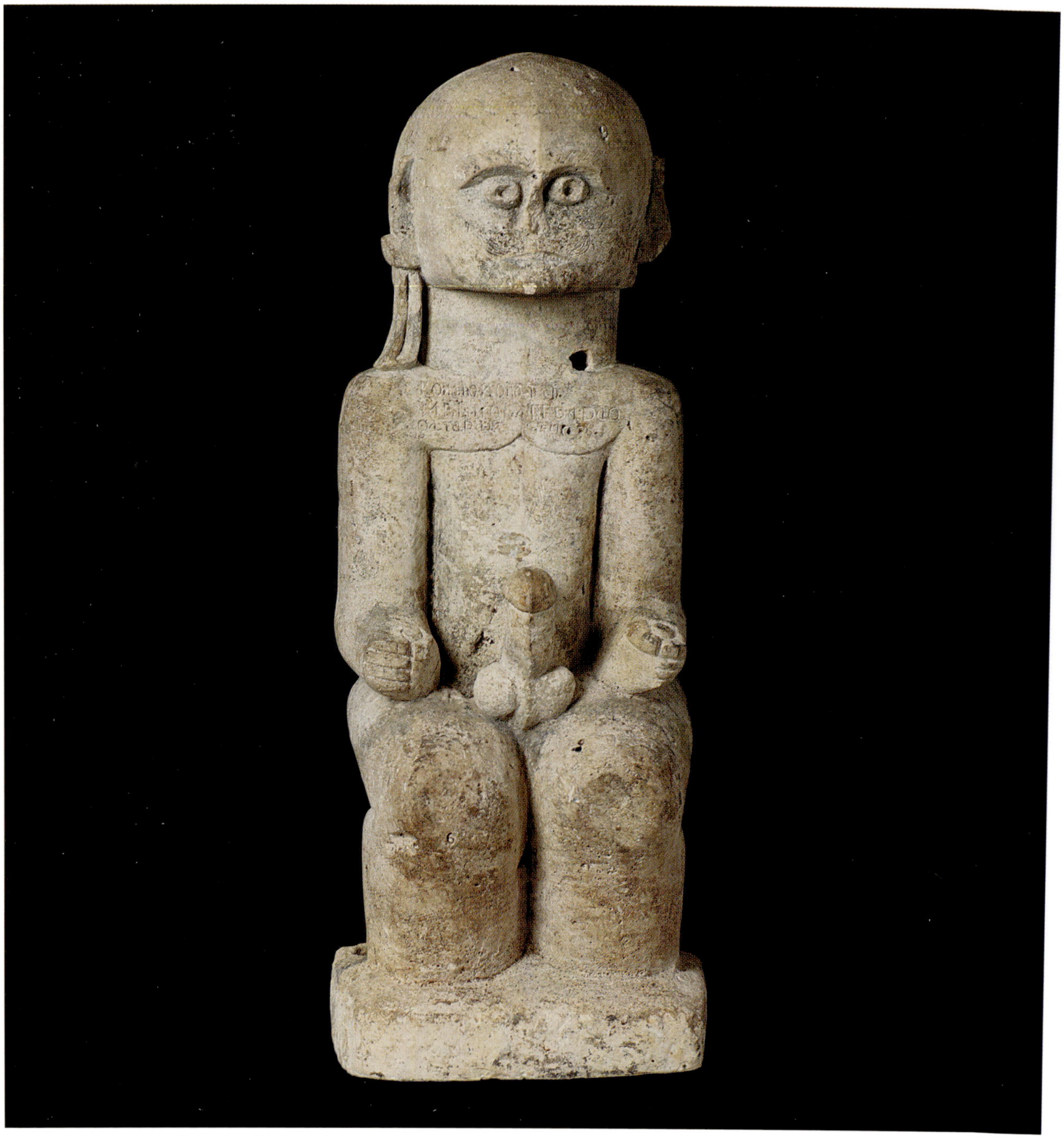

Statue *behu lawölö*

Indonesia, centre of Nias Island, Susuwa river region
Late 19th century
Limestone
122 x 35.5 x 33 cm
Former collection Barbier-Mueller Museum, Geneva
Inv. 70.2001.27.549

There is little information available on these *lawölö* anthropomorphic sculptures from the centre of Nias Island. They were generally placed in pairs near the village entrance.
This statue may represent a chief. Its only decoration is a ring in its right ear. There is a hole at the back of the plinth into which a spear or a banner may have been put. The torso features an inscription indicating the passage from one place to another and a date, 1908. These stone figures were often moved from one abandoned site to a new village under construction, to which they were supposed to bring peace and serenity.

The etymology of the term *lawölö* evokes the idea of strength and, above all, protection, and the disturbing glare and massive form are certainly enough to instil fear and keep any enemies at bay. MD

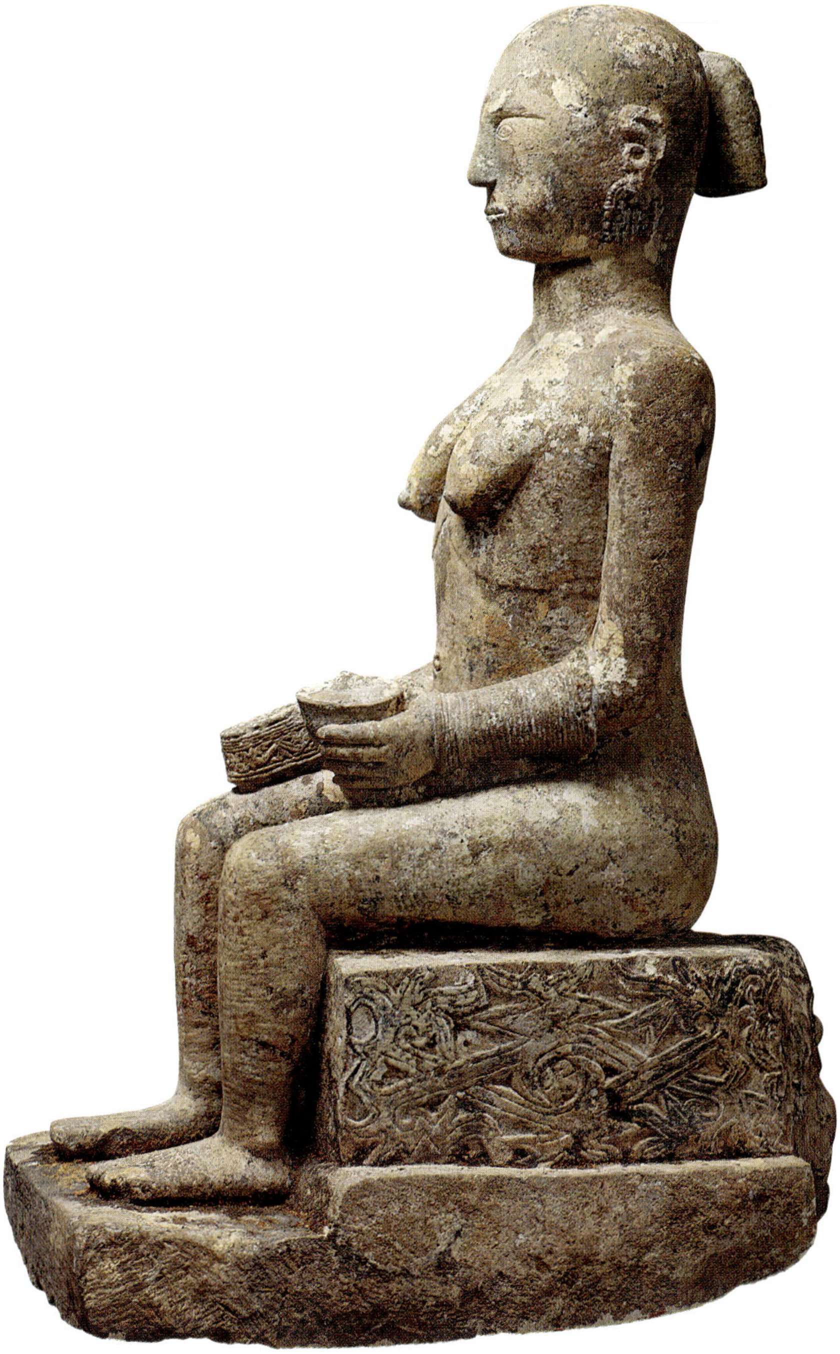

Ancestor effigy

Toba

Indonesia, Sumatra, Barus region
19th century
Stone
112 x 76 x 47 cm
Former collection
Barbier-Mueller
Museum, Geneva
Inv. 70.2001.27.585

The Toba of Sumatra are one of six groups belonging to Batak society. They have always attached particular importance to building stone monuments and large statues of a funerary character for ancestor worship or commemoration, as is the case here. Renowned "sculptor magicians" were called upon to create them. The sculpture of Ronggur ni Ari *boru* Barutu ("daytime thunderbolt") was created during her lifetime by an unidentified artist from the Barus region.
It was to honour his wife that Ompu Raja Ranjo Simanjuntak, whose reputation as chief and skilled magician was well-known, commissioned this effigy. He also possessed great wealth, symbolised particularly by the chair on which his wife is sitting. It features slightly raised curvilinear and foliated decoration which probably refers back to the Cosmic tree* and which was inspired by floral motifs from India and the Islamic world.
Boru Barutu is depicted naked, adorned with her jewels. She carries a box of ritual value in each hand: one for betel leaves and the other for lime. MD

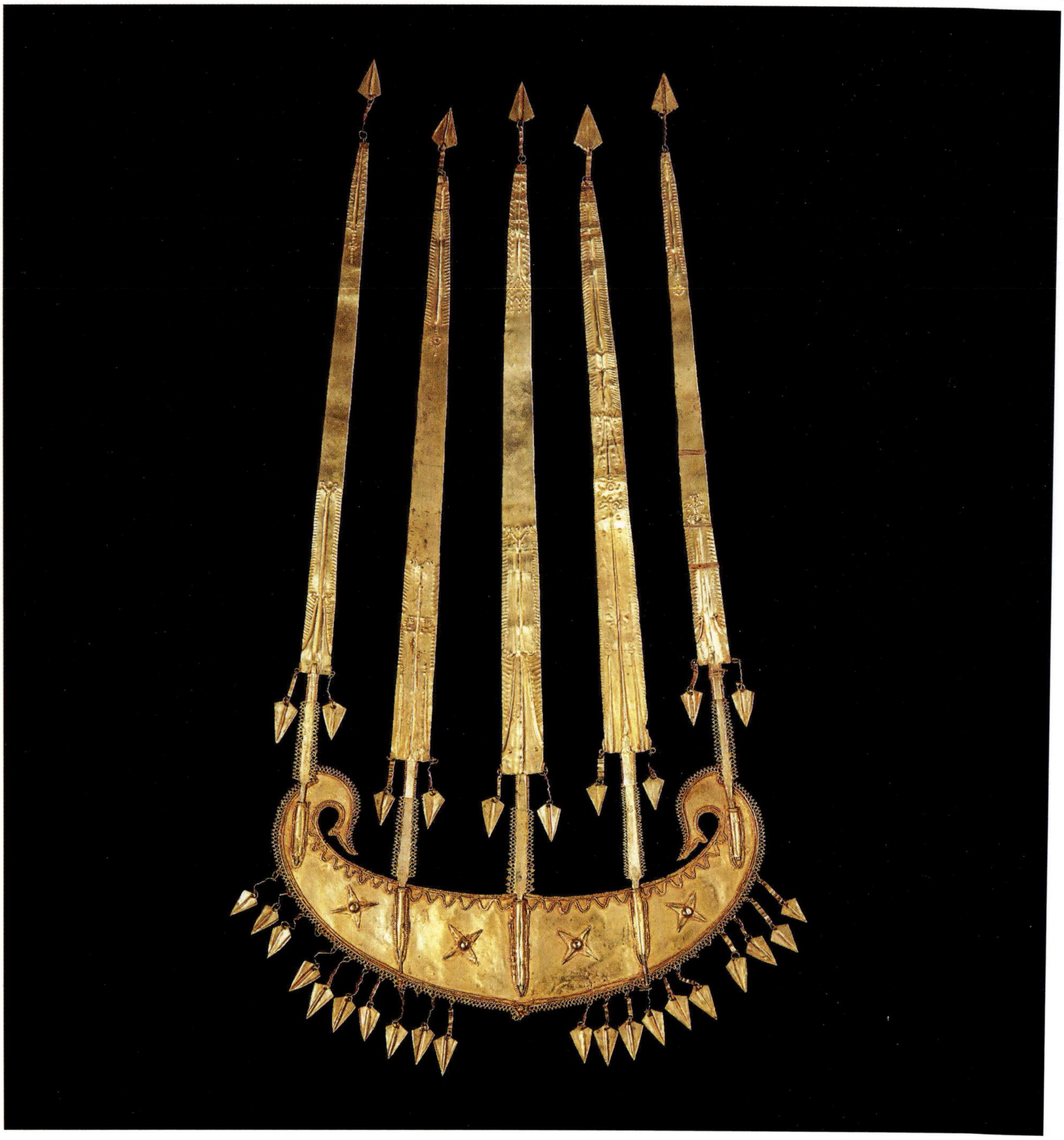

Lado forehead ornament

Nage

Indonesia,
Sonde Islands,
central Flores Island
20th century
Gold
50 x 26.6 cm
Donated by Monique and Jean Paul Barbier-Mueller
Inv. 70.2001.27.709

The Nage people live in the centre of Flores Island, in Eastern Indonesia. Their artistic creations were only really identified in the 1980s. In addition to wooden sculptures evoking the antagonism between the male and female principles, they created such jewellery as this gold diadem, or *lado wea*, undoubtedly the heritage of a prosperous colonial period, and a prestigious version of an older model made out of feathers and shells.

Symbolising ethnic identity and prosperity, these adornments, whose very manufacture required special ritual sacrifices, were passed down from father to son along with the family treasure. They were fixed to a headscarf and worn on the forehead by men of high rank, warriors or village chiefs, when new buildings or ceremonial poles were erected and buffalo sacrifices were organised. The base of the crown, in the shape of a crescent, evokes a boat as well as a buffalo horn. In Flores, buffaloes bring prestige to their owners and their blood is poured on the stones of the village altar to honour the ancestors. MD

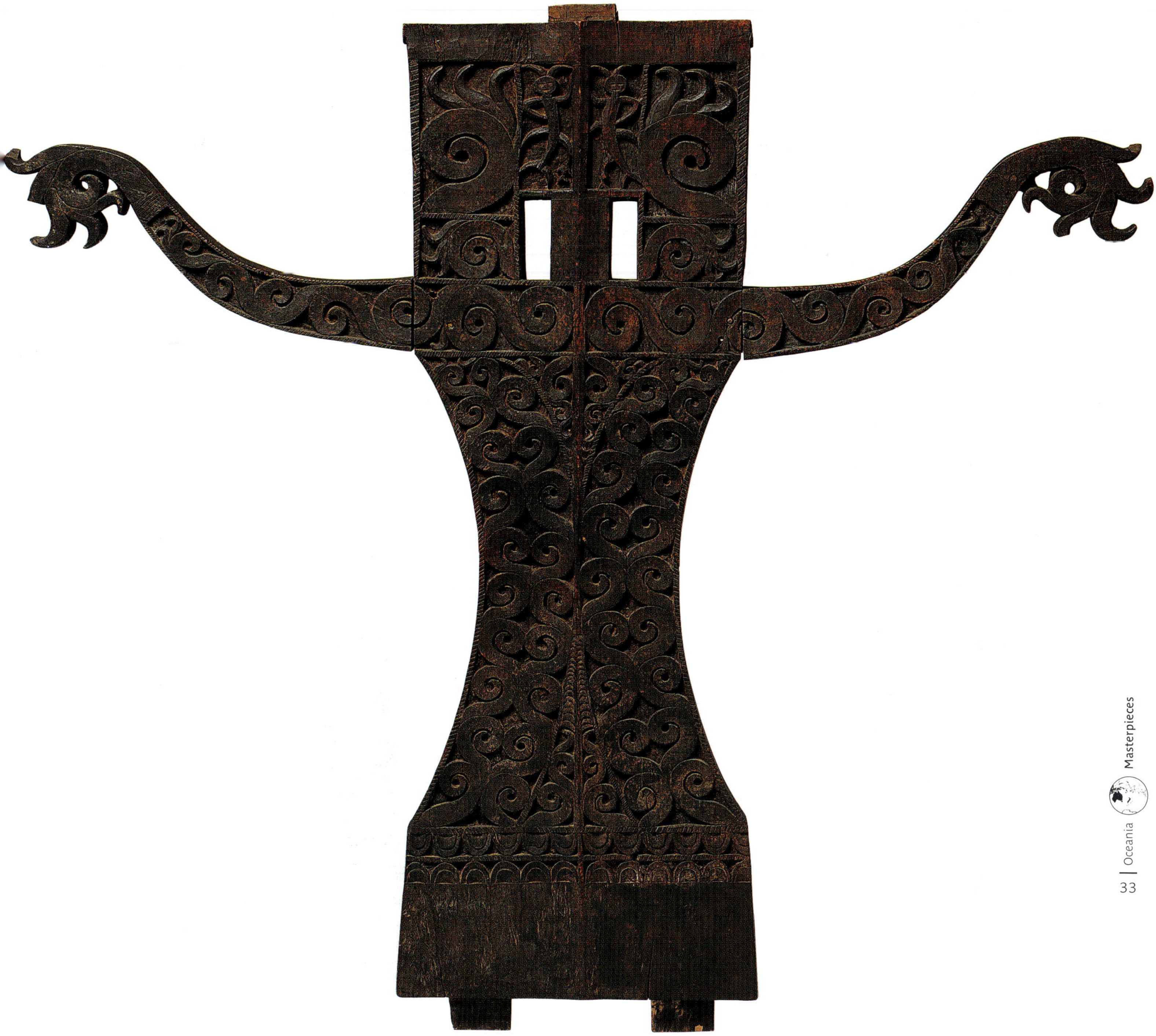

Tavu domestic altar

Indonesia,
Southern Moluccas,
Tanimbar archipelago
19th century
Clear patinaed
hard wood
236 x 146 cm
Former collection
Barbier-Mueller
Museum, Geneva
Inv. 70.2001.27.444

The face of Tanimbar archipelago, a Dutch colony and occupied by the Japanese in the Second World War, changed in the 20th century. The large decorated thatch and bamboo houses surrounding village squares gradually disappeared. The *tavu*, a domestic altar dedicated to ancestors, was placed opposite the front door. Very few examples still exist today and are on display in a handful of European museums.

Elegantly shaped and often decorated with spiral motifs, these altars, which evoked the body of an ancestor, supported one of the roof beams of the house. The wealth and prestigious assets passed down through a family were also included on the *tavu*. Certain animals – dogs, cockerels or fish, such as are seen here – may recall the deeds of the dwelling's founders. On a shelf above the altar lay the skulls of venerated ancestors, their first two vertebrae, the atlas and axis, and often their effigies.

The *tavu* was an integral part of the notion of lineage and sacred power. It was a clear link between the past and present, endowed with special spiritual power, a heritage of the "masters of the house". It was here that prayers and sacrifices were offered to promote fertility among people and harvests, ensure success in fishing or headhunting expeditions, and uphold the union between ancestors and their descendants. MD

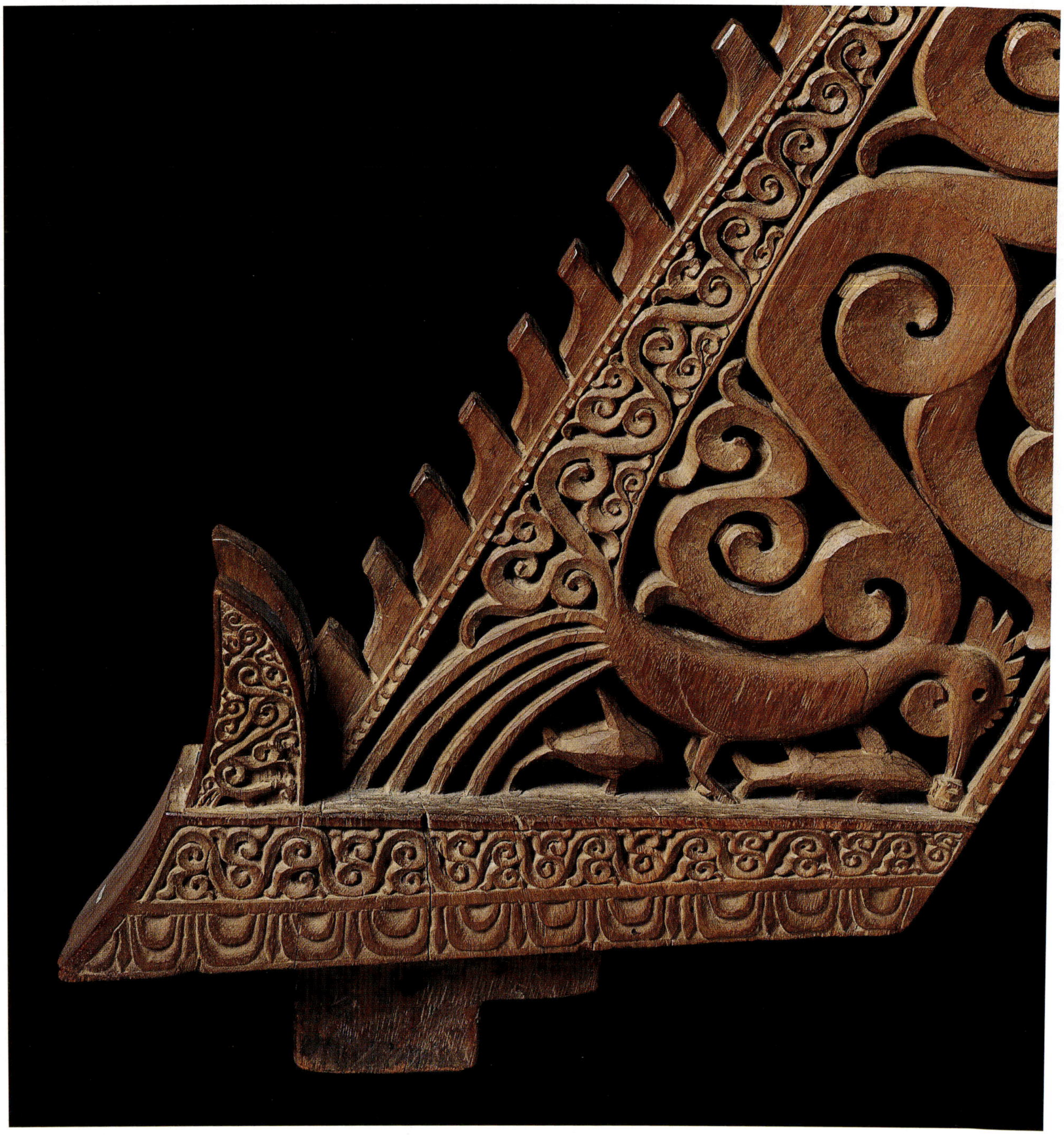

Prow of a pirogue

Indonesia,
Southern Moluccas,
Tanimbar archipelago
19th century
Wood
50 x 162.5 x 13.5 cm
Former collections
Jef van der Straete;
Barbier-Mueller
Museum, Geneva
Inv. 70.2001.27.520

The boat assumes great importance in many Indonesian islands, as much for maritime as symbolic and ritual reasons. Such is the case in Tanimbar, an archipelago in southwest Moluccas where some villages were organised around a stone platform whose end was shaped like a boat's prow. The inhabitants called themselves "the crew" and gathered there under the auspices of the supreme deity Ubila'a.

This wooden item, with an openwork design of single and double spiral motifs, forms the matching piece to the stone figureheads which were anchored in the social structure of the community. Paradoxically a symbol of movement, it adorned the bows of prestigious boats, metaphorically incarnating the ancestors that linked the world of the living to the world of the dead.

The fighting cock and fish, most probably sharks, represented on the lower part of the sculpture, may have symbolised the aggressiveness and predatory might of war expeditions against the enemy and the prestige of these boats, which also set sail in search of trade partnerships. MD

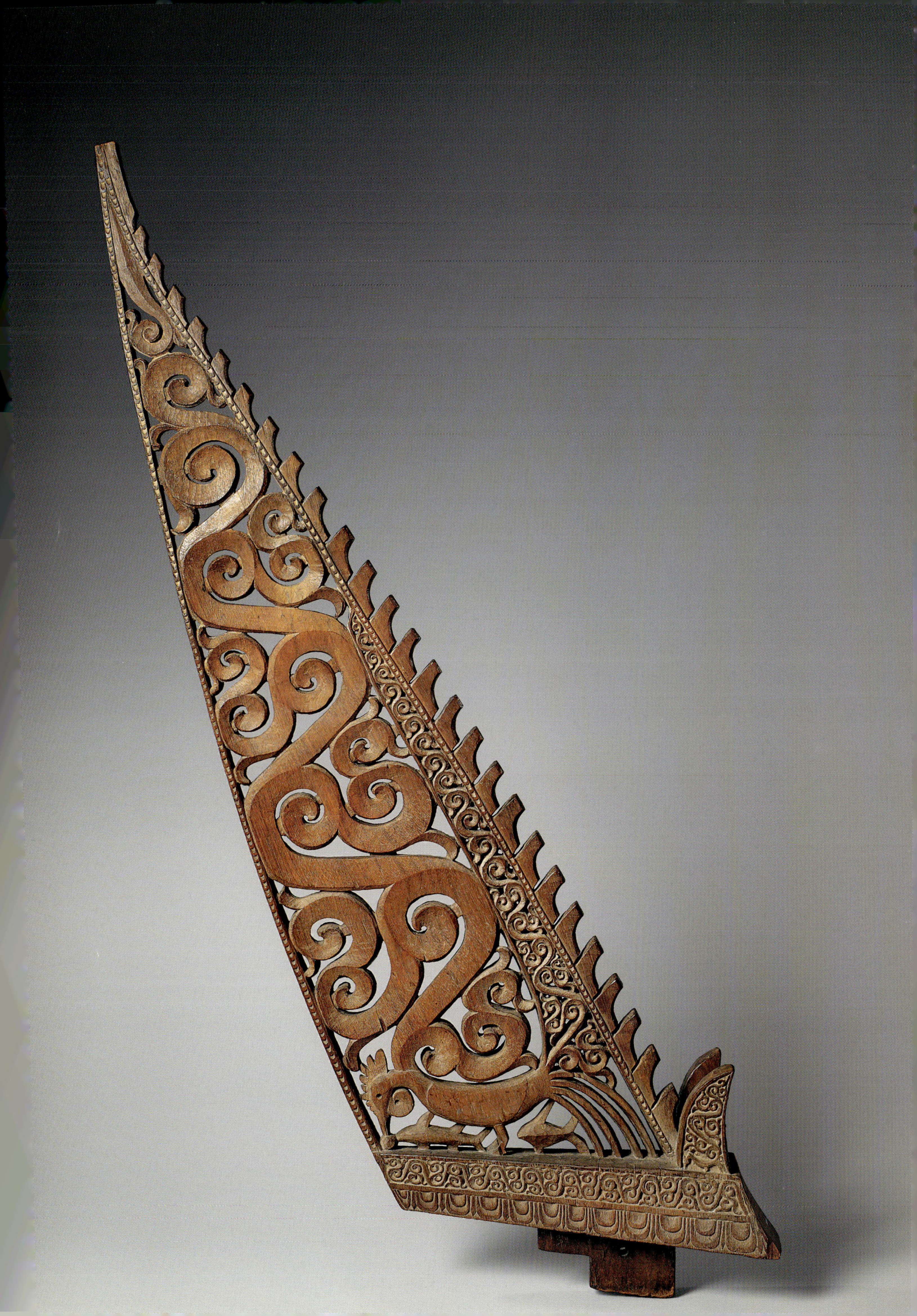

The Arts and Civilizations of Africa, Asia, Oceania and the Americas

The musée du quai Branly collection has a rich museal history, whose path was first traced by explorers during the last quarter of the 19th century. Following in the footsteps of these adventurers, and also of the artists, ethnologists and collectors who have gradually built up this field of reference, the permanent collections invite visitors on a journey of discovery across the African continent and Madagascar, following a geographical and cultural itinerary highlighted by trans-cultural themes.

The many institutions entrusted with these extraordinary objects – from the musée d'ethnographie du Trocadéro and the musée de l'homme, to the musée de la France d'Outre-Mer and the musée national des Arts d'Afrique et d'Océanie – have undergone a series of metamorphoses over the years. Testimony of the myriad cultures of this vast continent, most of the works in the collections represent the "traditional" ways of life and of thinking encountered during the 19th and first half of the 20th century, the period in which the majority of them were produced and collected. The history of these encounters, which is marked by its share of violence, also shows how strong the bonds created by two-way cultural interactions can be.

After over a hundred years of contacts, the emergence of masterpieces, representative works on both the aesthetic and the cultural levels, has fostered recognition of the quality of African sculptures and the expressive powers of the continent's artists. Everyday and ritual objects alike blend beauty with functionality, in which regional styles, and sometimes the work of a specific studio or even the hand of a particular artist can be discerned – as is evidenced by these images selected from among the finest items contained in the collection, and presented in homage to the genius of the peoples of Africa.

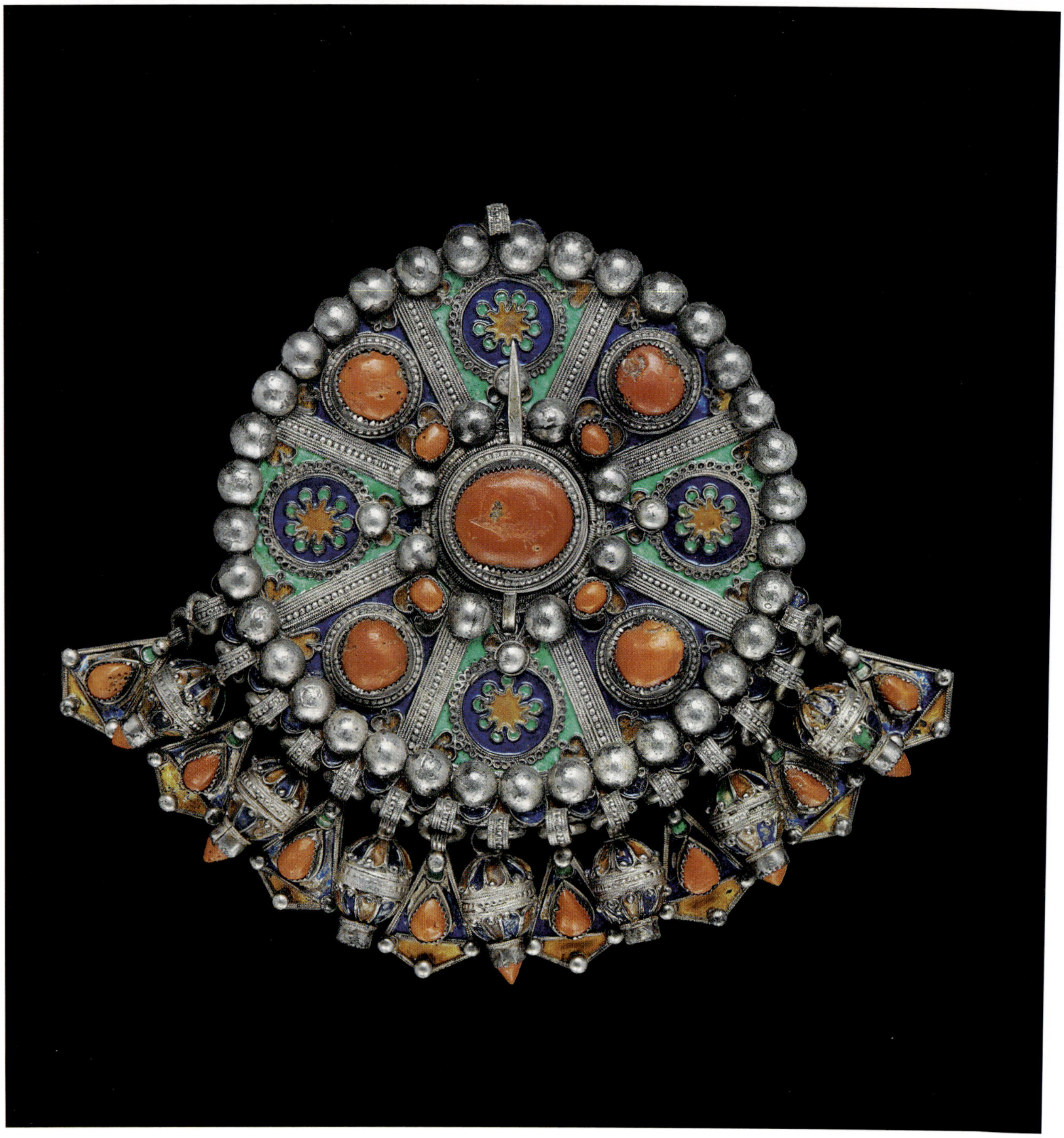

Tabzimt fibula

Ait Yenni and Ait Hichem tribes

Algeria,
Great Kabylia
19th century
Silver, enamel, coral
23 x 18 x 3 cm
Former collection
Paul Eudel
Inv. 74.1968.4.6

The Ait Yenni, Muslim Berbers with two hundred years of silverworking to their credit, use an age-old technique originating in Persia and developed by the Byzantines. Spread throughout Spain by the Arabs, it was introduced by Jewish craftsmen who left Spain for Algeria, Morocco and Tunisia.

This type of fibula, richly decorated on either side, was worn as a pendant by young Kabylian women on their wedding day and upon the birth of their first child. Their finest piece of jewellery, it could be quite large in size if the firstborn was a boy, upon which occasion it was worn on the forehead as a sign of joy. It was also used in a number of magical rites to protect against the evil eye. In this case, it was pinned to the little boy's chest on the day of his circumcision, and was kept fastened on his back during the month that followed.

This piece of jewellery comes from the collection of Paul Eudel, a French writer fascinated by North African urban and rural silverwork. Having undertaken a mission to Algeria in 1895, he studied the country's art and history and was the author of two works on the subject, still considered authoritative today. MD

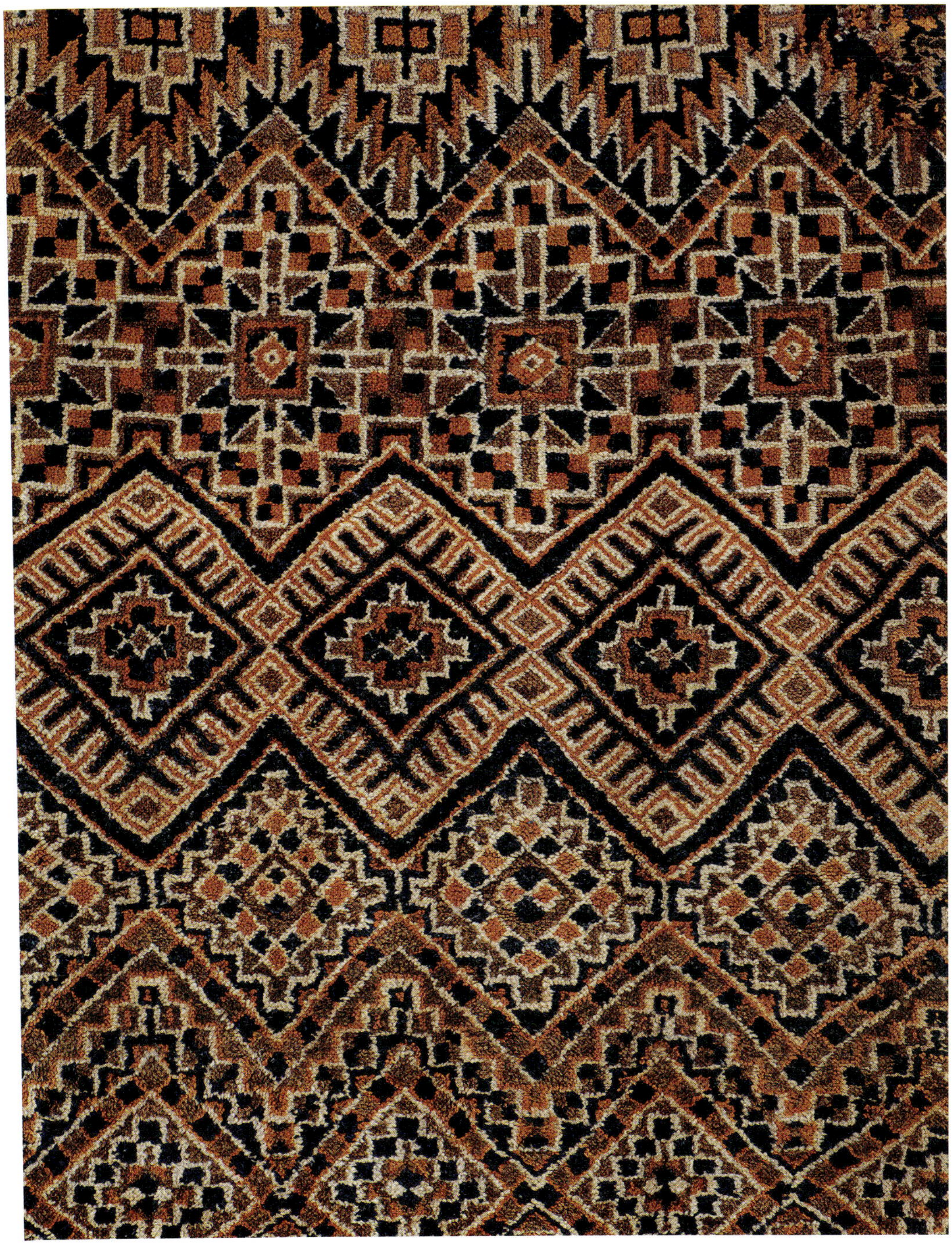

Zerbiya knotted carpet

Ait M'Guild tribe

Morocco, central Middle Atlas
Late 19th century
Wool, vegetable and chemical dyes
496 x 168 cm
Former collection Lelong
Inv. 74.1977.4.6

Produced on the plateaus and high slopes of the Middle Atlas mountains, *zerbiya* Berber carpets, although varying greatly in design from tribe to tribe, are always decorated with geometrical motifs in muted colours and without a border. Such is the case with this multicoloured carpet, whose basic motif is a lozenge and whose main weft is a dominant reddish brown.
The technique used is that of the Berber knot, specific to the Middle Atlas region. This exceedingly strong knot, which holds together three warps, encourages dynamic design and composition, which is asymmetrical and highly inventive.
These carpets, which protect against the damp, are part of the traditional furnishings of settled populations and nomadic peoples alike, acting both as mattresses and as blankets. They were woven by the women on a high-warp loom*, following strictly ordained rituals reflecting ancestral beliefs. Considerable skill and know-how was required, particularly for the beaming*. Their authenticity and originality remained unaffected by outside influences until the mid-20th century. MD

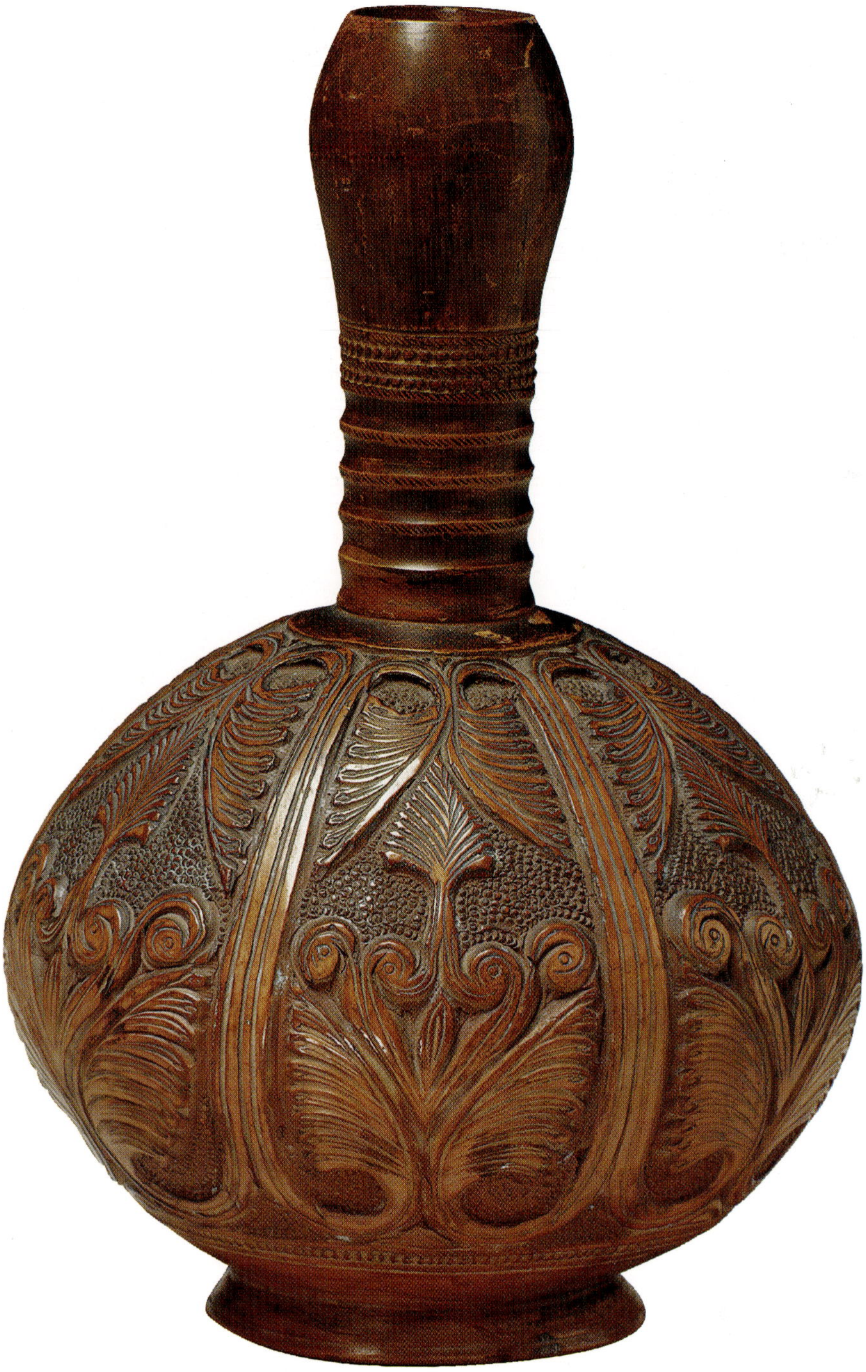

Qolal opium bottle

Ali Yunuth
Egypt, Asyut
Circa 1840
Terracotta coated in brown slip*
20.5 x 12.8 x 12.6 cm
Inv. 74.1985.4.3.1

This streamlined rather long-necked, round-bellied ceramic is sculpted in champlevé*, decorated with waves, palmettes, and flowerets in relief on an unpolished matt background* that gives it the appearance of wood.
It was used to carry medicinal opium, which was readily available throughout the Mediterranean Basin, not only as a painkiller but also for the pleasure of its smokers.
It was made by the master potter Ali Yunuth around 1840, using a technique dating back to the 3rd century BC, but which seemed to have disappeared.

This type of bottle, similar examples of which are to be found in the National Ceramics Museum in Sèvres, was manufactured in Asyut, the largest commercial crossroads in High Egypt, a city enjoying permanent relations with foreign countries and much appreciated for its textiles and opium. MD

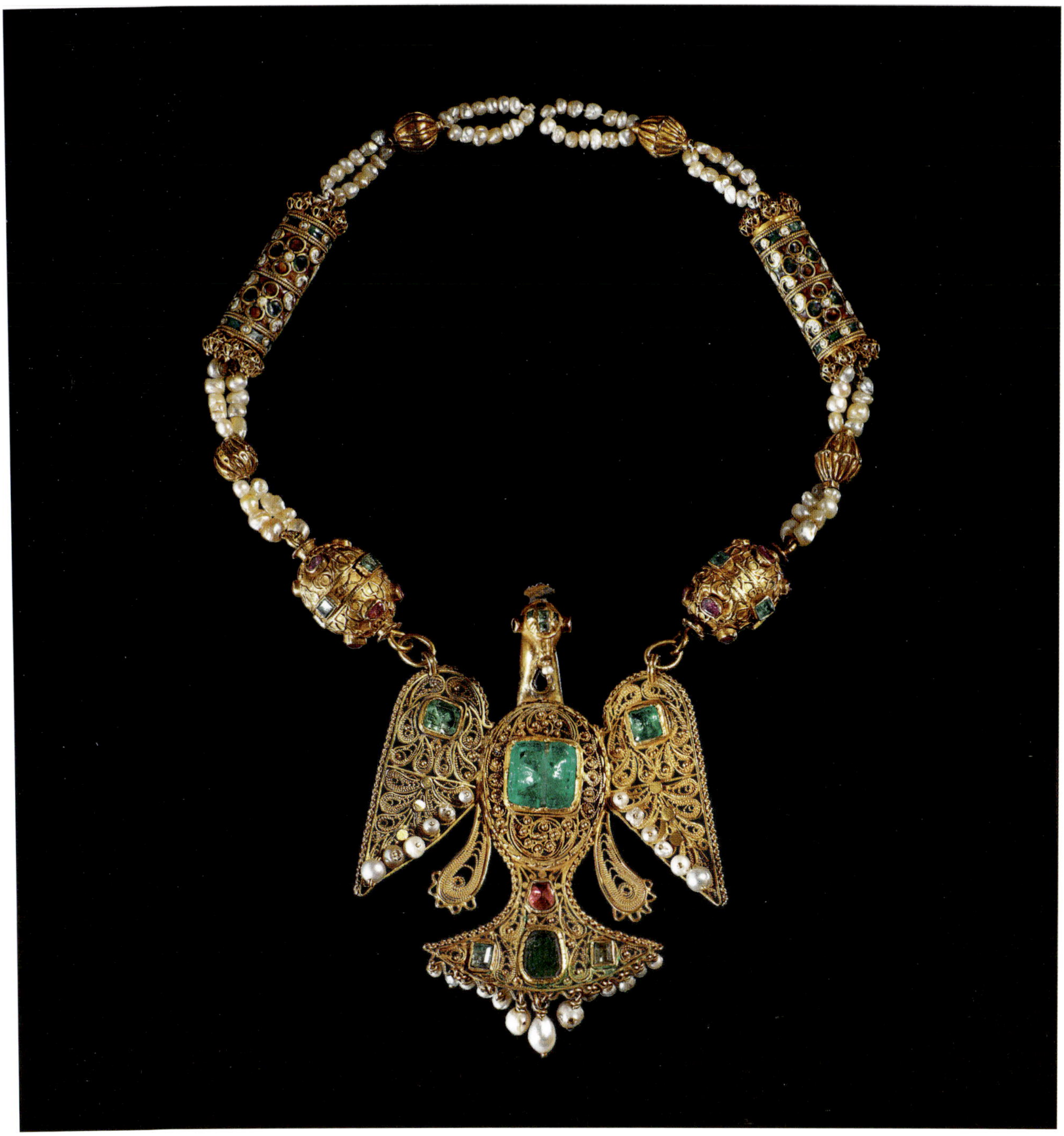

Bird necklace

Morocco, Fez
1012 H-1603 AD
Gold, emeralds, amethysts, natural pearls, enamel
40 x 8.2 x 2.9 cm
Donated by Mme Gradis-Koecklin
Inv. 74.1969.6.1.1-2

This delicately worked necklace comprising a pendant in the shape of a peacock (symbol of married bliss) is of ancient craftsmanship. The bird's head and body are embedded with emeralds, while its tail, adorned with a ruby and a sapphire, is a fan of tiny natural pearls.
This piece of jewellery evokes Andalusian goldworking in both form and technique, more specifically that of 14th and 15th century Grenada – Nasrid* necklaces in particular, with their enamelled tubular components decorated with floral motifs and patterned on the cases in which rolls of the Torah* were kept, a similarity which conferred sacred, talismanic power upon them.
The precious stones set side by side are also reminiscent of the jewellery introduced across the Muslim world by India and Turkey.
Such highly valuable adornments were mainly worn by Jewish women. Only five pieces of this kind are listed in private and public collections.
MD

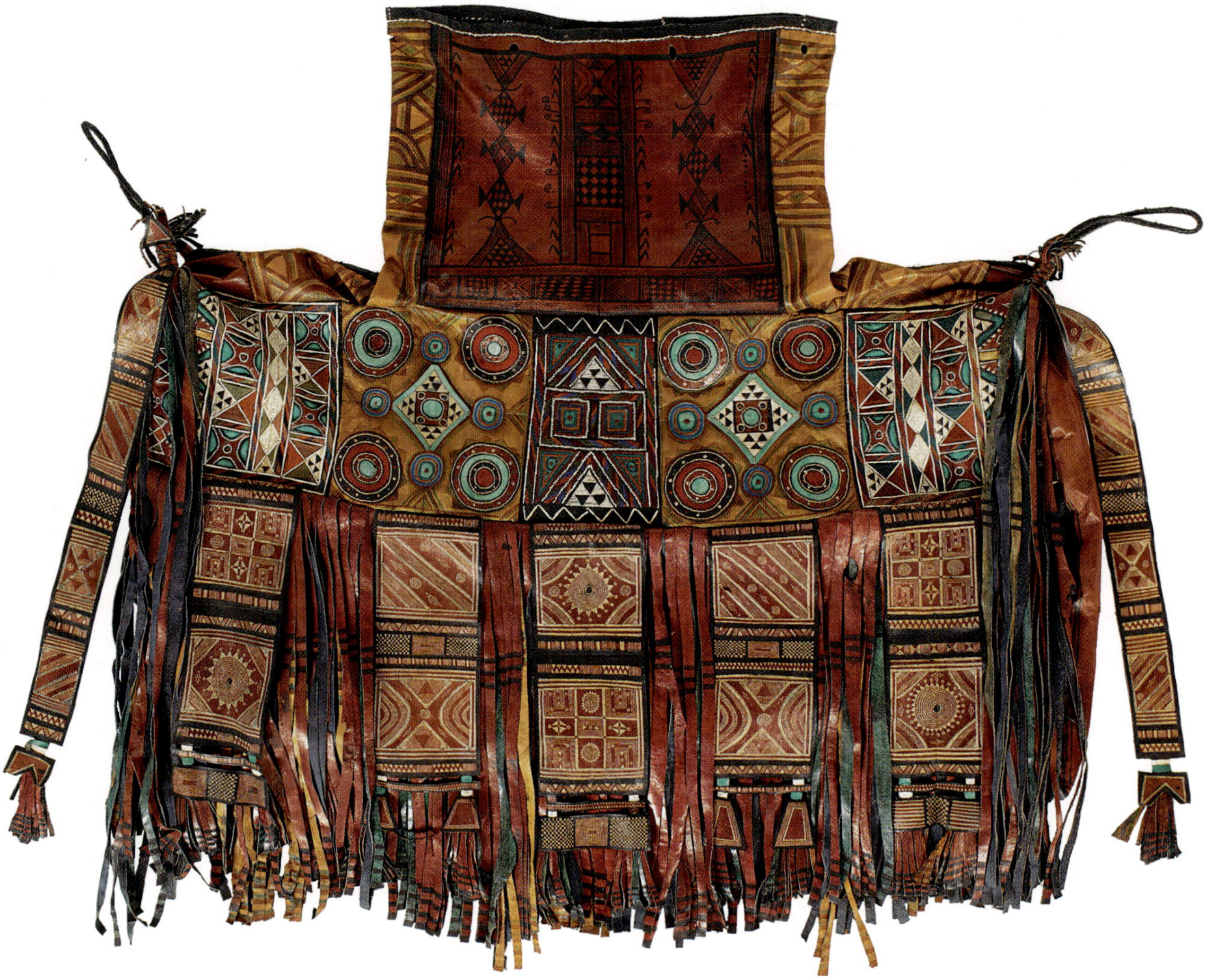

Tehaithait saddlebag

Touareg, Kel Ahaggar tribe

Algerian Sahara, Hoggar
Late 19th/
early 20th century
Leather, silk,
vegetable dyes
92 x 115 x 8 cm
Donated by
Georgette Soustelle
Inv. 71.1967.40.1

The Touareg were and partly remain nomadic stockbreeders. They live in the western and central Sahara, and in the Sahel. Of Berber origin, they are a mixed group, combining Mediterranean and African typologies.
Women enjoy a privileged position in their society. It is they who, making use of the few available resources but working in strict adherence to tradition, create the goods necessary to a life of travelling – these bags, for example, in which valuable clothing, jewellery and tea are stored, and which are carried on the side of the camel, then hung from tent pegs in the space reserved for their use.
Their preparation is a lengthy and meticulous collective operation: skins are degreased and desalted, then washed. When they are dry, they are tanned, then dyed – dyes are synthetic, giving a wider range of colours to work with – and finally glazed.
Decorative techniques are rich and varied. Red silk embroidery, for example, is the specialty of Haussa* women, who today teach it to their Touareg counterparts. Geometrical motifs have kept their prophylactic power*. MD

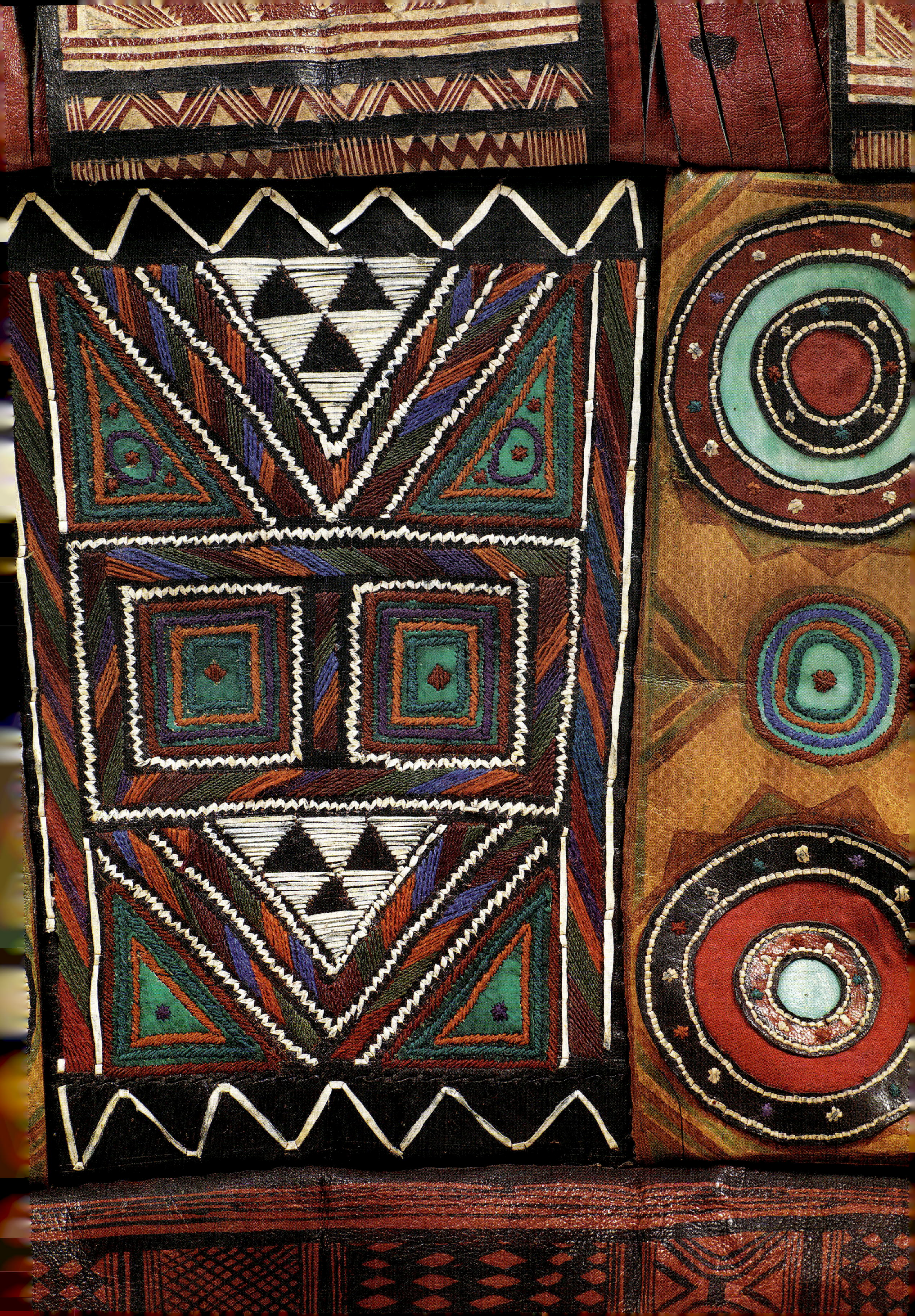

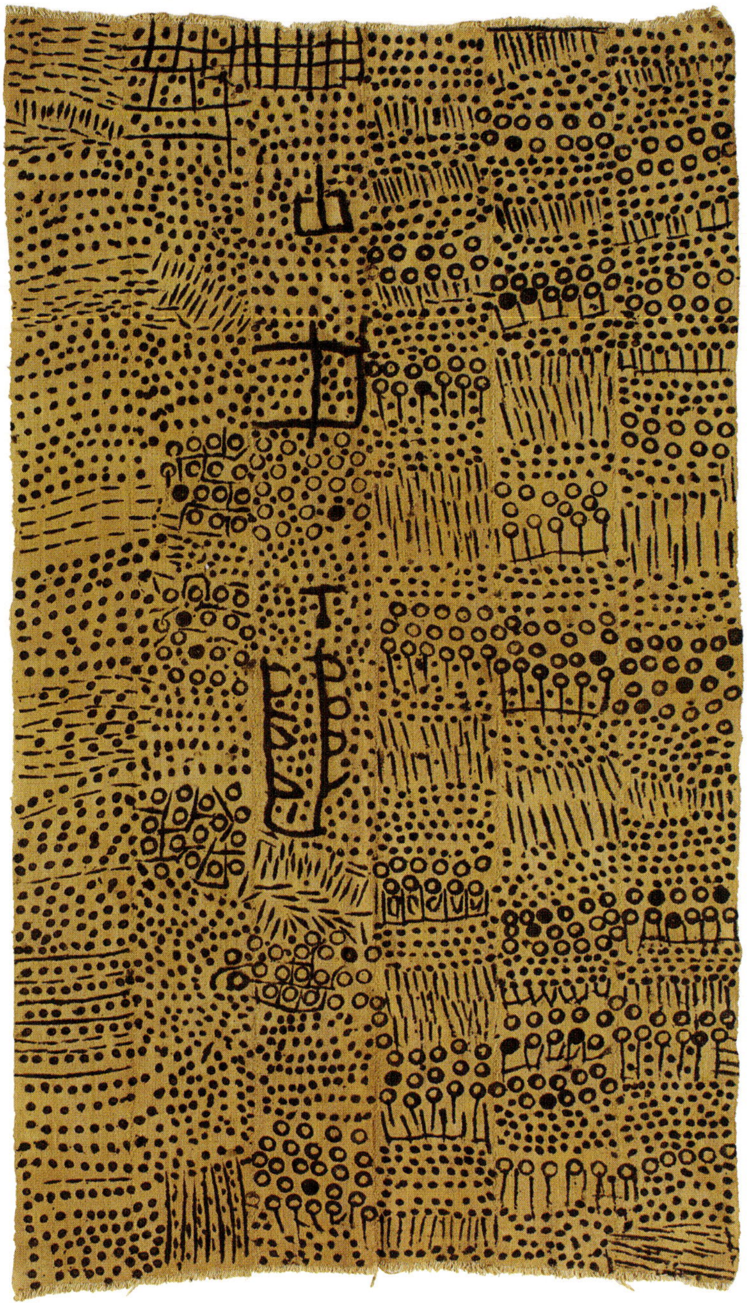

Hunting garment

Bamana

Mali, Segou region
Early 20th century
Cotton, dye,
bogolan clay
136 x 75.5 cm
Bequeathed by
François de Zeltner
Inv. 71.1930.61.908

This vintage *bogolanfini* (the term is Bamanan for "textile painted with earth") comes from southern Mali, although its light background colour and dark motifs, regularly spaced and covering the entire surface, are atypical of this region of West Africa.
This is a hunter's loincloth, made from strips of cotton hand-woven by the men and painted by the women, using a vegetable dye to produce its ochre colouring. It was long and arduous in the making. Fermented clay from backwater beds was used for the designs traced out with a metal stylet, replaced nowadays by a brush or craft stick.
The repertoire of abstract signs can be interpreted as actual writing celebrating an historical event or exalting the qualities of a man known for his bravery.
The hunter who wore it was protected from the malignant influences of the bush and the dangerous vital forces escaping from the body of the slain animal, as the fibres of the textile soaked up the blood.
This type of loincloth could also be worn by women at the religious ceremony marking their passage into adulthood. MD

Androgynous statue Djennenke style

Pre-dogon

Mali,
Bandagiara plateau,
Damagari village (?)
10th-11th centuries
Wood
191 cm
Acquired by patronage, AXA
Inv. 70.2004.12.1

Its imposing size, remarkable age and artistic qualities make this statue one of the masterpieces of world art.
The chequered scarifications on the face, similar to those found on Djenne statues in the Niger interior delta, identifies it as being in the Djennenke (literally, "those from Djenne") style. The figure seems to be an incarnation of dignity. It raises its arms to the sky, either in prayer for rain or in the gesture of apology common among the Tellem*, then the Dogon, in both statuary and mythology.
Its many necklaces and regal expression are evidence of high social status. It has the face of a chief of long lineage or a great king, as evidenced by the beard and the small chignon adorned with ribbons. The bust, however, is a woman's, with heavy breasts symbolic of the nourishing mother. Two figures are sculpted in rounded relief* upon the stomach, possibly representing twin foetuses.
These two principles, male and female, are attested by the seven wrist bracelets: the number of perfect union. MD

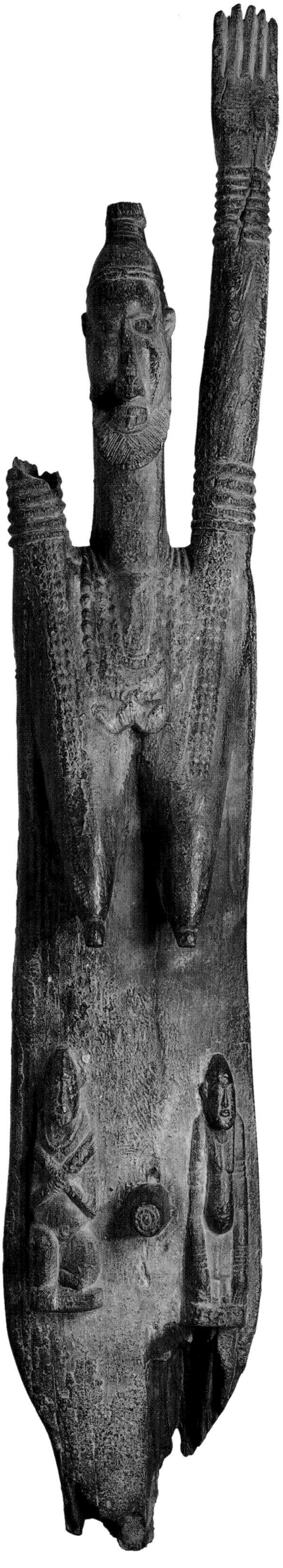

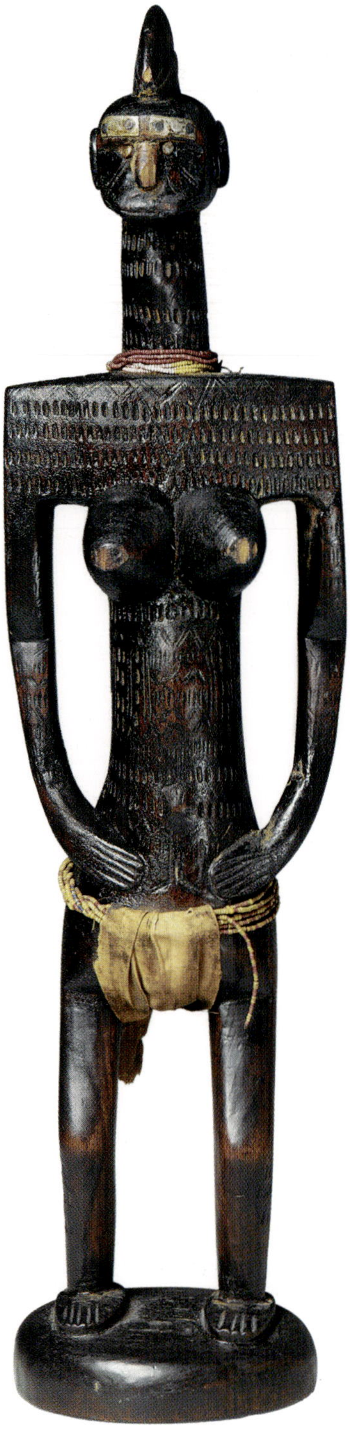

Jonyeleni female statue

Bamana

Mali,
Bougouni
or Sikasso region
Early 20th century
Wood, cotton, pearls, string
64 x 15 x 12 cm
Donated by
Georges Henri Rivière
Inv. 71.1935.16.1

Among the Bamana* of West Africa, initiation societies were responsible for acquisition of knowledge throughout a lifetime. One such society was the *jo*, a seven-year initiation cycle, characterising an ideal society of order and structure.

Jonyeleni figurines – the term can be literally translated as "beautiful young *jo* women" – are associated with this society. They reproduce an aesthetic ideal of female beauty, and are put on view during ritual ceremonies. Young initiates travel with these sculptures, broadcasting their newly acquired adult status and their desire for marriage.

This *jonyeleni* statue is remarkable for its size, sharply defined geometry, pearl adornments, crested hairstyle, tubular neck and tattoos, which are marks of beauty likely to attract widespread attention and admiration. Scarifications provide information on age group, social status and stage of initiation. MD

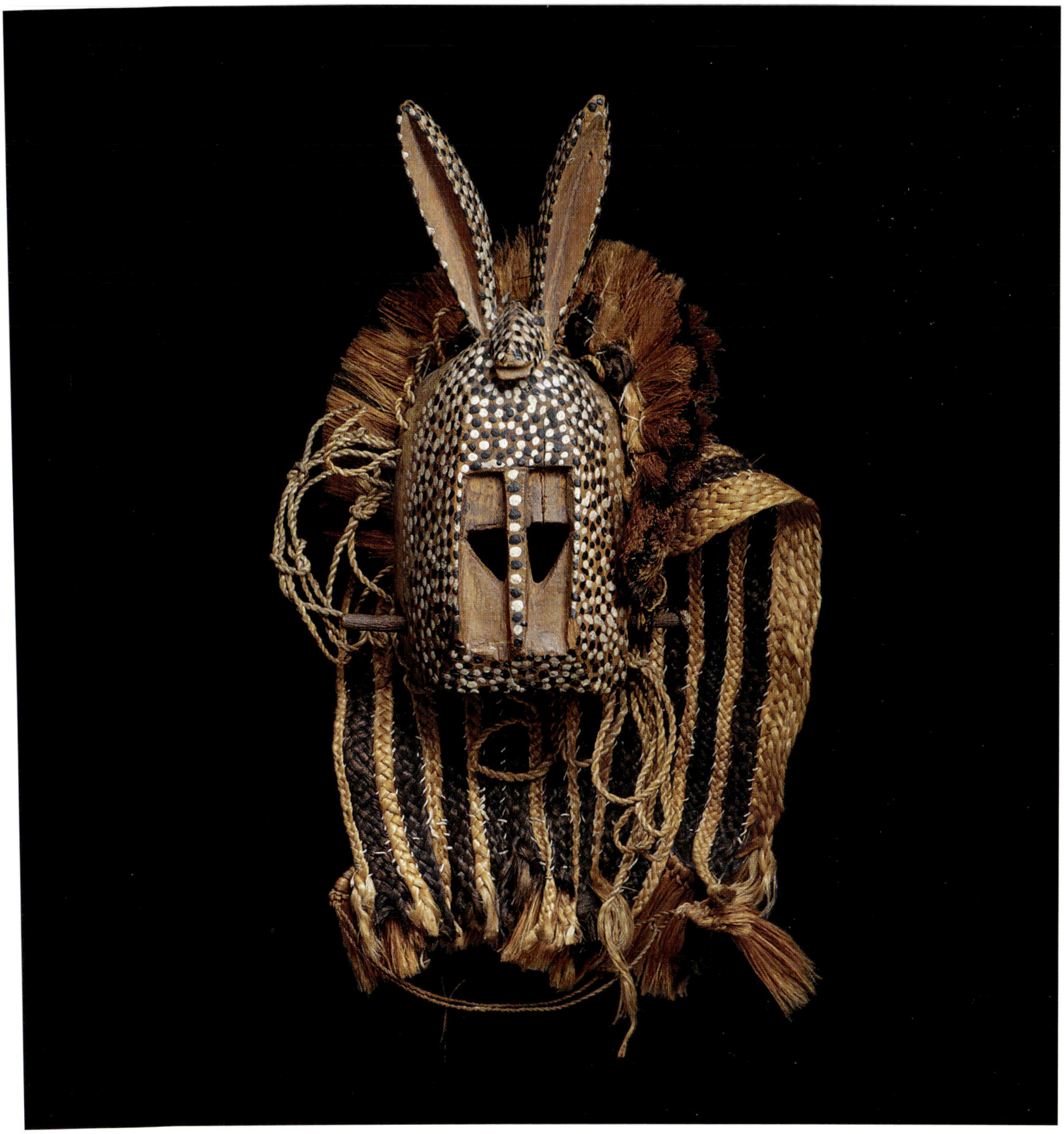

Hare mask

Dogon

Mali,
Bandiagara region
Early 20th century
Kapok wood, pigments, vegetable fibres
54 x 35 x 11 cm
Donated by Georges Henri Rivière
Inv. 71.1931.49.28

Since the 1930s, through the impetus of Marcel Griaule*, Mali's Dogon culture has been a focus of interest for French ethnological research.
A huge variety of masks exists in the cosmogonic vision of the Dogon, who thus sought to represent the world in its entirety. These artefacts are characterized by their geometric form and the three colours in which they are painted: black, white and red.
This sculpture was made by a member of the *awa*, the mask society of which all circumcised men were members. It was carved outside the village itself, well out of sight of women and children, and would have been discarded in a secret spot when it was judged to be too old or in too poor a condition to be used. It was worn at funerals, and end-of-mourning ceremonies* known as *dama*.
The dancer, usually a young initiate, head and neck completely covered by this hare mask, would mime the hunted animal, then finish by collapsing on the ground. The movements of the dance would be dictated by the accompanying song. The dance told the story of a myth according to which a hunter, whose dog had caught a hare, carved a wooden effigy of the animal before killing and eating it. MD

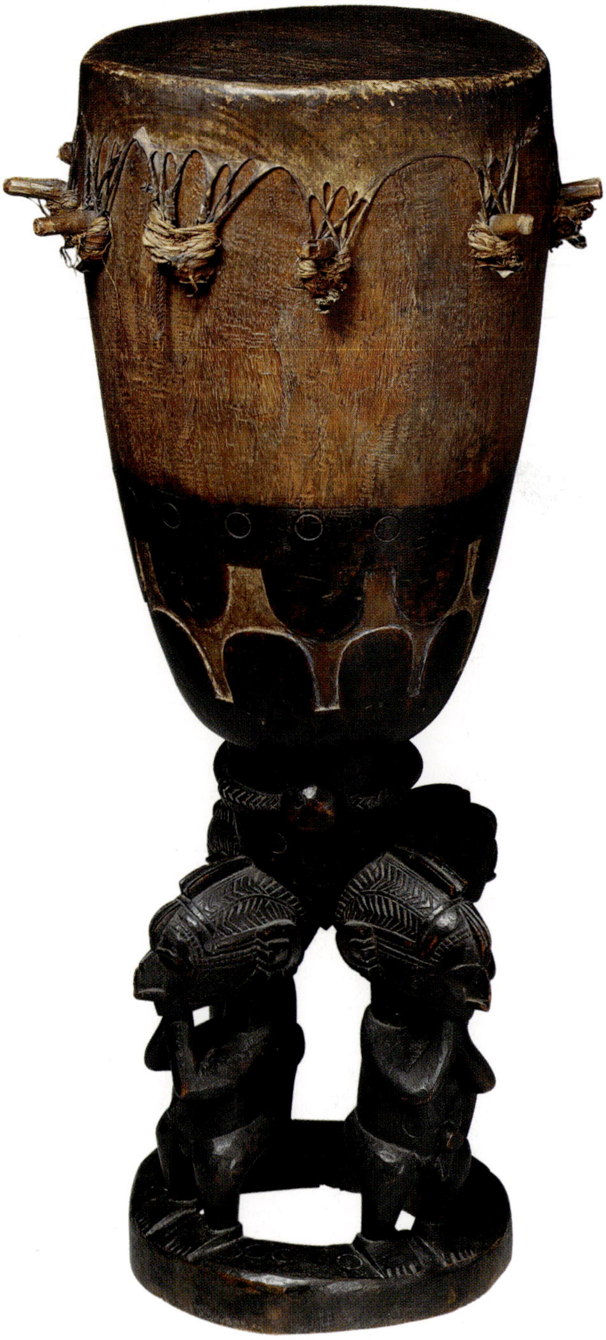

Timba single-skin drum on caryatid

Baga

Guinea,
Rio Nunez lowlands
Late 19th/
early 20th century
Wood, skin, pigments
120.2 x 49.5 x 49.5 cm
Donated by A. Chevrier
Inv. 71.1928.26.1

The Baga are made up of a number of groups scattered all along the Guinea coastline.
These skin drums, known as *timba*, were played at wedding or funeral ceremonies, where they symbolically reproduced the voices of the dead, but were associated above all with initiation rites, which generally took place at night.
Such drums were large in size – some as tall as 1.7 meters in height – and the musician, always male, often had to stand on a stool to be able to play them, which he did with a pair of wooden drumsticks.
This antique caryatid* drum comes from the Rio Nunez lowlands. It is supported by four figures, similar in style to *d'mba* shoulder masks. Two are male and two are female, an image of completeness also referring to procreation, and all stand with chin raised, drawing attention to the mouth and consequently to the importance of speech.
The instrument's elegant beauty is enhanced by its dual colouring, which highlights the purity of the whole. MD

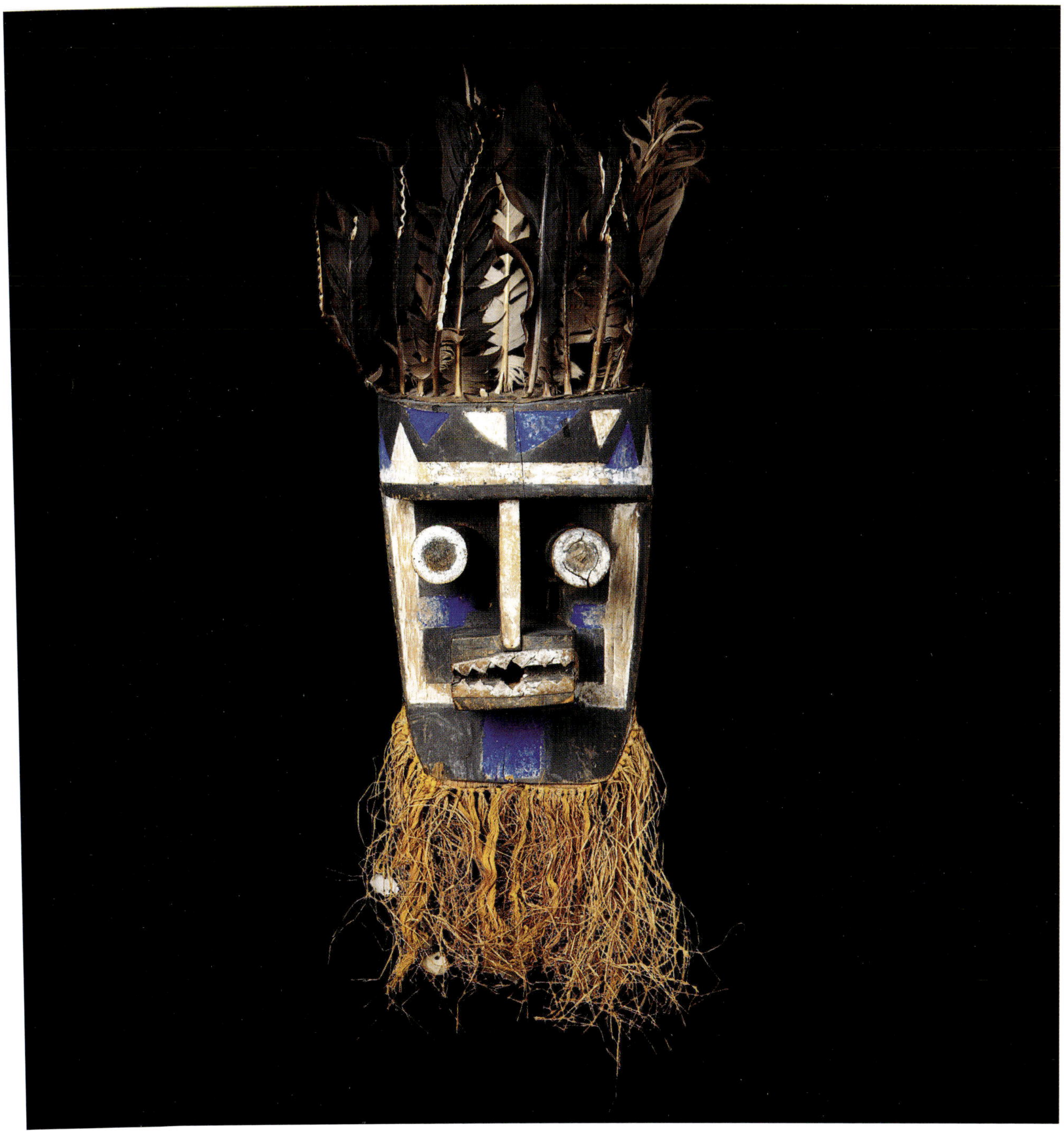

Anthropomorphic mask

Krou

Ivory Coast, Sassandra region
Late 19th century
Wood, pigments, feathers, straw, cotton, shells
68 x 20 x 17.5 cm
Donated by the Ivory Coast Committee, Universal Exhibition of 1900
Inv. 71.1900.44.103

Divided into clans, the Kru inhabit the southwestern coastal region of the Ivory Coast. Geographically and typologically, they resemble the Grebo*, with whom they have often been compared.

This surprisingly modern-looking mask might well have represented a forest spirit from the invisible world. It is remarkable for its polychromy, with colours obtained from kaolin, coal extract and, most important, blue from imported lye, which was put to this somewhat unusual use. Its fibre beard and feather crown are the attributes of a chief.

Artefacts of this kind were commonly found in both public and private collections in Europe in the first decade of the 20th century, and partly contributed to providing answers to artists in search of new artistic forms. The grouping together of disparate elements, along with an almost cubist geometric approach to volume, attracted the attention of Pablo Picasso who, before 1912, had two Grebo masks in his studio. They acted as inspiration for his *Guitar* sculpture (New York, Museum of Modern Art), in which there is the same use of superimposing and interplay of cylinders. MD

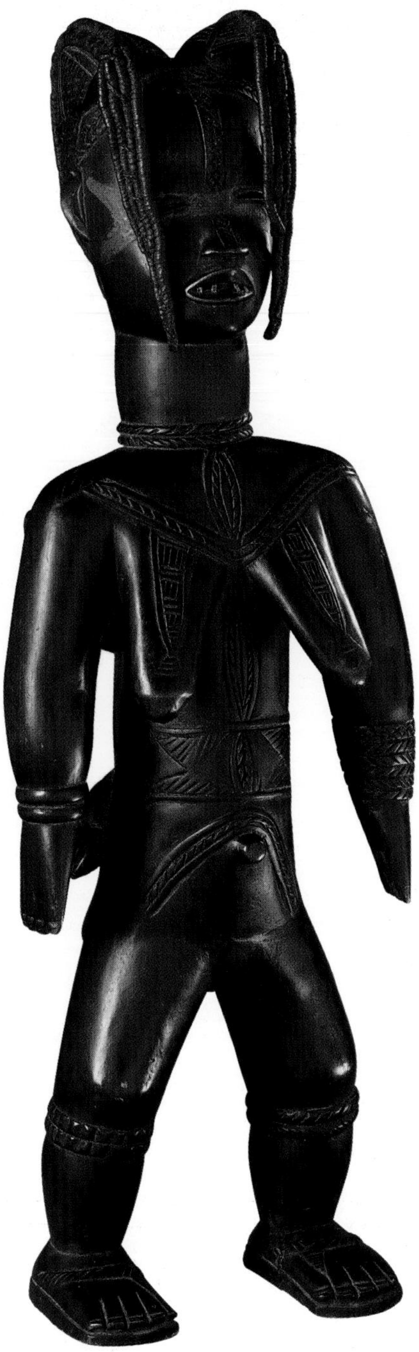

Mother and child

Dan

Work attributed
to the sculptor Zlan
(early 20th century-1960)
Ivory Coast
20th century
Wood, aluminium,
vegetable fibres,
pigments
63.5 x 20.3 x 16.6 cm
Inv. 73.1963.0.163

The Dan live between northeastern Liberia and the northwest of the Ivory Coast.
Lifelike representation of the human form plays an important part in their visual arts. This is true of this mother carrying her child on her back. There exist many such effigies of deceased wives and mothers, commissioned by their husbands to keep their memories alive and increase their prestige, all displaying the same characteristic traits: rounded arms and legs, bracelets and necklaces, chief's sandals, scarifications on the chest and stomach, lips parted to show metal teeth, eyes underlined with the white kaolin paint worn by initiated women, rounded forehead, and complicated double-looped hairstyle on a vegetable fibre wig.
This statue, with its beautiful black sheen, possessed spiritual power to bestow fertility. It is attributed to a We* artist by the name of Zlan, whose work was discovered in the 1960s. His name refers to the first sculptor who, according to Dan mythology, carved the universe. MD

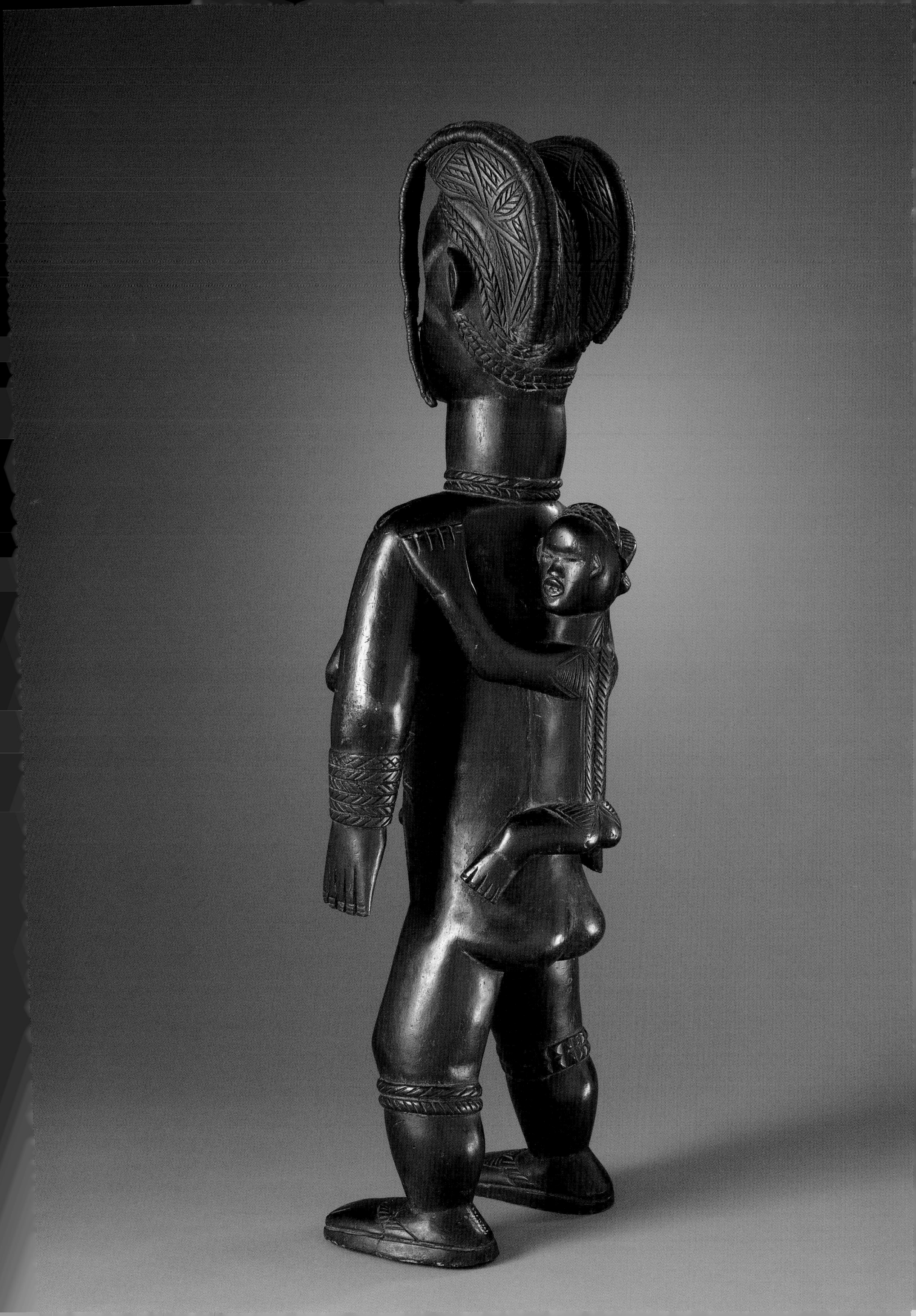

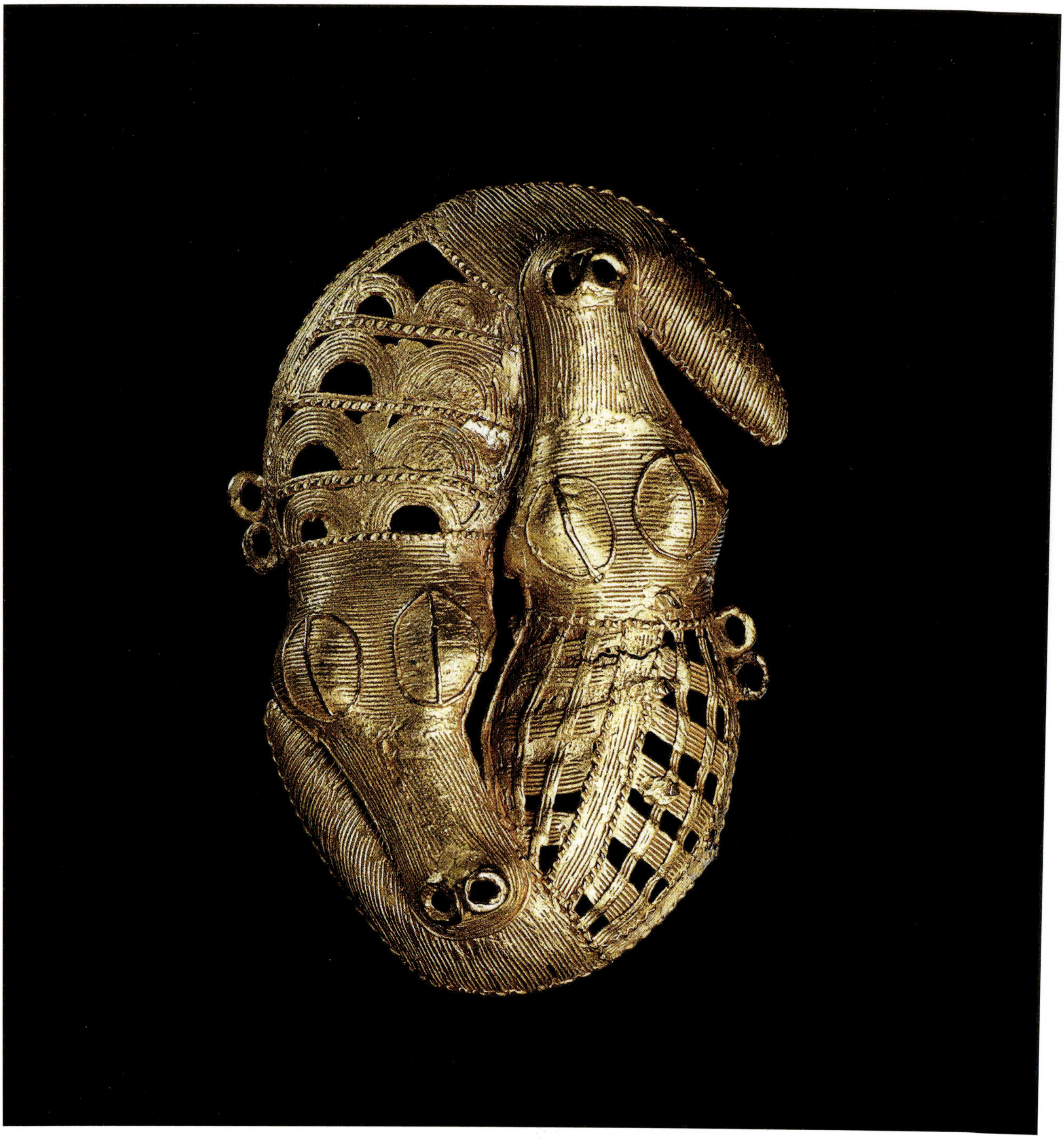

Ornamental two-crocodile brooch

Baule

Ivory Coast
19th/ early 20th century
Gold, cast using
the lost-wax technique
6.7 x 9.8 x 1.7 cm
Former collection
Roger Bédiat
Inv. 73.1966.9.2

Originally from Ghana, a region long known to European travellers as the "Gold Coast", the Baule belong to the Akan peoples. In the 18th century, they migrated to inland areas of the Ivory Coast.

They would have learned lost-wax casting from the Mande* peoples of Mali and Guinea. The process creates original pieces, as the mould is broken after use. The technique has survived, as can be seen from this delicately worked piece of jewellery. Gold, however, is not only used for adornment, but is also considered to be living matter, endowed with a soul and possessing spiritual power.

Stitched onto a headdress or bonnet, or woven directly into the hair, such artefacts, originally of abstract design, began to employ figurative motifs over the course of time, while preserving their magical protective properties.

The crocodile, a strong, fast-moving animal feared for its power, represented as it is here with its twin, head to tail, symbolizes twins as an ideal of completeness and perfection. It could also seal clan or family solidarity or, worn by the monarch, act as a sign of royal authority. MD

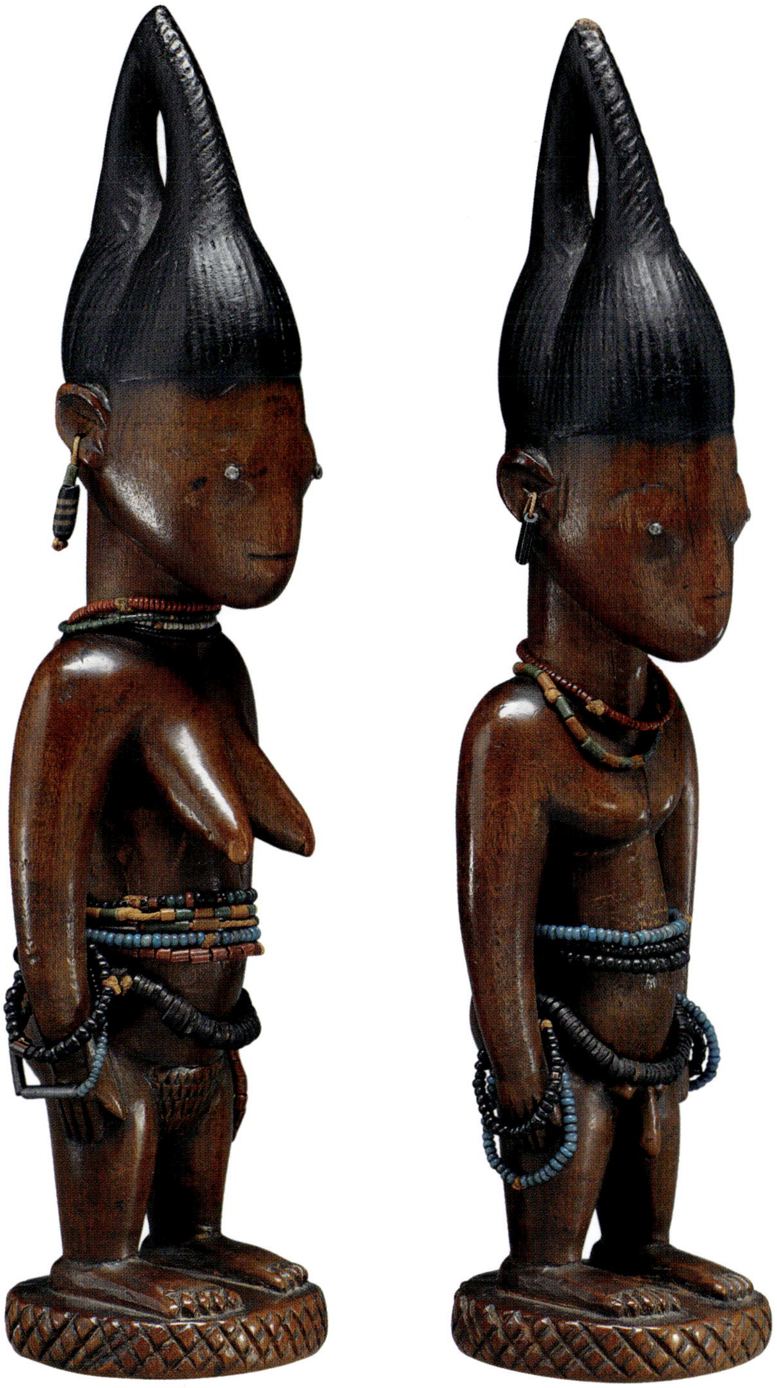

Ibeji pair of twins

Yoruba

Nigeria, town of Shaki
Early 19th century
Wood, pearls, and metal
29 x 7.5 x 6.2 cm
Former collections
Behanzin;
Charles Ratton;
Georges de Miré;
Louis Carré;
Hubert Goldet
Donation
Inv. 70.2003.3.7.1-2

This pair of elaborately coiffed gold figurines was made in Nigeria, in northwestern Yoruba country, but ended up as part of the personal treasure of the Fon of Abomey* (now Benin), King Behanzin*. He was deposed in 1894, and they were absorbed into major French collections.
The cult of the twins, powerful divine beings, spread throughout the west coast, from Togo to southwestern Nigeria, in the first half of the 19th century. Up until that time, twins were feared and put to death, but in 1820 a royal decree forbade killing them, and henceforth they were honoured by their families, with twin births bringing the prospect of enrichment and a rise in status. The death of one twin was therefore always feared, as it might endanger a clan's harmony. *Ibeji* statuettes (in Yoruban, *bi* means "born" and *meji* "two") are the cult's material support, and much care is lavished upon them. They are adorned, washed, cherished, coated with palm oil and, when deaths occur, continue to protect the families concerned. MD

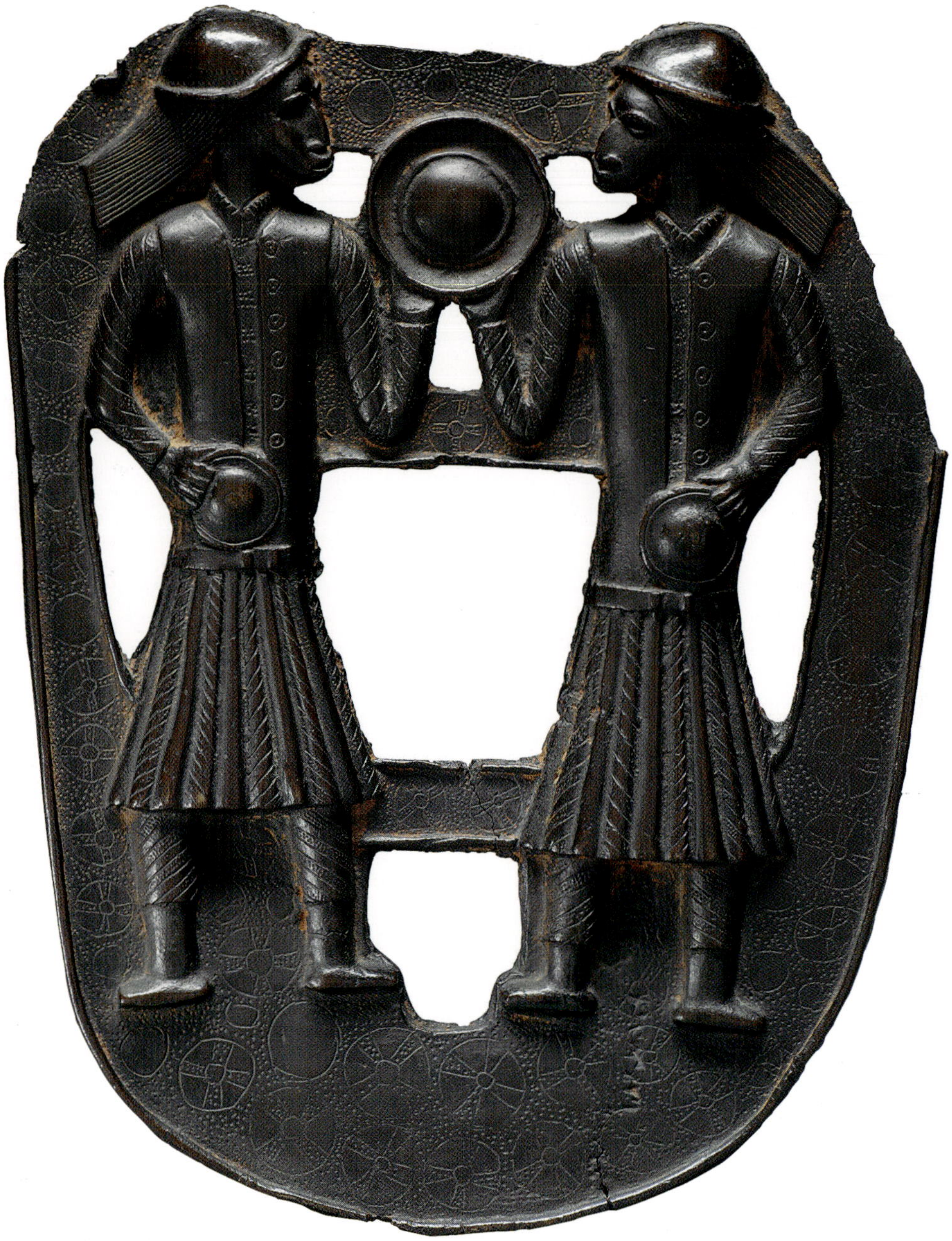

Bas-relief representing two Portuguese warriors

Edo

Work attributed
to the Master
of the Circled Cross
Nigeria,
Kingdom of Benin
16th century
Brass
39 x 29 x 5.3 cm
Inv. 70.2002.4.1

The Portuguese started trading with the Kingdom of Benin at the end of the 15th century, usually exchanging copper for slaves. This contact led to a period of intensive production of two-dimensional metal works of art, brass plaques, supposedly bronze but actually composed of a zinc and copper alloy.

Within the palace, they served decorative and commemorative purposes. The King of Benin, the *oba*, was regularly represented in royal apparel. Courtiers and animals were sometimes featured and, less frequently – although such is the case here – Portuguese sailors, recognizable by their long hair, helmets and pleated skirts. The work is atypical in other ways: its openwork circular form is unusual, as is the shallowness of the relief, and profile rather than full-face depiction is also rare. Only the symmetry of the design conforms to tradition in this piece dating from the earliest contacts with Westerners. MD

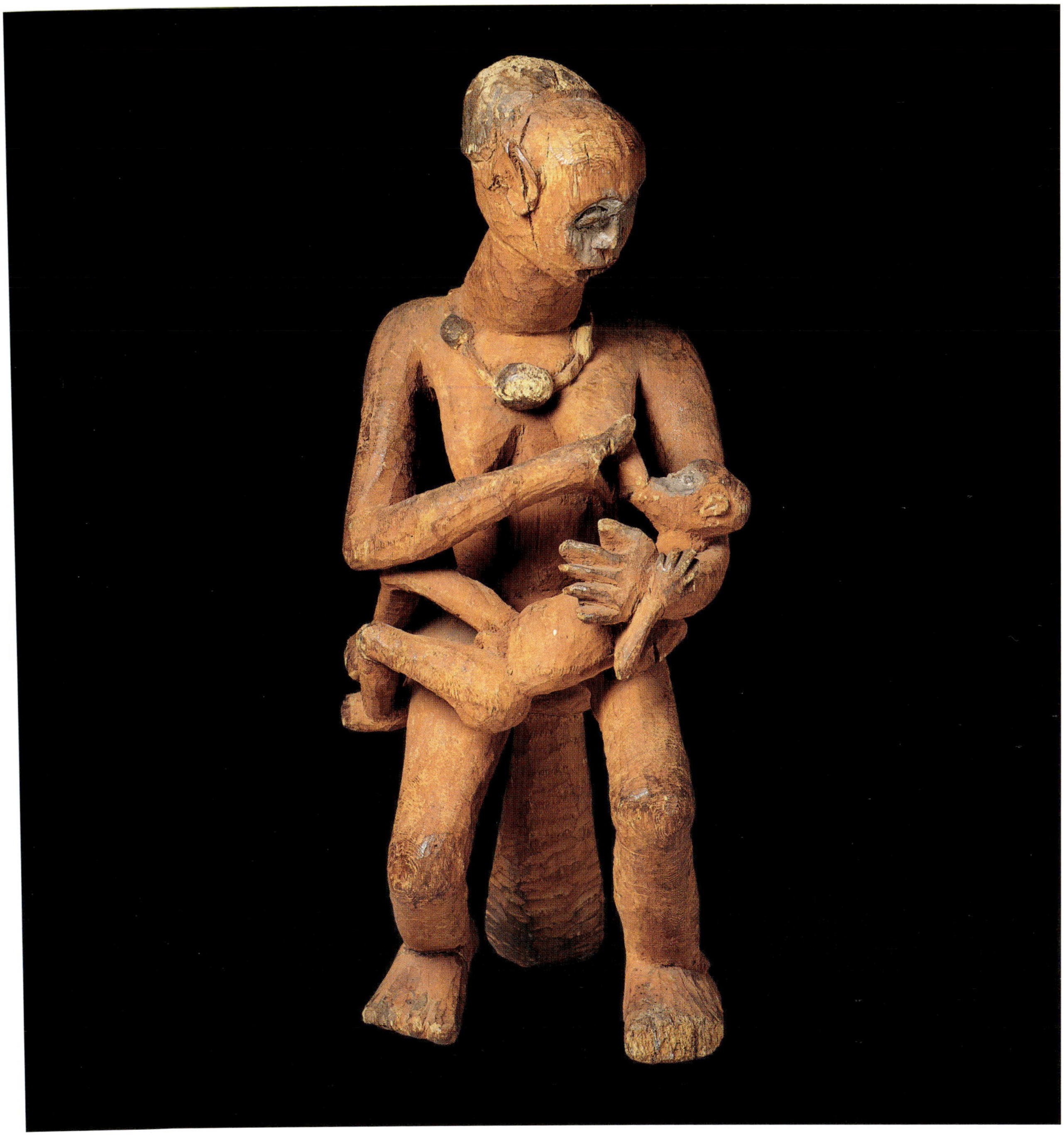

Mother and child

Bamileke

Work attributed
to the sculptor Kwayep
Cameroon
Circa 1912
Wood, pigments
61 x 24.9 x 35.3 cm
Henri Labouret Mission,
1932
Inv. 71.1934.171.607

The term "bamileke" refers to the native peoples of the Cameroon grassland*, whose society is organized into a multitude of chiefdoms.
As a collective symbol celebrating the power of the deified king, the *fo*, and of initiates, art forms an integral part of beliefs. It is the very core of the royal treasure, a vast collection of artefacts with which the powerful surround themselves, including commemorative statues such as this queen and her son, whose birth was honoured by its creation.
An emblem of fertility and survival of the royal line, the woman depicted here, gazing down at her child, is also an image of loving tenderness. Such an attitude is rarely seen in African mother-and-child images. Traces of makeup are apparent on her face, evoking enthronement* rites, and she wears a headdress emphasizing her eminent position in the Kingdom.
The statue's spatial characteristics are highly original, and the strength evident in its subject's gaze shows how much care the artist, Kwayep, put into its creation. MD

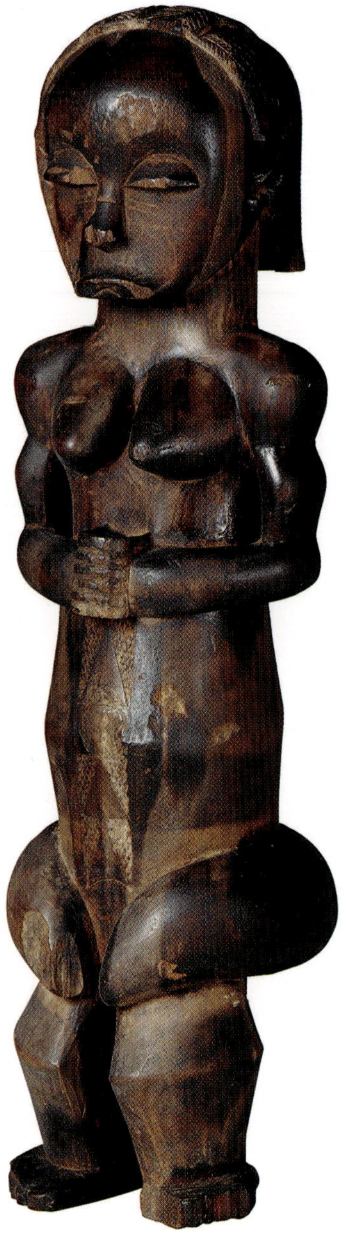

Eyima byeri reliquary guardian

Fang

Gabon
19th century
Wood
56 x 15.9 x 14.5 cm
Former collection
Paul Guillaume
Donated by
Mme Paul Guillaume
Inv. 71.1941.13.16

Scattered across Cameroon, Gabon and Equatorial Guinea, the Fang are famed for the vast amount of art they produce. Their works, much sought after by collectors, have been available in Europe since the second half of the 19th century.

Byeri, the name given to such reliquary figures, refers both to the statuettes themselves and to the contents of the tree-bark boxes upon which they stand – the cleaned and sometimes painted bones of ancestors. These are kept safe by the head of each family, although a single item (a tooth or phalanx, for example) might be carried by a man to ensure protection when leaving his native village.

The *byeri* is consulted in cases of sickness, conflict or sudden death, and also to forecast the outcome of hunting or fishing expeditions. The skull and other parts of the skeleton are brought out and sprinkled with the blood of sacrificed animals, and the statuettes guarding the reliquaries are coated with palm oil to purify the wood and foster the figure's powers of intercession with the ancestors. Often fully preserved and highly stylized, as is the case here, they are carved from light-coloured, lightweight woods and then coated to give them the traditional dark, gleaming patina. Only initiates may attend such rituals. MD

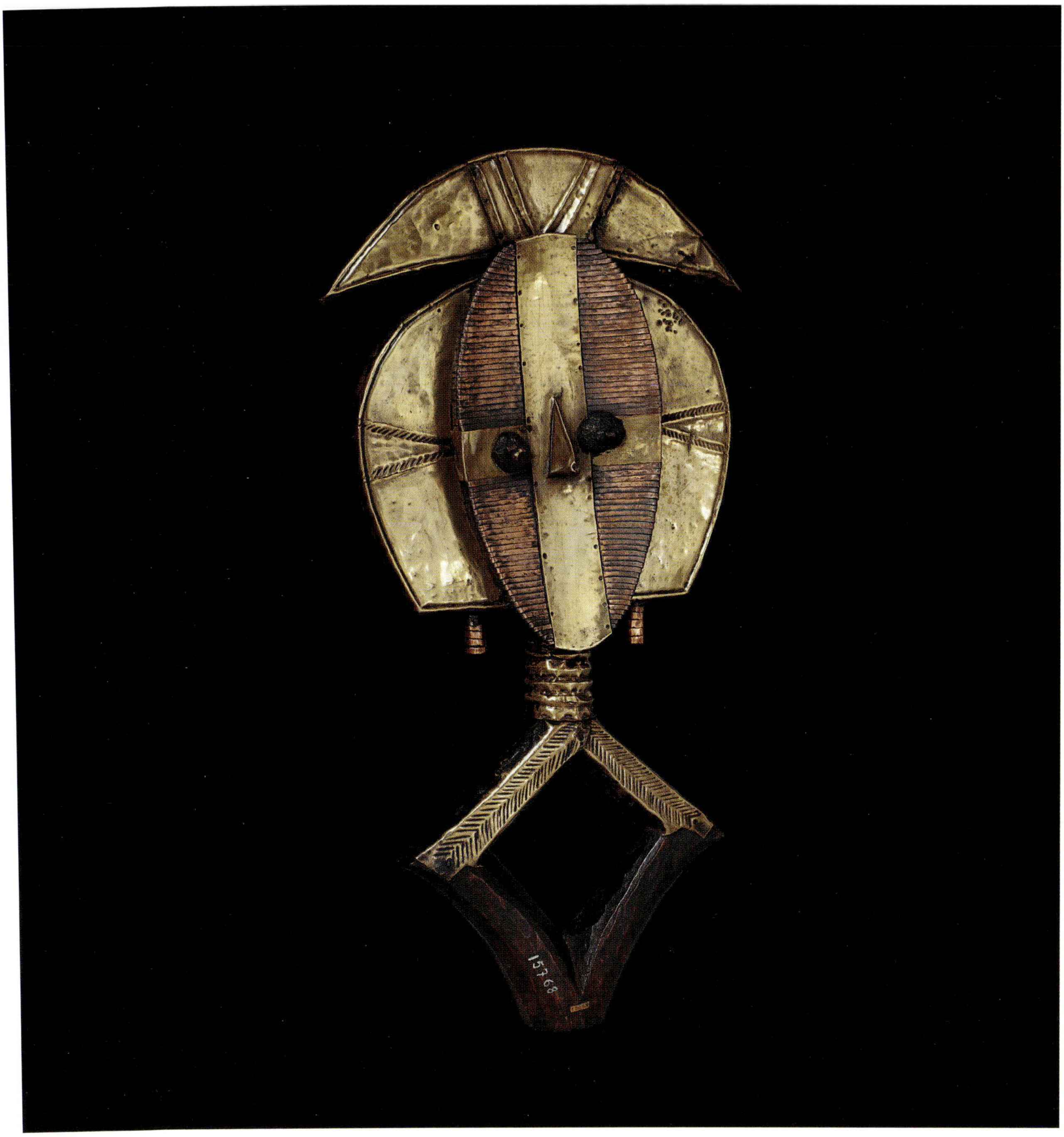

Ngulu reliquary guardian

Kota

Gabon,
Haut-Ogooué region
19th century
Wood, brass, copper
63.6 x 29.5 x 11.6 cm
Donated by Jacques Savorgnan de Brazza and Attilio Pecile
Inv. 71.1886.79.4

The Kota of eastern Gabon practise the ancestor cult *bwete* – ancestors who are feared but whose protection is also sought.
After the death of an illustrious member of the community, his bones are cleaned and carefully preserved in a woven fibre basket placed beneath a flat wooden core* covered with brass and copper plates and wires – the stylized effigy of a human figure, the *ngulu*, guardian of the reliquary. The jutting nose throws the two studs of its eyes into relief and, beneath the head, a shimmering metal lozenge used to fix the sculpture to the basket, and doubtless also serving as a handle, forms a rudimentary body.
During initiation rites presided over by the family priest, the relics are nourished with sacrificial blood and presented with food that is later consumed by the living.
The sculptures themselves are rubbed with sand to keep their sheen before being brandished by the men in their ritual dances. Women, children and outsiders are forbidden to view these sacred ceremonies, which are only open to initiates.
MD

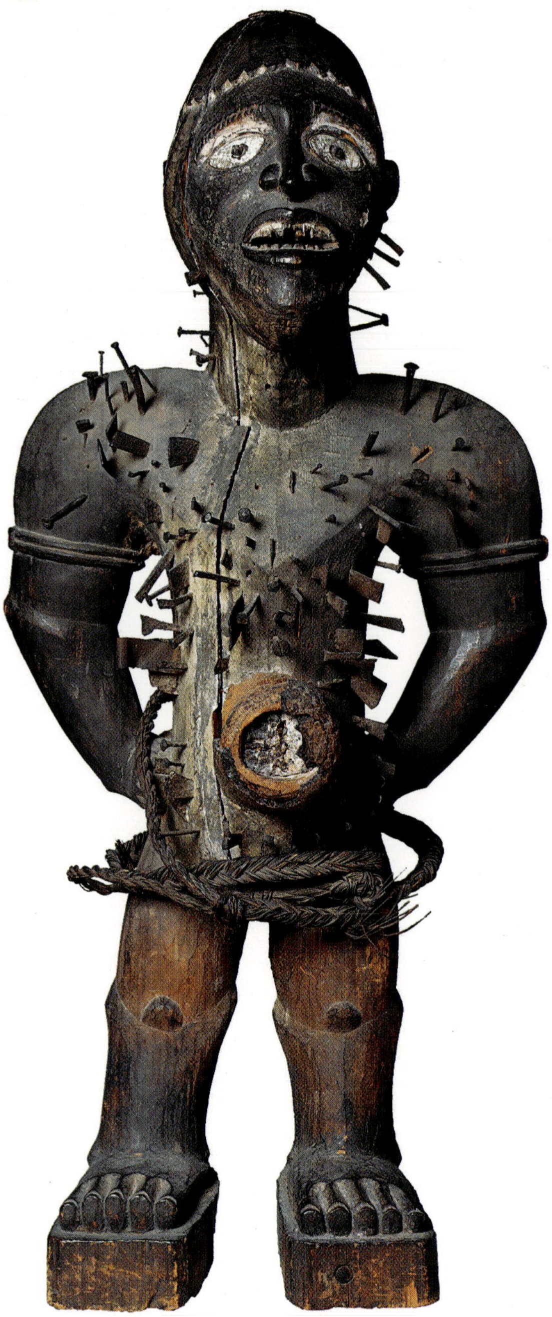

Nkisi nkondi statue

Vili

Work attributed
to the Master
of the Chiloango River
Angola
Late 19th/
early 20th century
Wood, iron, pigments,
cord, enamelled sheet
metal, resin, clay,
organic matter
110 x 50 x 32 cm
Donated by M. Lang,
1935
Inv. 73.1963.0.175

Living around the mouth of the River Zaire, the Kongo people believe in an invisible world peopled by spirits, *nkisi*, with supernatural powers, which can choose to help human beings, or be prevented from doing so.
Statuettes, which are the repositories and receptacles of such powers, bear the same name. They contain a "magical charge" in the navel, concealed by a piece of mirror or shell which are more important than the sculpture itself. This "charge" is composed of white clay, earth – associated with the world of the dead – leaves, blood, hair and various natural substances consecrated by the priest, the *nganga*. It is he who, acting as intermediary, uses dances, songs and ritual artefacts such as whistles and bells to ensure that the magic works.
Nkonde statues of men or dogs are larger in size and for collective use. These "nail fetishes" may be consulted by the community as a whole. The nails embedded in the wood by the *nganga* put their symbolic powers into effect with each appeal made to him. Besides their curative properties, such artefacts are used to bind agreements or seek out guilty parties. MD

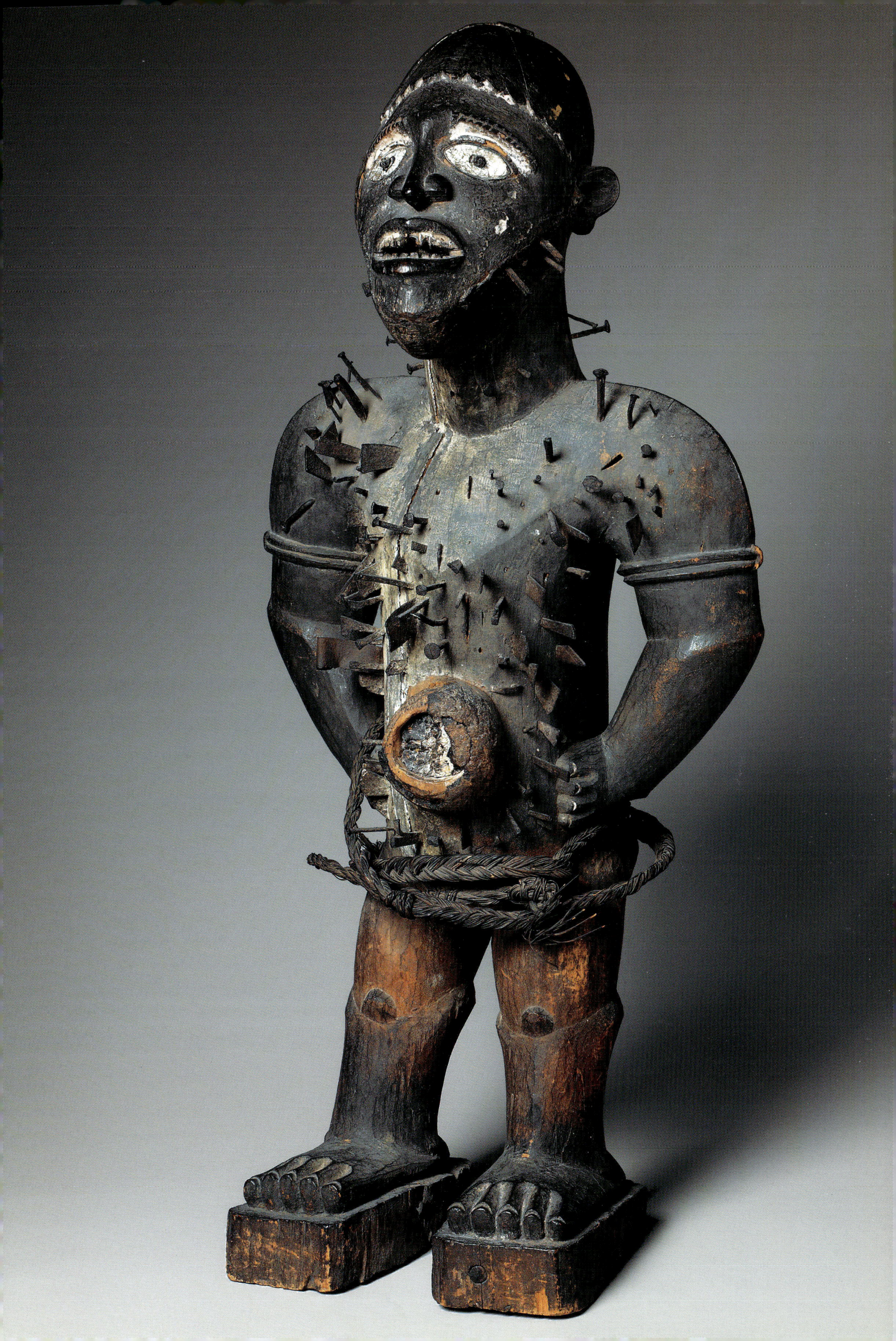

The Arts and Civilizations of Africa, Asia, Oceania and the Americas

The world's largest and most highly populated continent, Asia is a plurality, a human mosaic where almost two thousand living languages are spoken today. The Asia collections date from the late 19th and above all, from the 20th century, and are a memory of this too often forgotten multitude of peoples. Complementary to the Louvre and Musée Guimet collections, which focus on the past, they shed light upon contemporary societies, presenting a very different world from the nostalgic view of an exotic and backward-looking Asia. These objects testify to contacts between cultures, to exchanges, influences and transformations over the course of time – for these peoples have not remained trapped within traditional culture, beyond the reach of history.

Composed of antique and historical items (from royal embassies, and for universal and colonial exhibitions), the earliest collections were assembled by great travellers at the turn of the 19th century: the Lapicque mission aboard the *Sémiramis* in the 1890s; Joseph Martin, who was present at a number of shamanic ceremonies in Siberia; Jacques Bacot in the Tibetan Marches, Alexandra David-Néel in Tibet; Auguste François in China and Vietnam; and the members of the "Croisière jaune" in 1931 and 1932. The missions undertaken by Bernard Dupaigne in Afghanistan, Jacques Millot in India, and Dominique Champault in the Near East enriched the collections with new items – some now unique – bearing witness to the cultures from which they originated. The richest and best-documented groups of objects were the results of extensive scientific research and put together by ethnologists in the field – among them, Georges Devereux, Jeanne Cuisinier and Georges Condominas, who produced in-depth studies on the village peoples of South-East Asia.

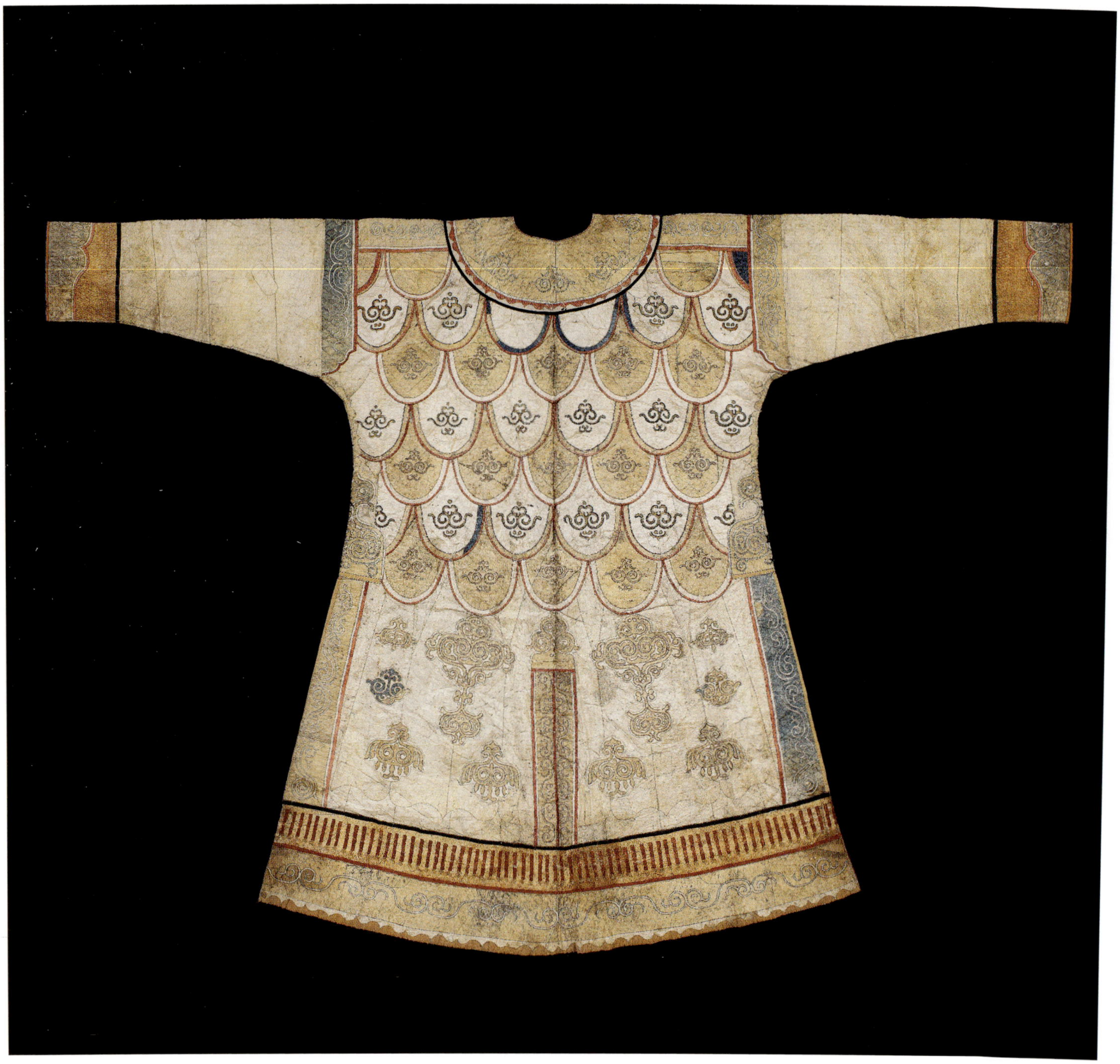

Woman's ceremonial dress

Nivkh

Russia, Far-East Siberia, Amur Basin
Late 19th/
early 20th century
Salmon skin
H. 120 cm
Georges Montandon Mission
(collected in 1919-1921)
Inv. 71.1934.15.105 D

The Nivkh, called Ghiliak in the past, live in the Russian Far East, in the Amur Basin and Sakhalin. Traditionally, they hunt marine mammals, fish for salmon and hunt in the forest to live.
This ceremonial dress made of salmon skin is cut in the style of Mongolian and Manchu dresses. It was worn by a bride on the day she left her father's home to be with her husband and could also be worn at funerals.
At bear festivals, this dress was worn during ritual dances when women mimed the movements of a bear on its hind legs. The dancers took care to display the embroidery on the back of the dress relating to bears, represented by their rolled fur in the place of honour. A particular use of this embroidery was as symbolic protection against the attack of evil spirits, and it featured various stylised animals. The upper back of the dress is made of small pieces of fish skin, arranged as scales and adorned with decorative patterns, forming a sort of armour. In the centre of the scales and on the cuffs, the Nivkh embroiderer, associated with an enchantress*, has inserted curled motifs representing bears' heads.
JLL

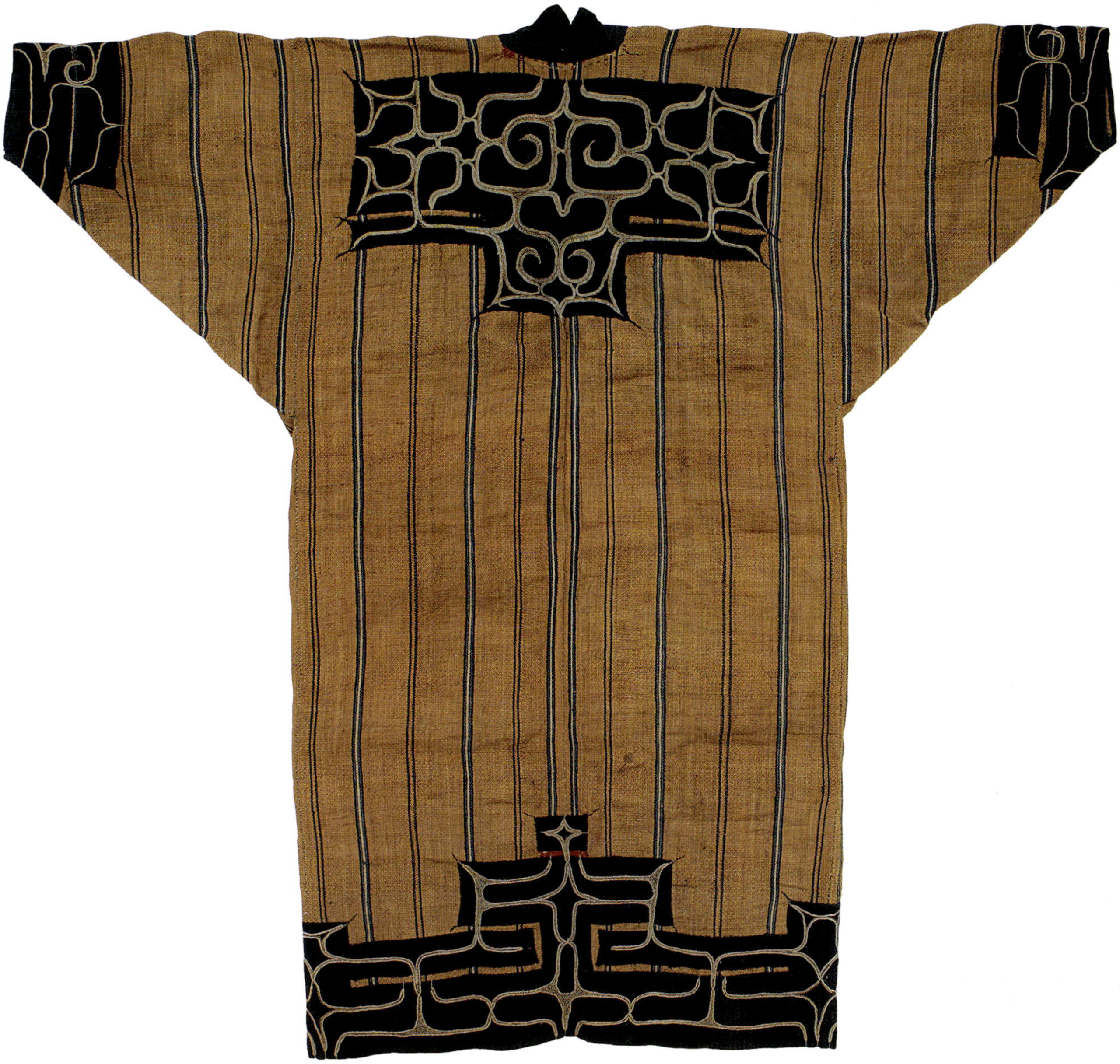

Man's dress

Ainu

Russia, Far-East Siberia, Sakhalin, Poronai Valley
Late 19th century
Elm bark phloem, cotton, striped cloth with appliqué decoration and embroidery
H. 122 cm
Donated by Paul Labbé
Inv. 71.1899.76.94

Although they now live only on the most northern island of the Japanese archipelago, Hokkaido, the Ainu also lived on other Far-East Siberian islands until the turn of the 20th century and the end of World War II.
The most exceptional item of Ainu clothing was a long coat, called an *attush*, that was kept closed by a belt. The material, cut and decoration attest to the originality of this culture and, at the same time, of contacts with Siberia, China and Japan.
As was generally the case, this coat is made of fibres from the inside layer of elm tree bark or phloem. The material produced is a brown cloth with fine indigo cotton stripes. The decoration is created from blue cotton cloth appliqué, imported from Japan, forming geometric shapes adorned with scrolled white embroidery. These stylised patterns play a protective role.
This coat was brought back at the end of the 19th century by Paul Labbé, a linguist and ethnologist who at the time was one of the leading experts on Siberia. He travelled there on numerous occasions and brought back major collections. FC

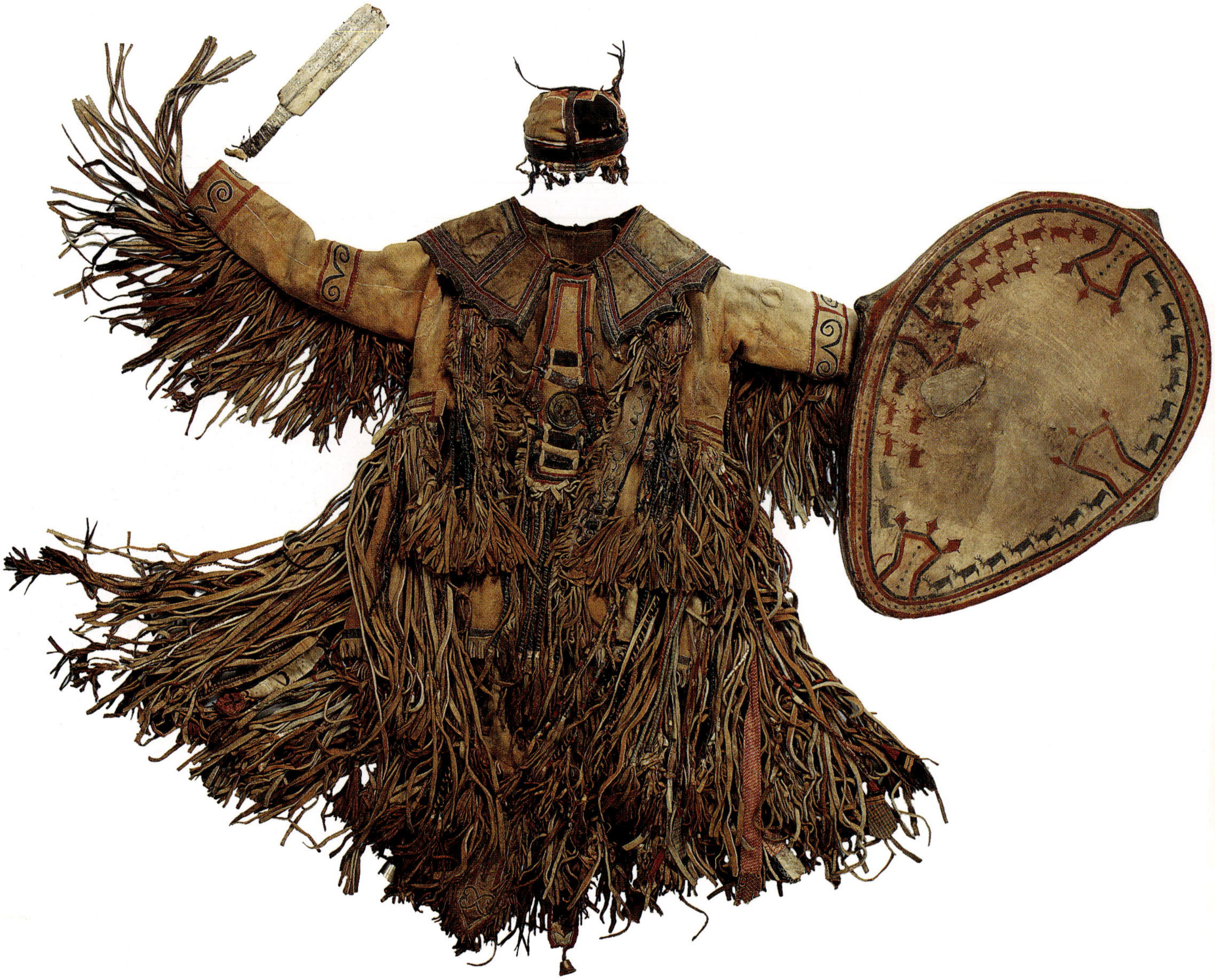

Shaman's costume

Evenk

Russia,
Eastern Siberia,
Stanovoi Mountains
19th century
Chamois leather,
metal ornaments
H. 133 cm
Donated
by Joseph Martin
Inv. 71.1887.42.1-10

The Evenk, formerly known as Tungusics, live throughout eastern Siberia. They are primarily hunters, but also breed reindeer depending on region. Their shamans are widely reputed.

The heavy dress of the Evenk shaman is richly symbolic. As a whole, it is considered as the body that the shaman is supposed to possess in order to evolve among the spirits. With the headdress dominated by metal antlers and the dress made of wild reindeer hide, it represents above all the image of a deer: the shaman was thus meant to be able to leap and, if necessary, defend himself like a reindeer using his antlers. The sleeve fringes evoke a bird's wings, the bones of which are represented by metal plates: they supposedly enable the shaman to fly. Three rows of metal accessories form a breastplate on the back of the dress, a protective symbol against evil spirits. Multiple pendants represent the numerous animal spirits – fish and aquatic birds in particular – who help the shaman during the ritual. JLL

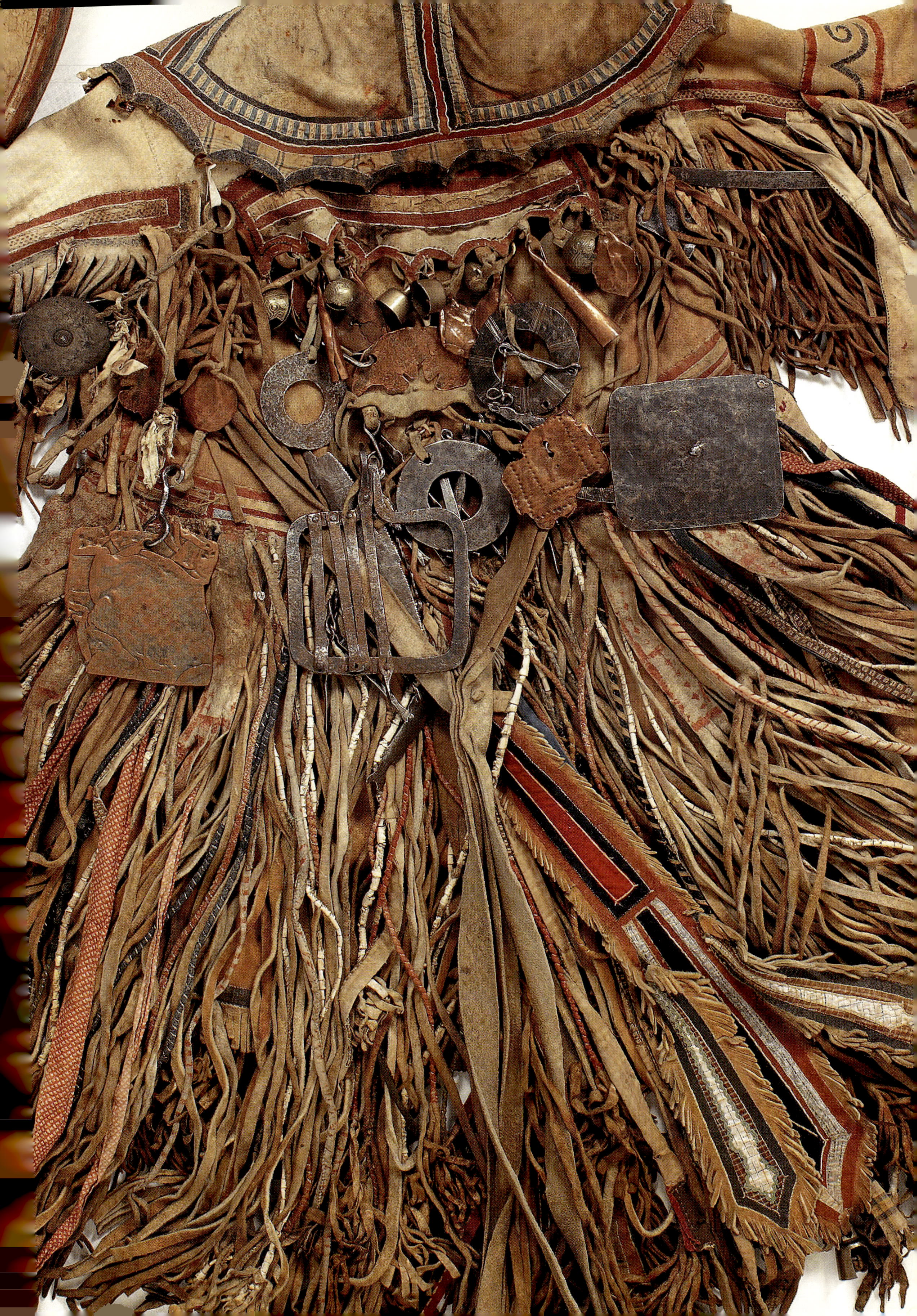

Viele and bow

Xalx

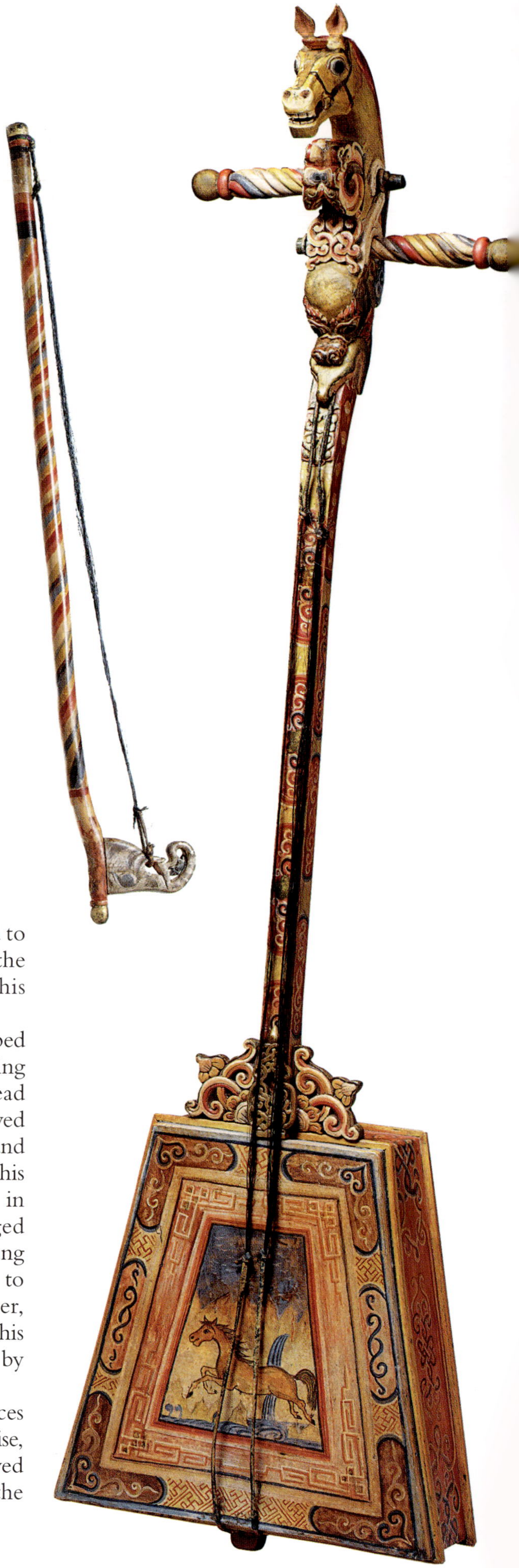

Mongolia
20th century
Painted and carved wood, hide, horsehair
H. 127 cm
Donated by Dangarsüren
Inv. 71.1957.61.3.1-5

This Mongolian viele is inextricably linked to a society of nomadic horsemen for whom the horse is primordial, and every part of this instrument is reminiscent of this animal.
On the decorated and painted trapezium-shaped case, there is a pastoral scene: a horse galloping in a mountainous landscape. A dragon head stands out at the top of the sleeve, and a carved horse head forms the top. The two strings and the bow are made of horsehair. Moreover, this instrument has been called a "horse-viele", in reference to the legend behind it: a winged horse, whose wings had been cut by a young woman to keep her lover by her side, is said to have combined lamentations for his master, through caresses, with a vibration caused by his mane, thus explaining the sound produced by the viele.
This instrument, played by men only, embraces a large repertoire of ballads, epic songs and praise, or long poems of incantation. It can be played by a soloist and lead a dance, or accompany the human voice in its melodic undulation. MD

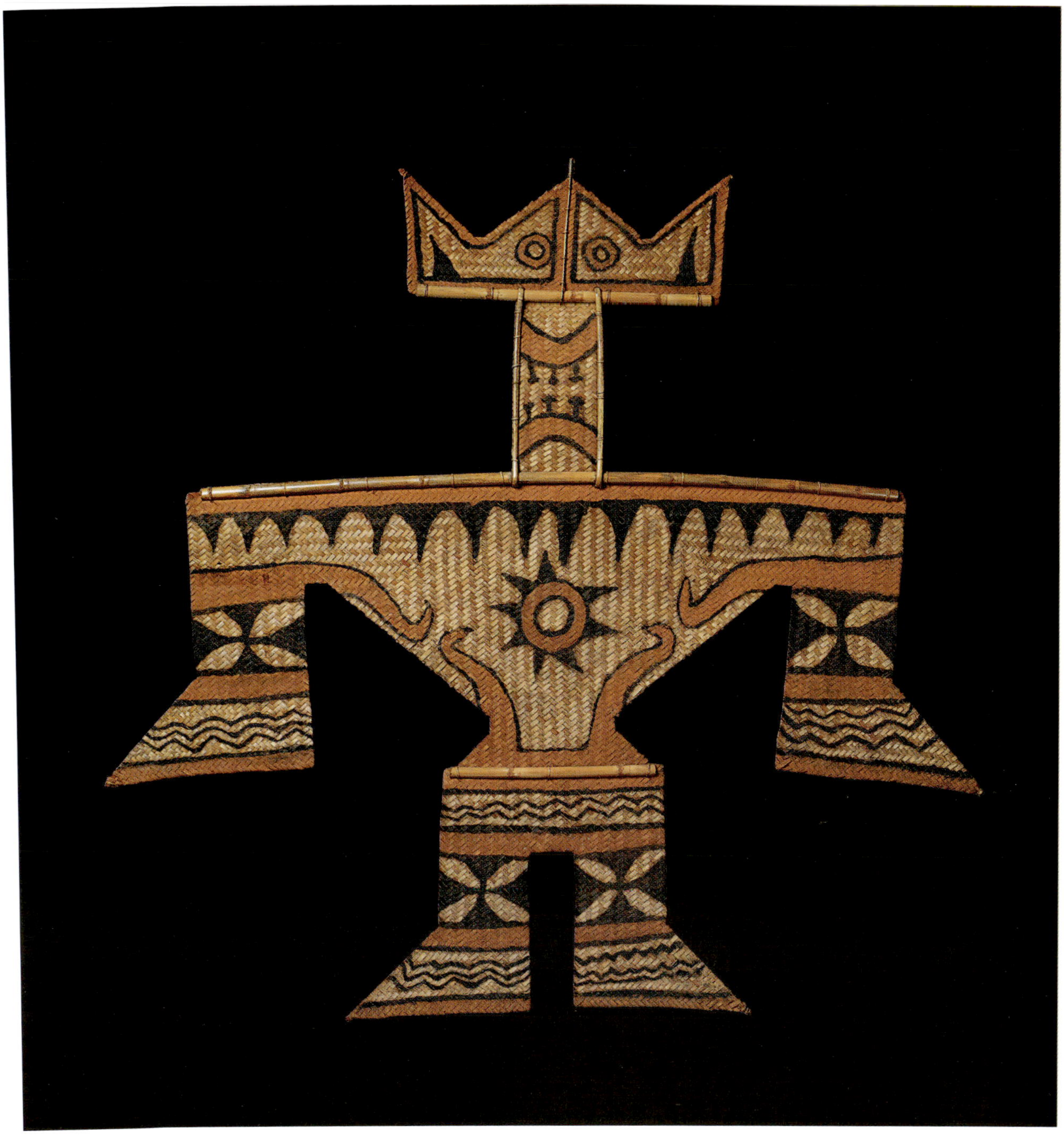

Field scarecrow

Gié/Jeh (Die)

Vietnam,
Kon Tum province,
Peng Sial Pen
Mid 20th century
Basketwork of twill woven bamboo strips, with red ochre and black decoration
132 x 126 cm
Donated by Frantz Laforest (collected in 1955-1956)
Inv. 71.1956.44.13

The majority of civilisations living on the High Plateaus in the centre of Vietnam practise dry slash-and-burn farming. Rice is grown during the rainy season until the start of the dry season when the harvest begins. To protect the crop, numerous rites are performed, along with the use of scarecrows, some of which contain moving sound elements activated by air or water. This scarecrow, made of bamboo strips, is hung from a tree by its head, at the end of a long string. The body, mobile around the bamboo separating it from the neck, sways above the rice fields. It derives its power against predators from its human form, its central motif inspired from Dongsonian* culture, similar to bronze drum motifs, and a small three-engine plane in particular, the image of war-time experience, drawn in black at the back of the head. This scarecrow, probably made around 1955, was still in common use at that time. CH

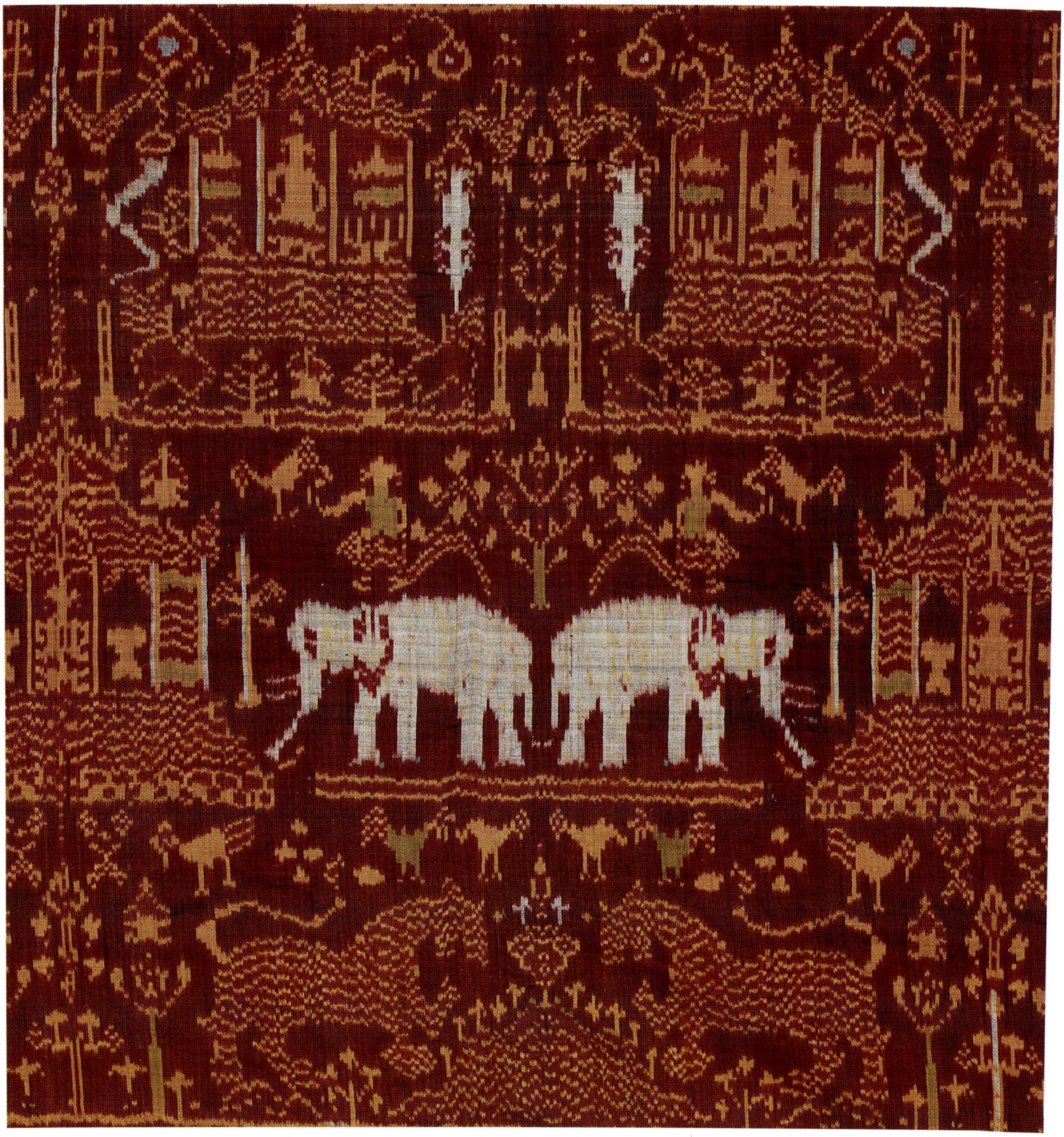

The Three Worlds

Khmer

Cambodia
Early 20th century
Silk, woven cloth,
tie-dyeing of weft yarn
(weft ikat)
83 x 164 cm
Collected for the
Colonial Exhibition
in Paris, 1931
Inv. 71.1962.22.224

These hangings, or *pidan*, were woven by women to be donated to the temple where they would adorn the altar of Buddha. Like other religious donations, a *pidan* offering was considered a source of merit taken into account in subsequent rebirths in theravâda* buddhism. Their main themes depict episodes in Buddha's life, his previous existences, the *jataka*, or Buddhist cosmology. The theme here is the Three Worlds, or the three "lands" of the universe. The row of temples and "crocodile banners" at the top evoke the world of the gods at the summit of Mount Meru. In the middle, the world of men and favourable reincarnations is represented by sacred white elephants facing royal residences with terraces and columns. At the bottom, leaping lions and trees of life represent the world of the damned, the domain of unfavourable reincarnations.

The iconographic wealth is enhanced by the use of motifs created by the weft ikat technique called *hôl*, where the yarn is resist-tied* before being dyed. The image appears during the weaving phase. CH

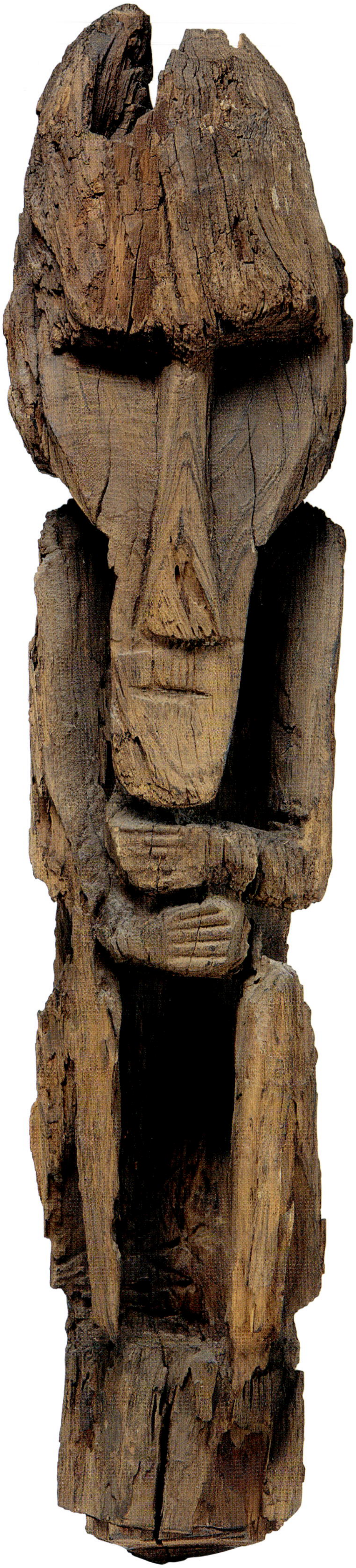

Tomb sculpture

Bahnar

Vietnam,
Kon Tum province
Late 19th/
early 20th century
Wood
154 x 29 cm
Donated by
Frantz Laforest
Inv. 71.1956.44.1

The civilisations living on the High Plateaus in the centre of Vietnam adorn their tombs with sculptures, the most remarkable of which are made by the Jörai and Bahnar people. They are carved during the "tomb abandonment" ceremony, marking the end of mourning several years after a person has died. Buffaloes are sacrificed and food and jars of alcohol are distributed, with dances and rituals using a gong. The tomb is made as new, decorated with sculptures, and then abandoned. The animals depicted, as well as the men and women who are generally represented naked, accompany the deceased in the afterlife.
The statues are carved out of a tree trunk by villagers renowned for their skill. The cut wood is worked immediately using a pendulum axe then finishing touches are carved with a knife. The parts to be hollowed out are drawn with charcoal. The face is concave, and the axe is used to hollow out the eyes and the mouth, leaving the nose long and straight.
At the turn of the century, the explorator Henri Maître described this figure, with hands folded on his knees, as a *bram*, a masked man who still plays a part in funeral rites today. CH

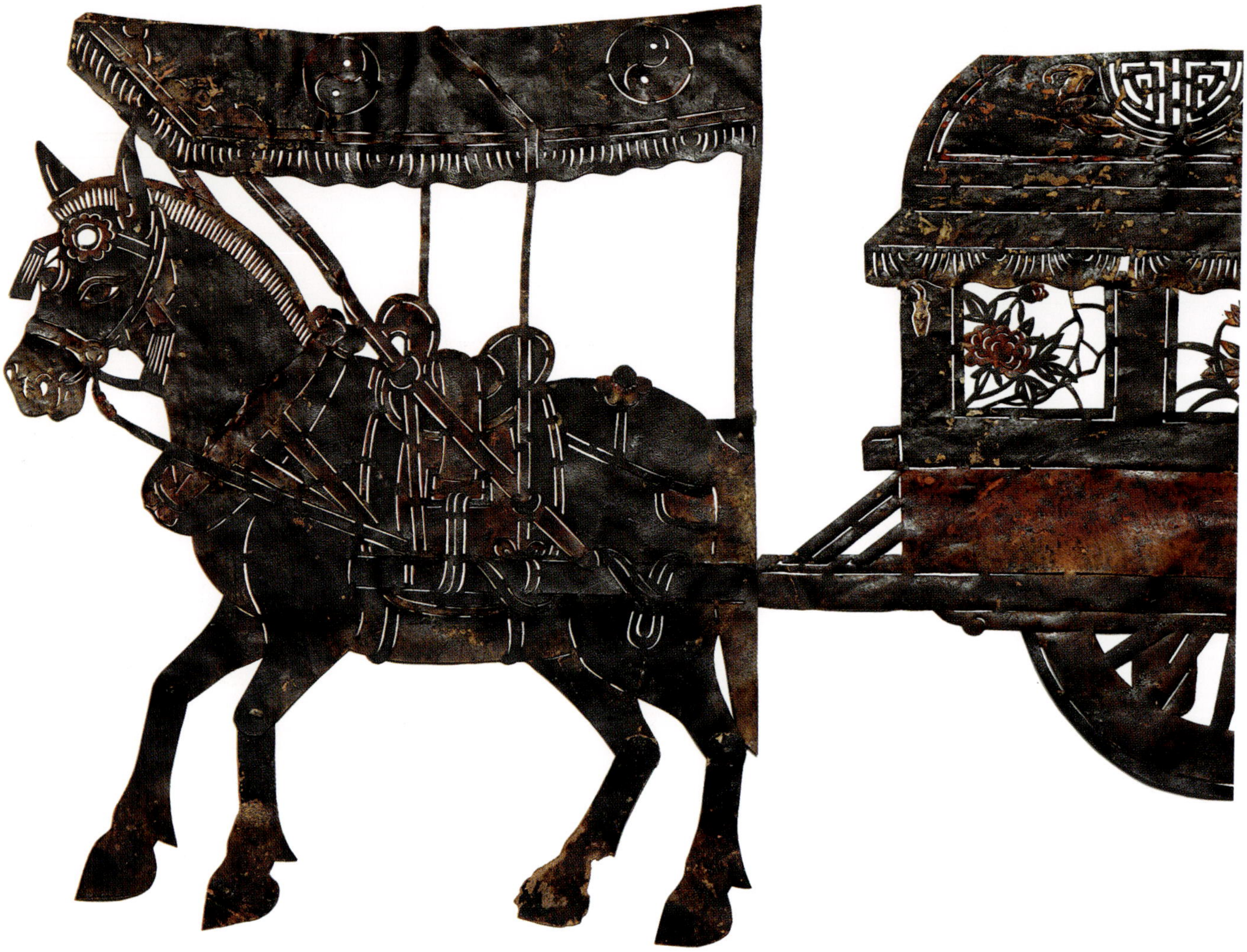

Cart

Han

Chine,
Hebei province
18th century
Donkey hide
L. 45.5 cm
Former collection
Jacques Pimpaneau
Inv. 71.1990.108.84

This cart made out of donkey hide is characteristic of the Hebei, an important centre of shadow theatre. It was part of a full 18th century theatre belonging to a famous master called Luan Zhou. As with all shadow theatres, the master moves the characters between a screen and a source of light. The figures are made of translucent hide which lets the colours through. Most of the characters are moved using three sticks, one for the body and two for the arms, all held by one master.

The repertoire is not specific to shadow theatre and uses themes and stories from normal theatre. In the same way as in classical opera, four types of main characters can be distinguished: male roles, *sheng*, female roles, *dan*, painted faces, *jing*, and clowns, *chou*. A small orchestra accompanies the movements, gives the rhythm (percussion instruments) or accompanies songs (wind or string instruments). Originally, shadow theatre played a key role in funeral rites or seasonal festivals. CH

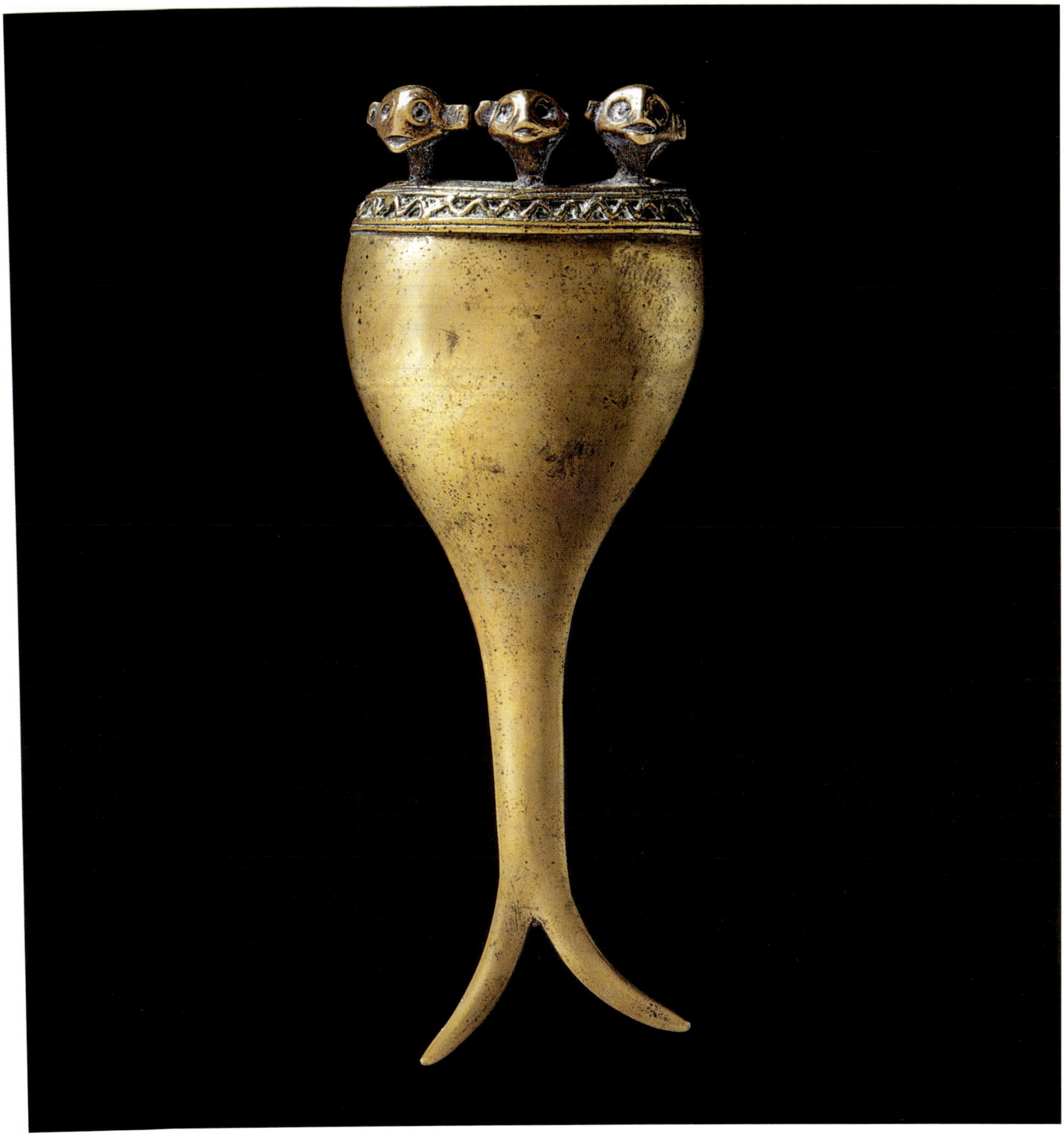

Chest ornament

Naga

India, Nagaland
19th-20th centuries
Brass
H. 17 cm
Donated by
Monique and Jean Paul
Barbier-Mueller
Inv. 70.2001.27.13

Located between India and Burma, the Naga are a mountainous people. After the 1830s, although under the control of the British authorities, they battled for almost another century to preserve their social organisation, particularly certain ceremonies such as festivals of merit* and ritual practices including headhunting*, inseparable from the notion of fertility.
This type of pendant, in the form of a conch cut in two culminating in a fish tail and topped with three heads, is associated with the tradition of headhunting. It is used as a substitute for brass carved heads indicating the headhunter status. Naga ornaments have a symbolic vocabulary value. The materials used to make them – pearls, cowrie shells, horse hair or brass, acclaimed for its rarity – are always the same. Put together in diverse combinations, their variants define the identity and status of individuals within one group. The right to possess and wear these adornments is strictly monitored socially because of the intrinsic symbolic power attributed to them. In the past, their importance was such that the ornaments contributed to the very definition of a human being and could only be removed after death.
DC

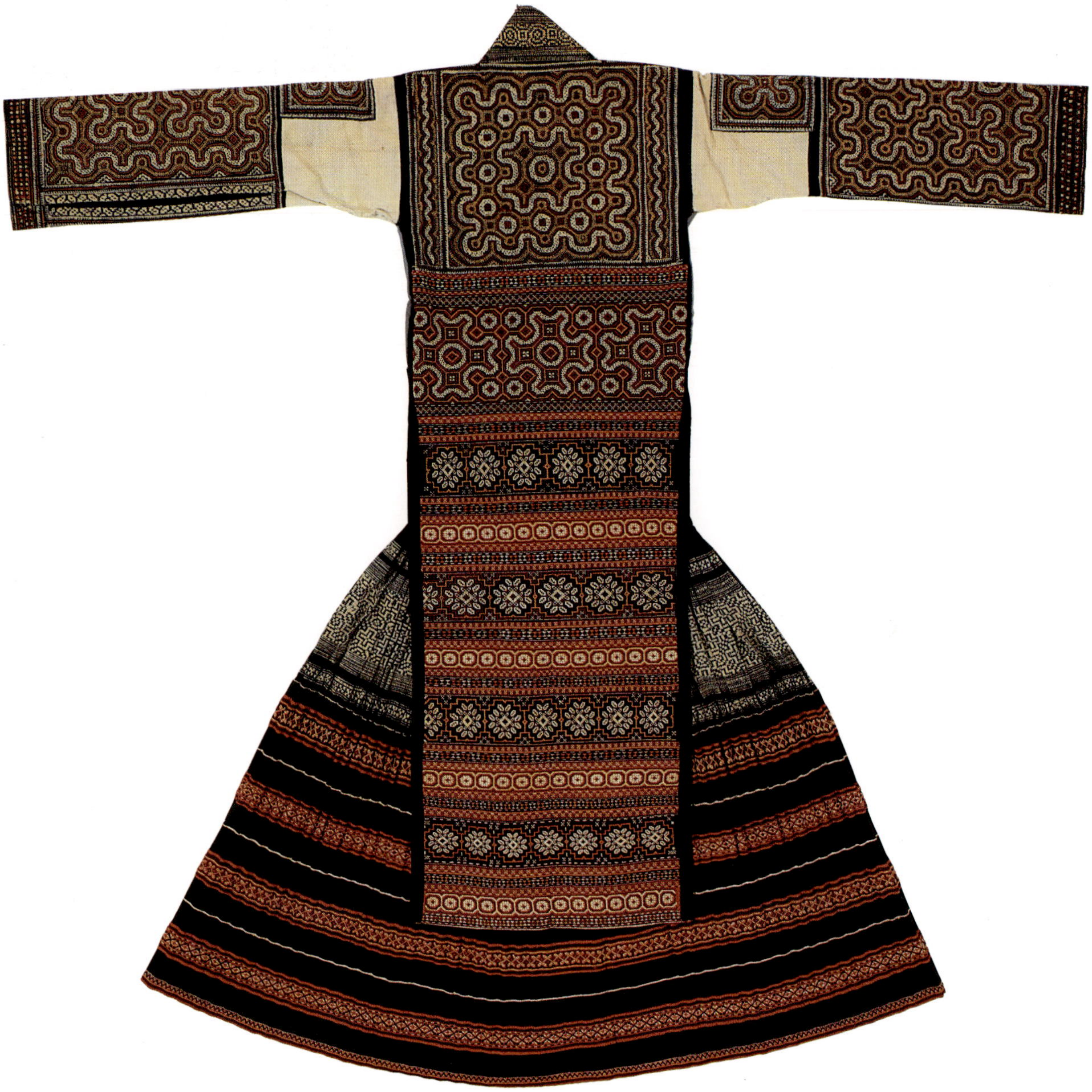

Woman's costume

Miao

China, Guizhou province, Liuzhi
20th century
Cotton, silk, hemp, felt, hair, wool, wood, brightly coloured batik decoration and embroidery
Inv. 71.1993.68.1-4

Miao women who wear this type of dress belong to a group of at least five thousand people spread over twelve villages and hamlets in the Zhijin and Liuzhi region, to the west of the Guizhou province. The Qing Miao, or Miao of the ravines, used to be named "Long-Horn Miao" after a large comb in the shape of buffalo horns on which women roll a wig of almost two metres of hairpieces inherited from their mother. This headdress, worn on festival or market days along with the dress, marks the moment when young girls become adults and are eligible for marriage.
This attire displays batik decoration, a resist-dyeing* technique, and coloured embroidery, the fine points and geometric motifs of which evoke a woven pattern. The blue and white batik on the gathered skirt is adorned with yellow and red on the jacket. The decoration on the upper part of the long back panel of the jacket is unusual in that the same patterns appear in batik and embroidery. The dress is worn with an indigo-tinted wool felt apron and white felt puttees. CH-FC

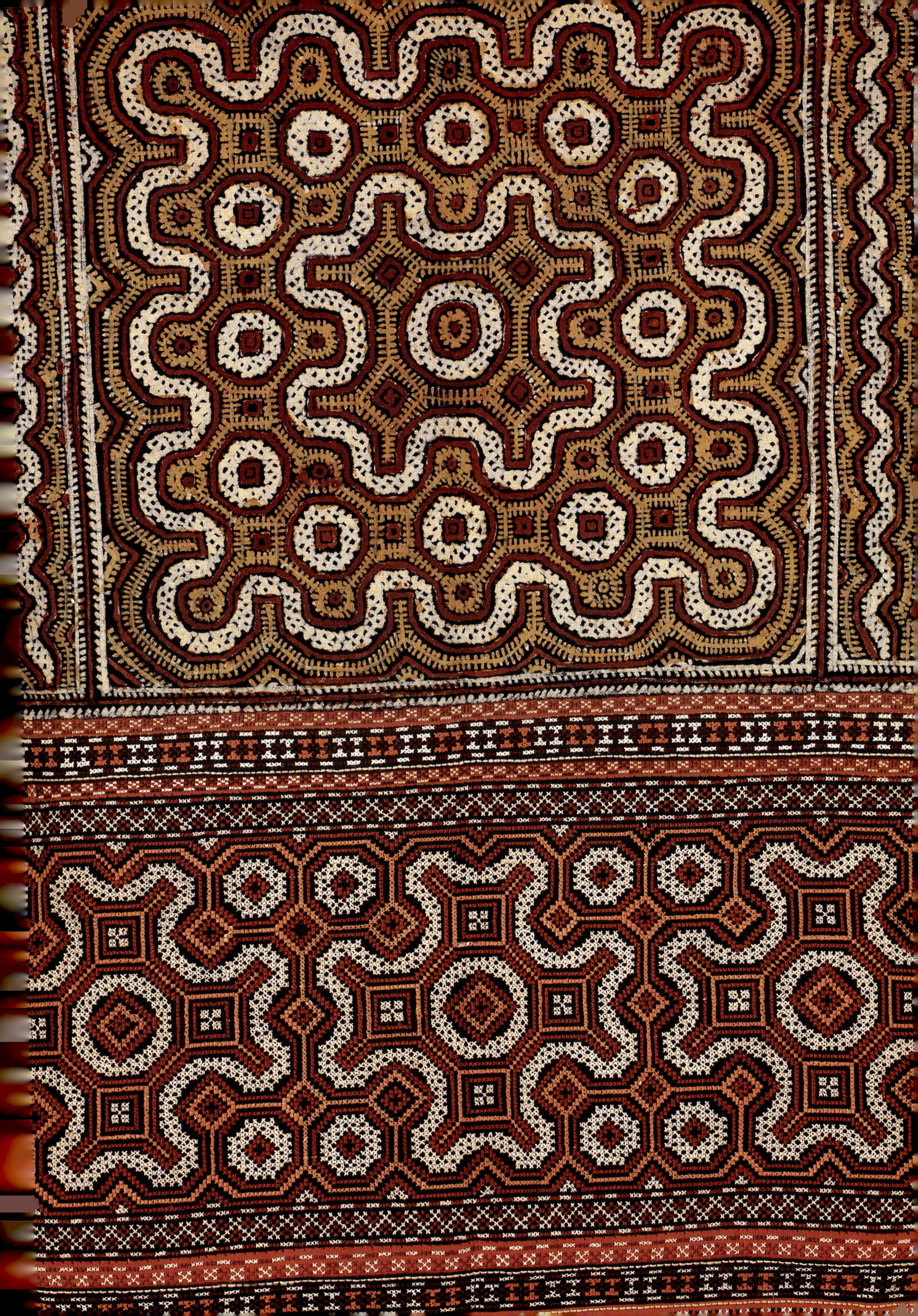

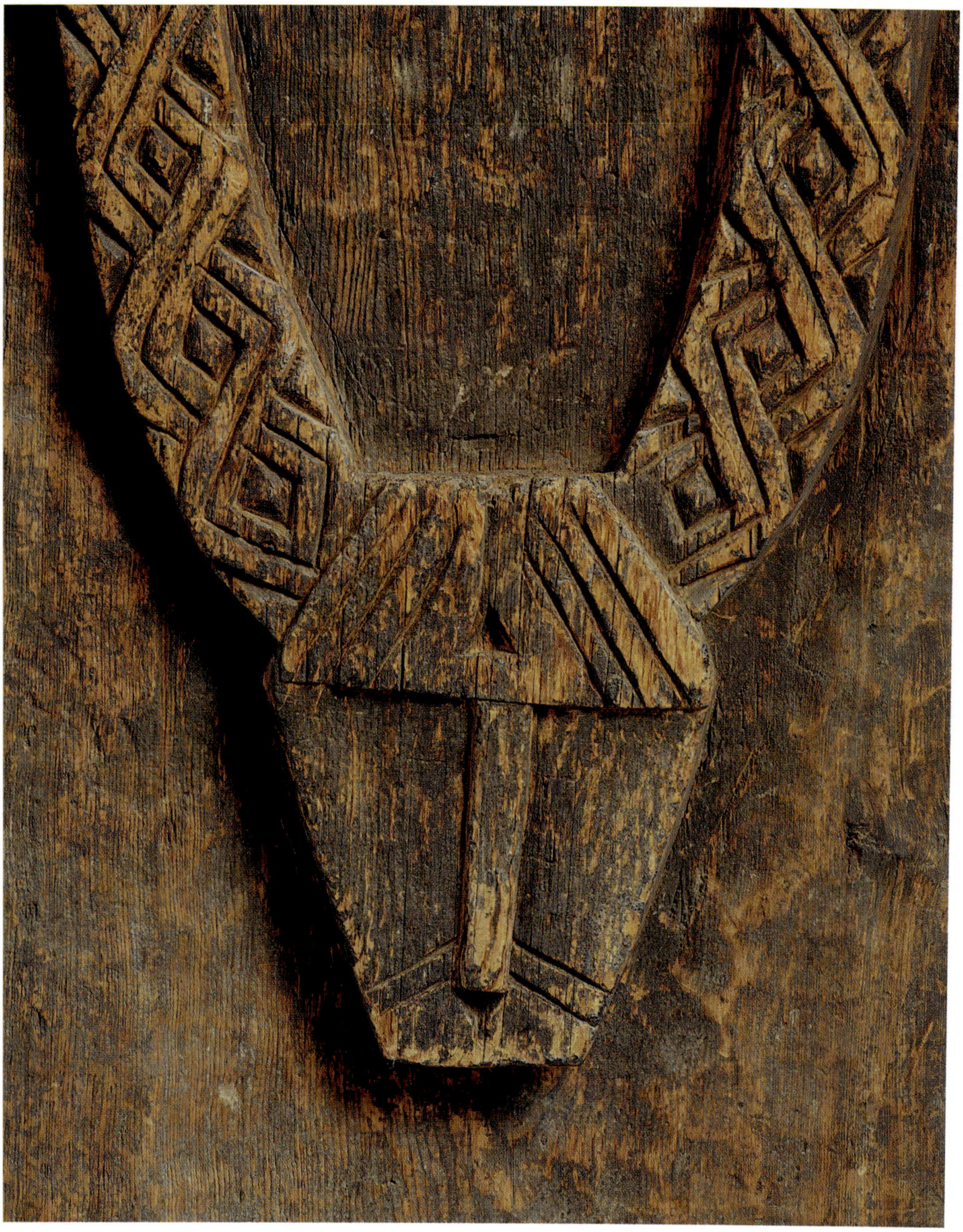

Carved door

Kalash

Pakistan, Chitral
19th-20th centuries
Wood
168 x 70 cm
Donated by Monique and Jean Paul Barbier-Mueller
Inv. 70.2001.27.508

Today, the Kalash ("man" in Kalashamon), the only non-Islamic population of the Hindu Kush, live in hamlets perched on the slopes of the narrow Chitral valleys, in north-west Pakistan. Their economic activity combines agricultural terracing and cattle, sheep and goat farming.
Cattle are sacrificed to the spirits during annual spring rituals associated with the farming cycle and intended to ensure prosperity and abundant harvests. The unsettled land in the inhospitable mountains surrounding them is inhabited by supernatural Kalash spirits (*pari*), which are alternately hostile or benign, and which have to be symbolically placated, particularly to ensure success when hunting. Wooden carvings of the heads of wild sheep and goats, obvious signs of these spiritual beliefs, feature on the doors of major dwellings and houses of worship. The door on display here is an striking example. The carved horn motifs and wooden edifices on stone bases are typical of the inhabitants and architectural style of the region. DC-FOA

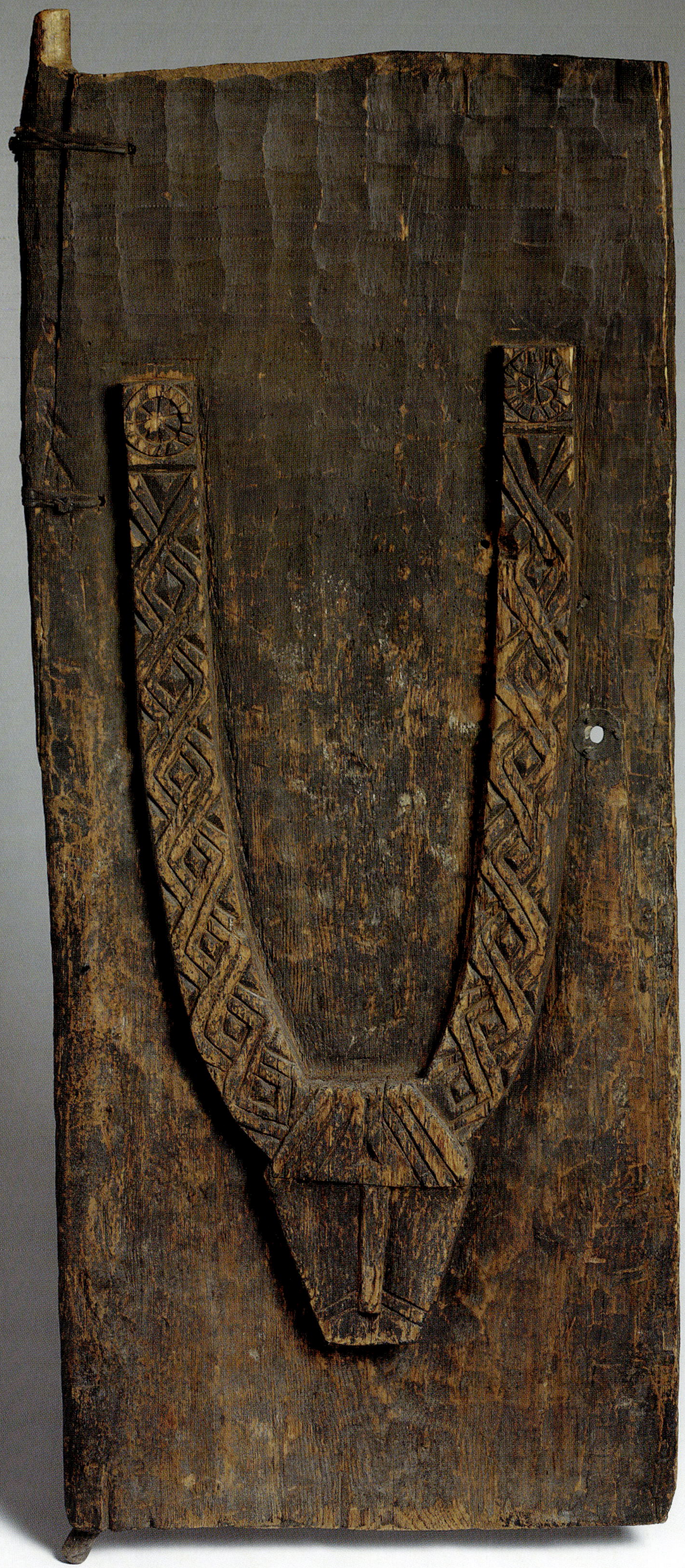

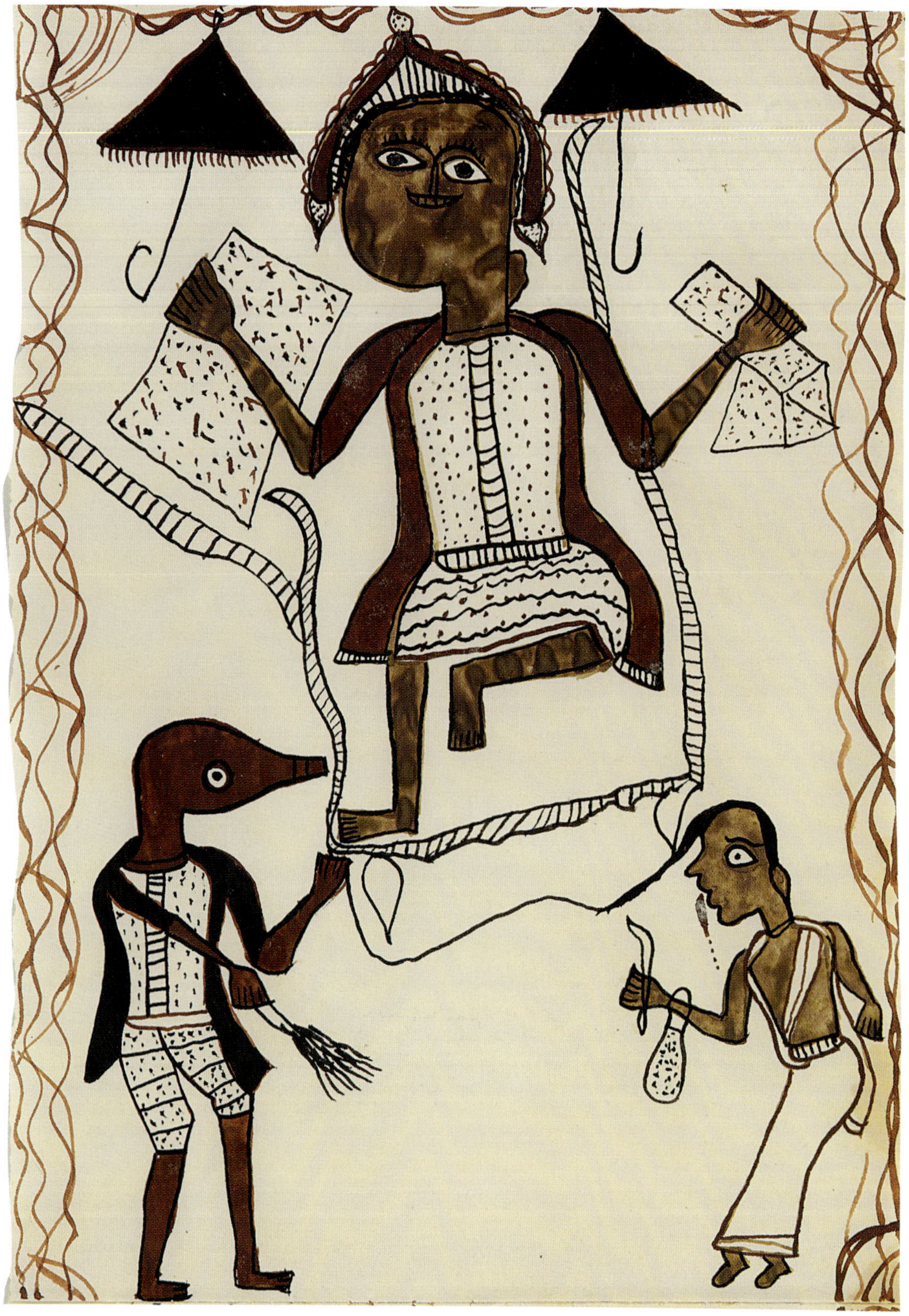

Yama painting

Santal Pargana

Lankeshwar Chitrakar
India, Bihar
20th century
Paper, cotton, wood, pigments and canvas
240 x 21 cm
Donated by Jean-Baptiste Faivre
Inv. 71.1981.59.119

Bengali scroll paintings are an original and enduring aspect of popular Indian art. Painter-storytellers visit villages daily to put on shows of these scrolls. As they unroll the painting, a story is told through the unfolding scenes.
The *chitrakar* ("people who make images") occupy a lower status in Hindu society. One of their main activities among the Santal (Non-Hindu civilisation) remains the parody of funeral ceremonies, which explains their name of painter-magicians (*jadupatua*) and the Santal's mistrust of them.
The recurring themes of the scrolls evoke the mythology of Kali and Yama, the creation of the world or the Santal Festival of Baha. Like all Yama paintings (*jom pat*), this one begins with a portrait of King Yama, Black King of Death, seated on his throne. The scenes which follow describe his kingdom where his acolytes try to torture humans. A great number of punishments focus on rice, the main currency in which painter-storytellers are paid. Here, a rice thief is punished by having his mouth pounded by a pestle. MC

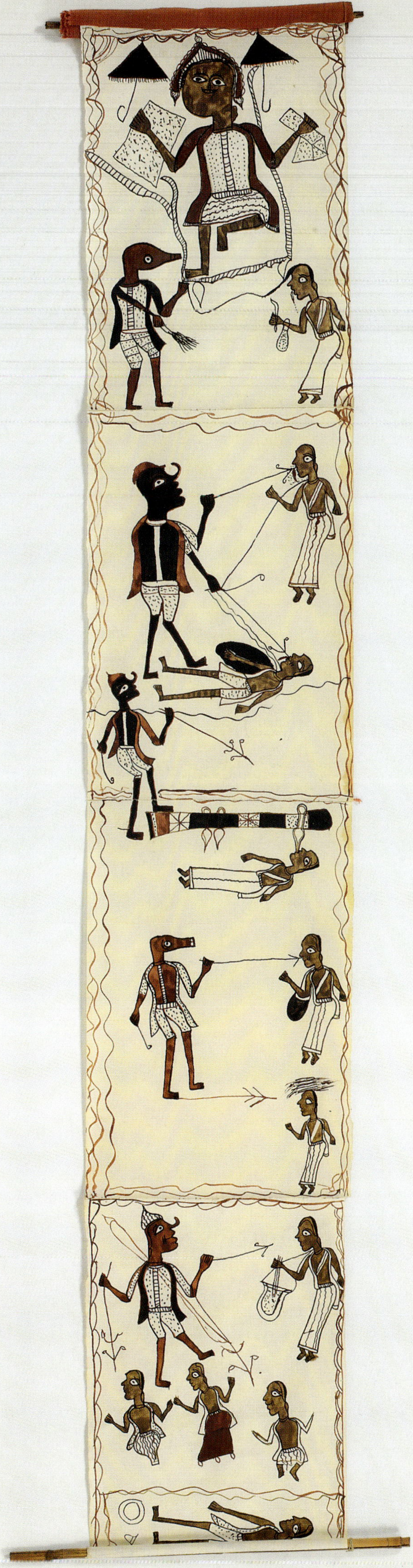

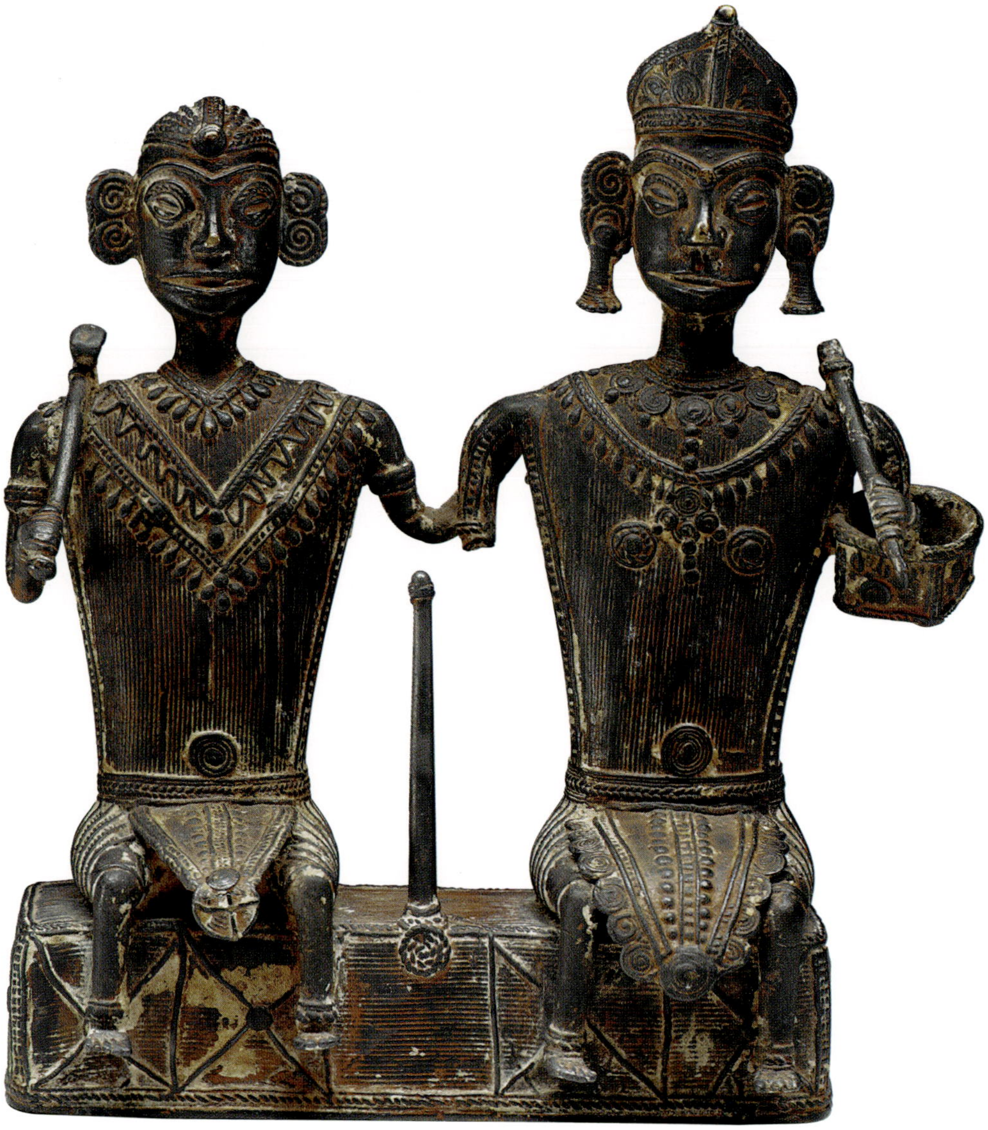

Jhitku and Mitki

India, Chattisgarh, Bastar
Early 20th century
Bronze
25 x 22 cm
Former collection
Christophe Niemoller
Inv. 70.2000.1.40

The Bastar village civilisations create traditional bronze statuettes using the lost wax technique. These figurines – people, animals, figures of fantasy – are usually placed on altars in the home or the village. Less often, they can represent clan divinities or folk Hinduism, as well as legendary characters who are worshipped so that they bring protection and prosperity to their owner and the village. As a symbol of the divinity being worshipped, if the statuette fails in its benevolent role it is immediately deemed ineffective and thrown away.

These bronze figurines, made by the master foundrymen caste, do not follow strict iconographic precepts, but are the expression of individual artistic skill. The attributes and settings of the divinities are nonetheless recognisable most of the time. This statuette represents Jhitku and Mitki, a couple of divine characters from a well-known Bastar folk legend. They are recognisable by their belongings, a shoulder axe for Jhitku and basket and spade for his wife Mitki. DC

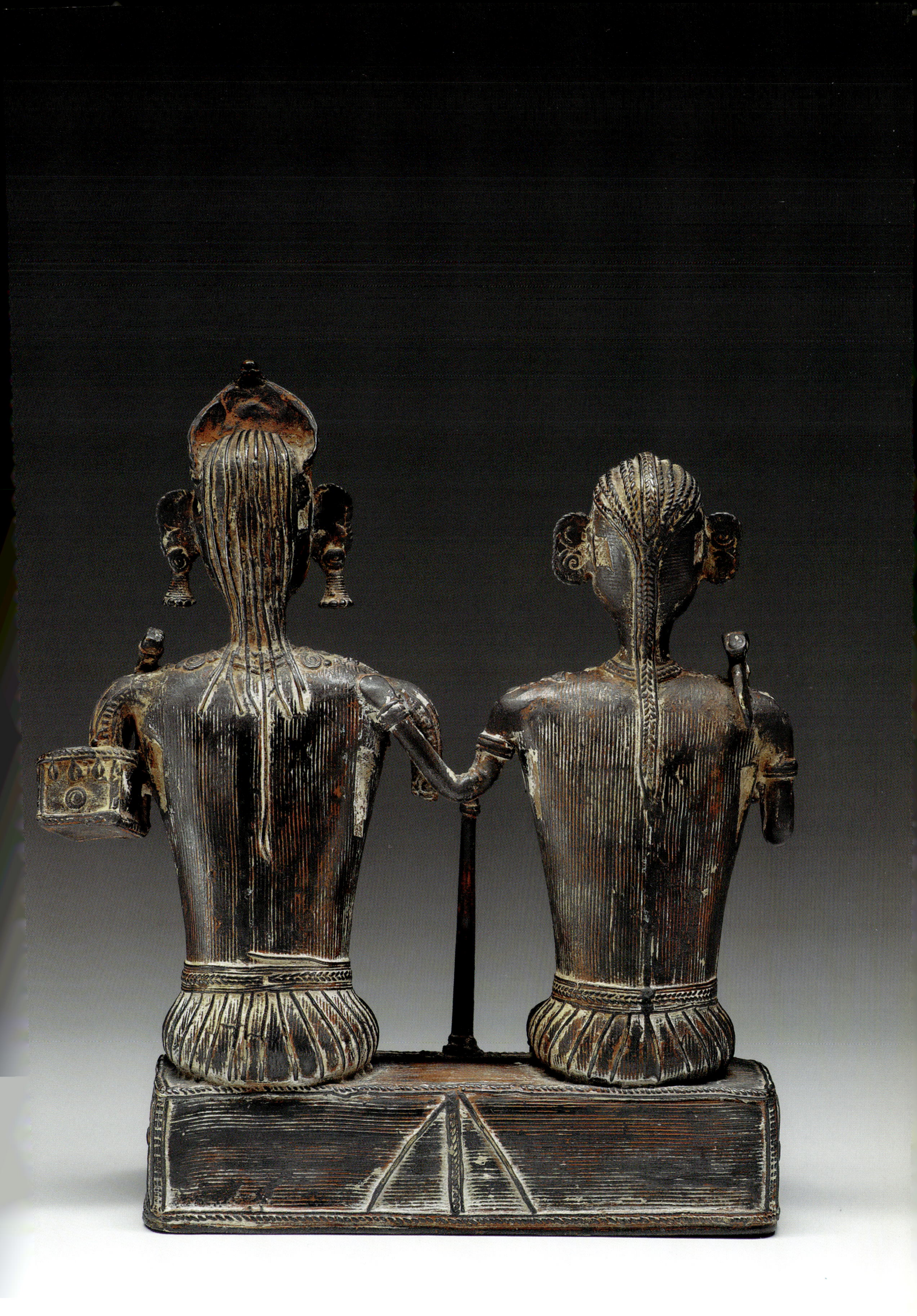

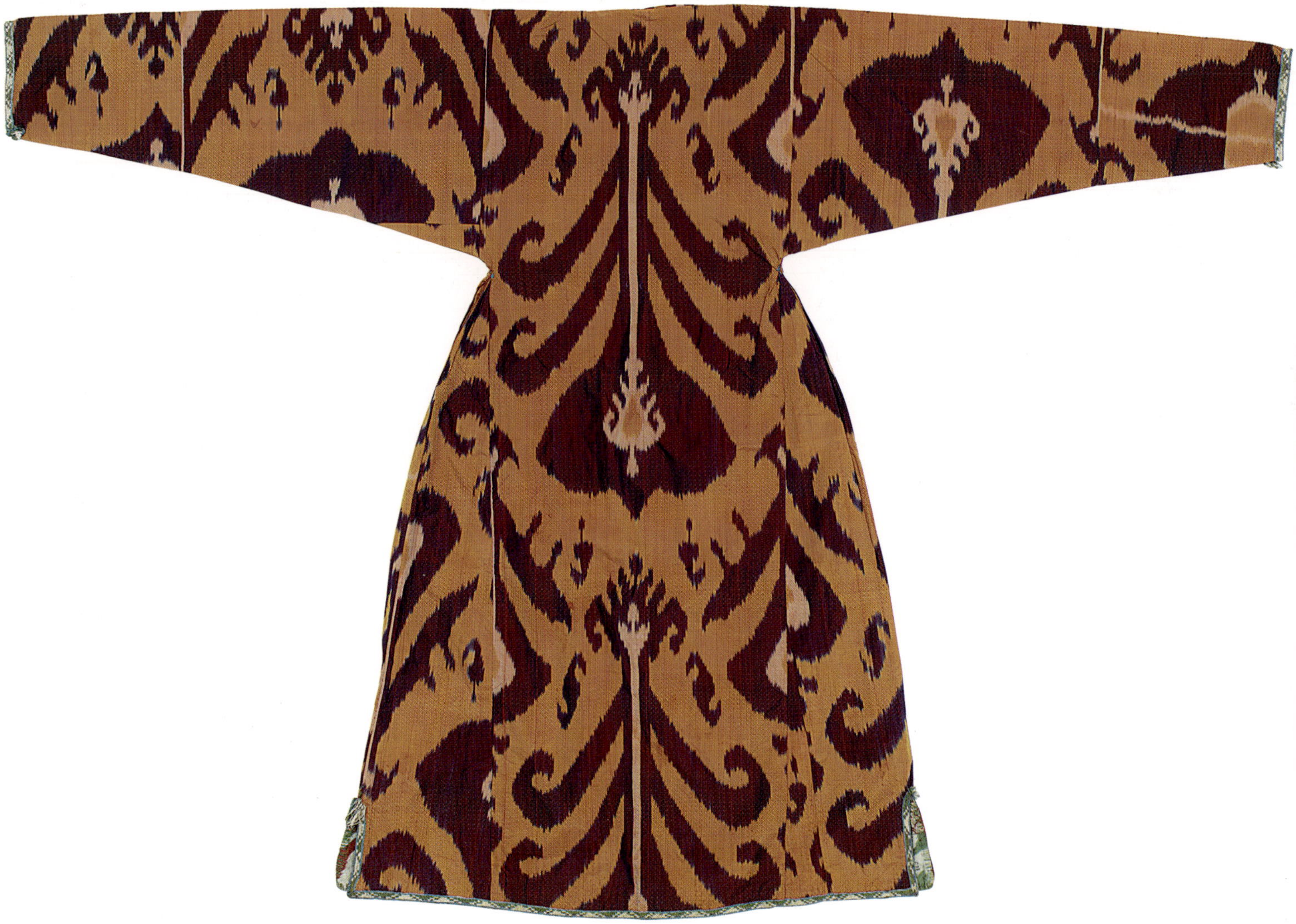

Woman's coat

Uzbek

Uzbekistan, Bukhara
19th century
Silk taffetas, warp ikat
H. 134 cm
Inv. 71.1989.24.31.3

Situated on the old Silk road, Central Asia became a region that produced silk goods in around 500 BC. The oldest fragments of ikat decoration to be found date back to 6th-7th century AD, but it is in the 19th century that the warp ikat technique, tie-dyeing of the warp yarn before weaving, underwent a decorative explosion with regard to motifs and colours. The combination of forms, boldness in tone repetitions and blurred contours created by the technique itself forms a unique whole.
The silk taffetas thus decorated, called *adras* in the local dialect, were used as hangings or to make clothes. Prestigious silk velvet, or *baghmal*, could also be adorned with ikat decoration. Present-day workshops are trying to revive this craft.
This coat, lined with industrial cotton fabric, is decorated with large violet motifs on a yellow background, while ikat facings with white and red motifs on a green background are sewn around the whole of the inside circumference. The roped warp binding fixed on the hem while it is being woven is applied using another original technique. FC

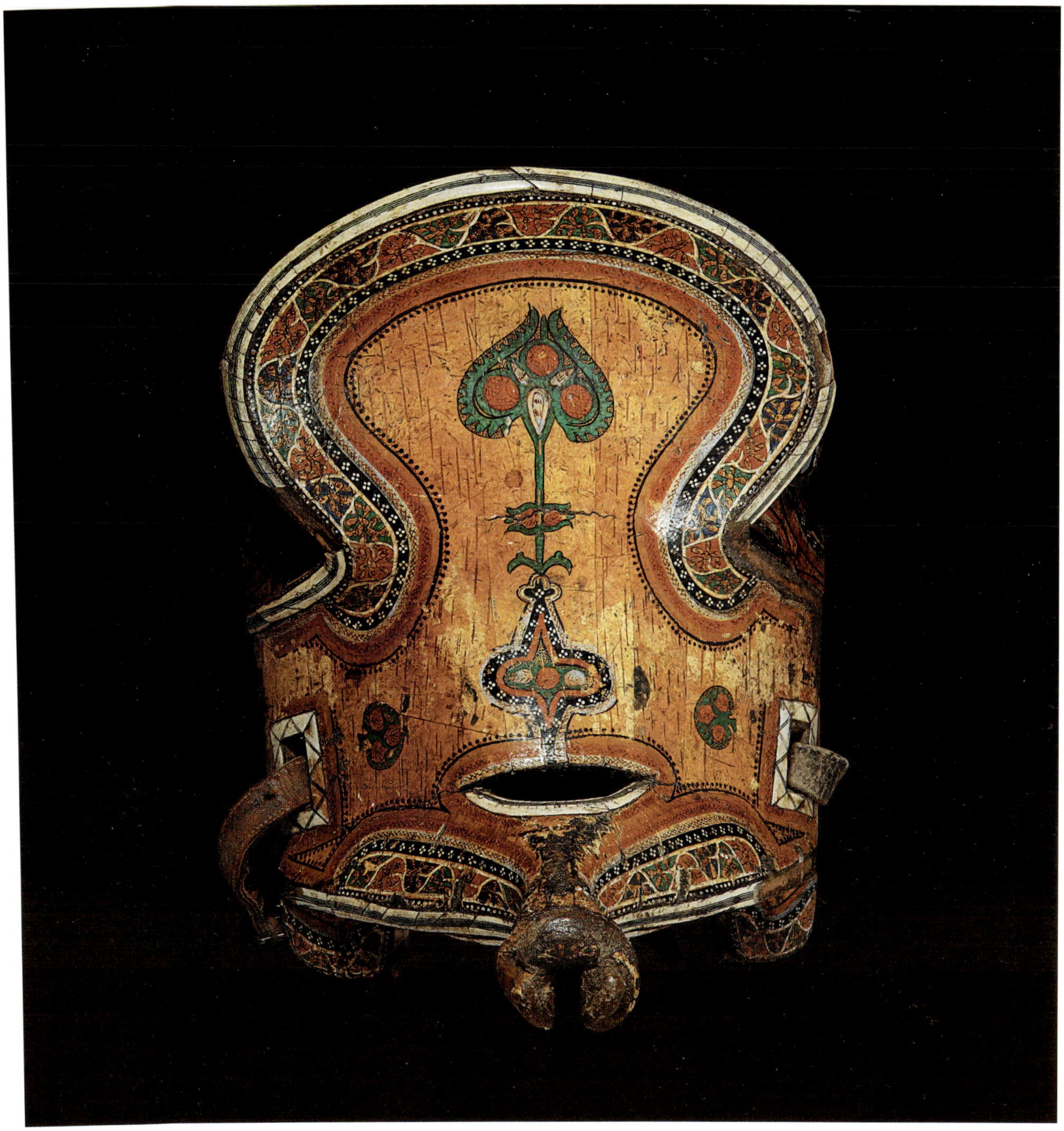

Horse's saddle

Uzbek

Uzbekistan, Bukhara
19th-20th centuries
Wood, birch bark, bone, leather, iron
45 x 35 x 88 cm
Donated by Citroën, "Croisière Jaune", 1931-1932
Inv. 71.1935.115.65.1-5

Carved out of a single piece of wood, this urban saddle has a raised pommel topped with a projection sometimes called a "duck's head". This is used for attaching the bridle and therefore for stopping the horse by pulling its head back without the rider having to look for a post. Since this saddle is for urban use, it has two metal rings enabling purchases to be attached or bundles to be carried. The saddle was placed on an embroidered caparison, made of silk or velvet, and could be covered with a cushion or rug, both for the comfort of the rider and the protection of the painted and varnished decoration.

This saddle also has a central floral motif (*anor gul*, "badge motif") in green and vermilion, repeated on the skirts* in a smaller size; a floral arabesque, in the same shapes and colours, runs around the edge of the pommel and sides; and contrast is provided by the ochre background and white bone plaques. These colours are a good example of decorative painting on wood, in which the craftsmen of Bukhara and Samarkand excelled. SJ

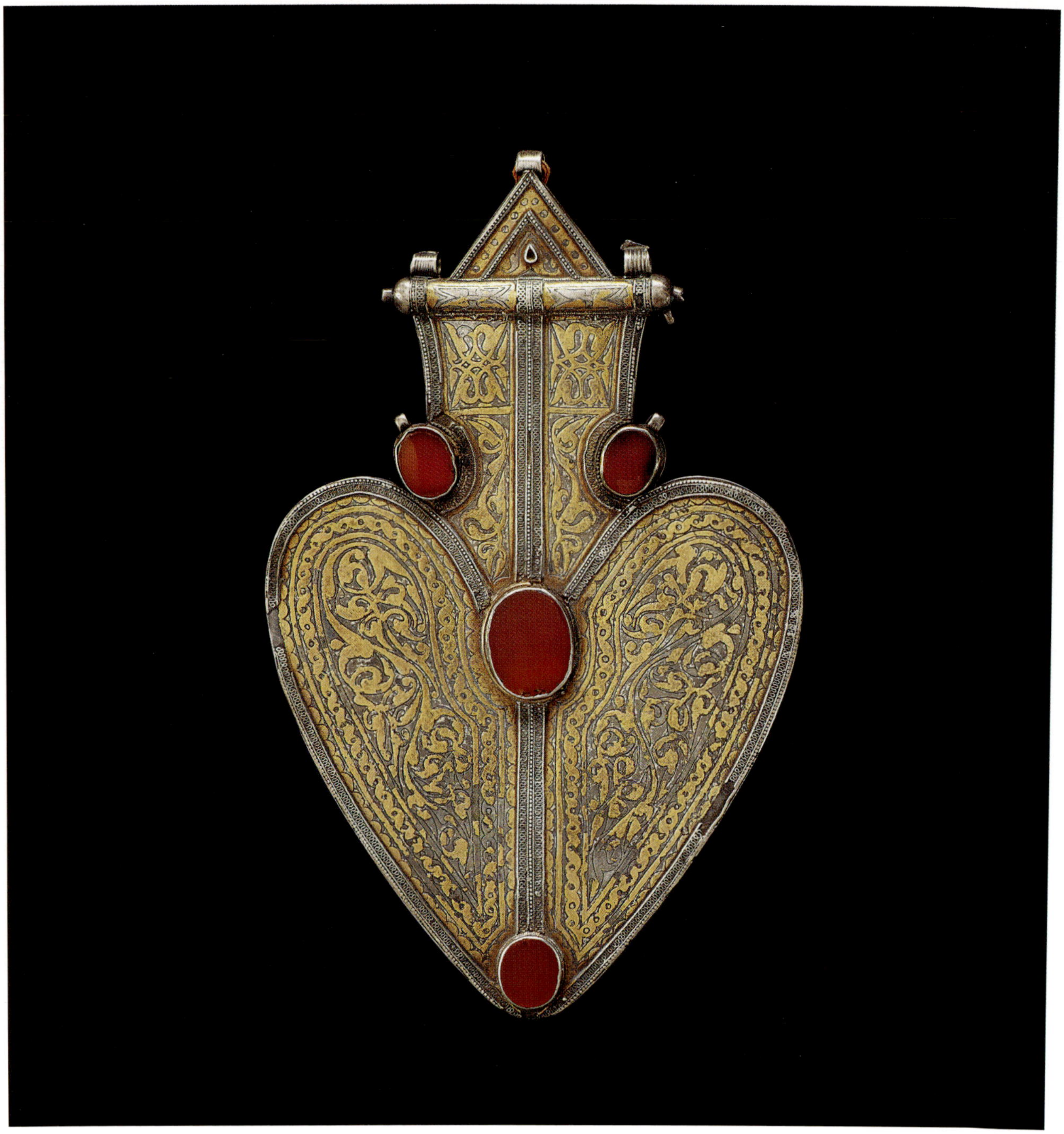

Back pendant

Turkmen

Afghanistan
18th-19th centuries
Gold-plated silver, cornelians
26.7 x 16.5 cm
Mission Bernard Dupaigne
Inv. 71.1972.12.195

Nomadic shepherds and farmers living on the stretches of desert to the east of the Caspian Sea up to the Khorezm oases in present-day Turkmenistan as well as the more fertile valleys of northern Iran and north-west Afghanistan, the Turkmen are celebrated for the quality of their crafts, knotted carpets and silver jewellery. This silver back pendant (*asyq*) inlaid with cornelians is a perfect illustration of their craftsmanship. It was presented to the bride by her husband's family and worn as an adornment on her wedding day, laden for the occasion with precious and heavy adornments, which belong by right to all married women.

Weddings are the occasion for major transfers of assets between two families. The bride's price is paid in cattle by the son-in-law's family to her family. She also receives a personal endowment, comprising rugs and matting on the one hand and, on the other, jewellery that has been given partly by her family and partly by her husband's family.

This pendant, bearing a cornelian that is believed to encourage the birth of children, also has the value of an amulet. It is therefore evidence of both wealth and fertility. DC-FOA

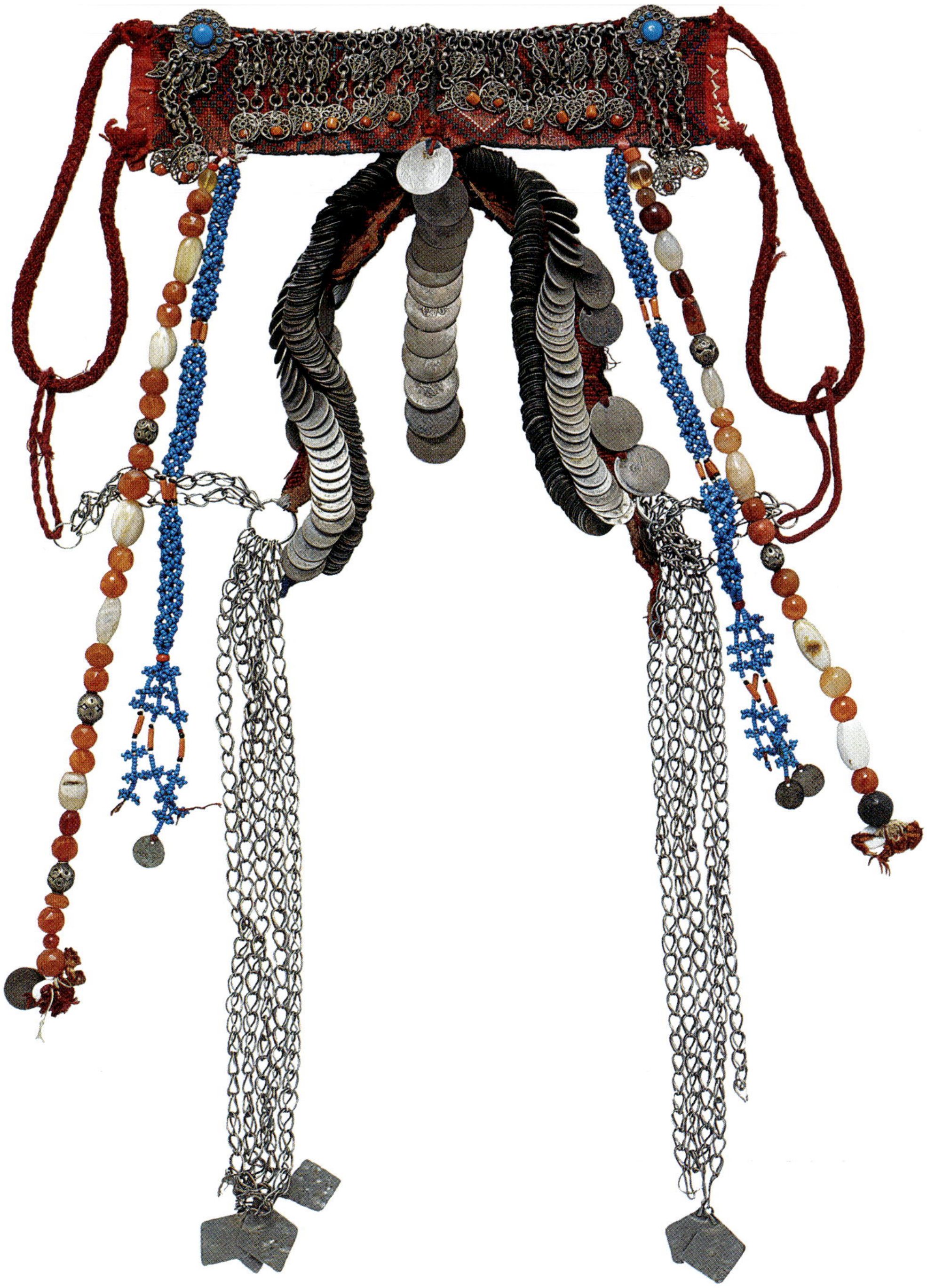

Face veil

Neguev Desert Bedouins

Palestinians Territories, Gaza
Early 20th century
Textile, coins, silver, glass, cornelian, agate, cowrie shell
60.5 x 29.5 cm
Donated by baronne Alix de Rothschild
Inv. 71.1973.51.1

The attire and face veil (*burqa'*) worn by Bedouin women are a sign of their tribal affiliation. For Bedouins living in southern Palestine, a married woman's wealth lies in her veil, worn as a piece of finery on which the jewellery and coins of her dowry are sewn. Around twenty years ago, only elderly Bedouin women still wore these frontlets which are on the verge of disappearing today.
While the place and date of the first appearance of the face veil are unknown, it is certain that draped garments covering the head were an integral part of Eastern women's attire in 1000 BC. The first laws obligating married women to cover their heads in public are attributed to the Assyrian king Teglath-Phalasar I (1115-1077 BC.). In biblical times, women wore a veil, even if the Torah did not make it a legal requirement, and Saint Paul exhorted women to cover their heads when praying. The veil of Roman vestals (chaste priestesses of the Goddess Vesta) is at the origin of Christian religious veils. In Pre-Islamic Arabia, as attested by Tertullian, a priest from Carthage (circa 200 AD), respectable women covered their head with a veil in public, and sometimes even their face. Just as in Judaism and Christianity, Islam assimilates these customs from the Ancient Near East, keeping their meaning sacred. HC

The Arts and Civilizations of Africa, Asia, Oceania and the Americas

For millennia, the Americas had a history apart, unaffected by events on other continents until the blow inflicted by the European conquest. The dynamism and creativity of American civilisations is evident in every field of human activity – social, political, economic, architectural, and aesthetic – and took innovation in the plastic arts to its outermost limits.

The musée du quai Branly's rich ethnographic and archaeological collections bear witness to the inventiveness of the Amerindian world. Inherited from the King's Cabinet constituted in the 16th and 17th centuries, they were enriched by 19th century explorers and scientists, then by research missions on behalf of the musée de l'Homme, before being completed by recent acquisitions.

Twenty artefacts from different millennia and cultural areas have been selected as illustrations. Pre-Columbian stone sculptures and ceramics from Mesoamerica, the Caribbean and the Andes stand alongside wooden masks from Alaska, painted hides from Mississippi and feather adornments from Amazonia dating from the last three centuries. Through the interplay of colours and materials, and a subtle balance between figurative and abstract, these objects evoke the major preoccupations of Amerindian societies: ensuring that the world remained in balance, and affirmation of identity. Animals, often hybrid, are omnipresent – they may be a relation, a double, a god, or represent a part of the universe. Beyond their apparent diversity, these works confirm the unity and uniqueness of Amerindian cultures.

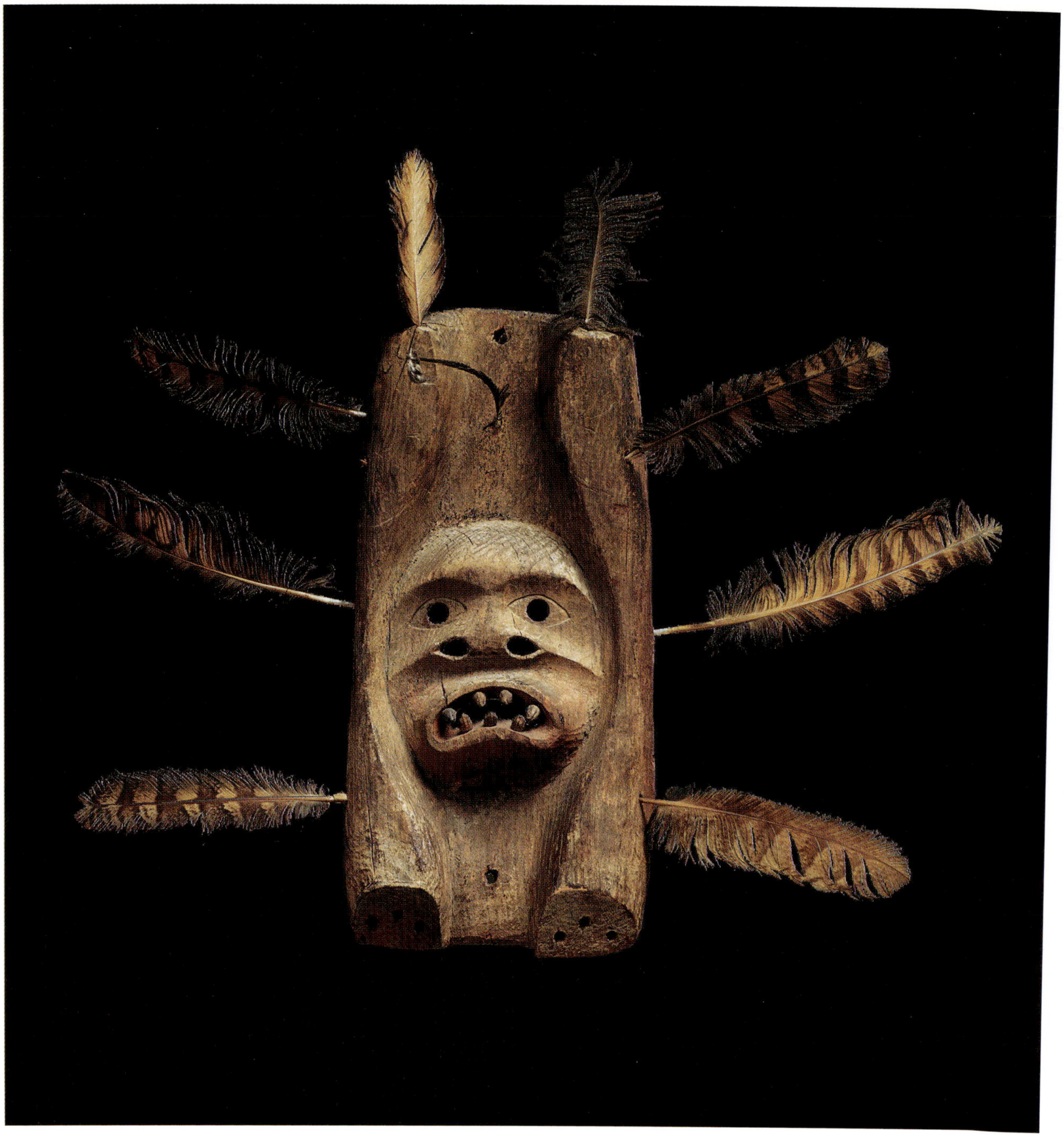

Anthropomorphic mask

Yup'ik

United States, Alaska, Kuskokwin Bay, Quinhagak village
19th century
Wood, feathers,
red colours, aged patina
60 x 21 x 8 cm
Former collection
André Breton
Inv. 70.2003.9.3

The Yup'ik Inuit live along the coast of the Bering Sea, Alaska. They used to wear masks on the occasion of winter festivals, during ceremonies held in honour of certain totemic animals. Through his mask, which hid his human identity from view, the Shaman could communicate with the spirit world and make predictions.

Yup'ik art is distinctive for its ingenious composition and the way in which its features emerge from the materials employed, both these characteristics being evident in this exceptional, if incomplete, sculpture of a face, carved out of monoxylic* wood. The combination of feathers and wood evokes seabirds afloat, while the face, half seal, half man, seems to strive painfully to achieve existence.

This mask, which had been part of the Heye Foundation collections since 1901, was acquired by the New York merchant Julius Carlebach during the Second World War. He later sold it to André Breton who kept it in his studio, along with other Alaskan artefacts, until his death. Surrealists gave this particular region of the world special consideration. MD-ED

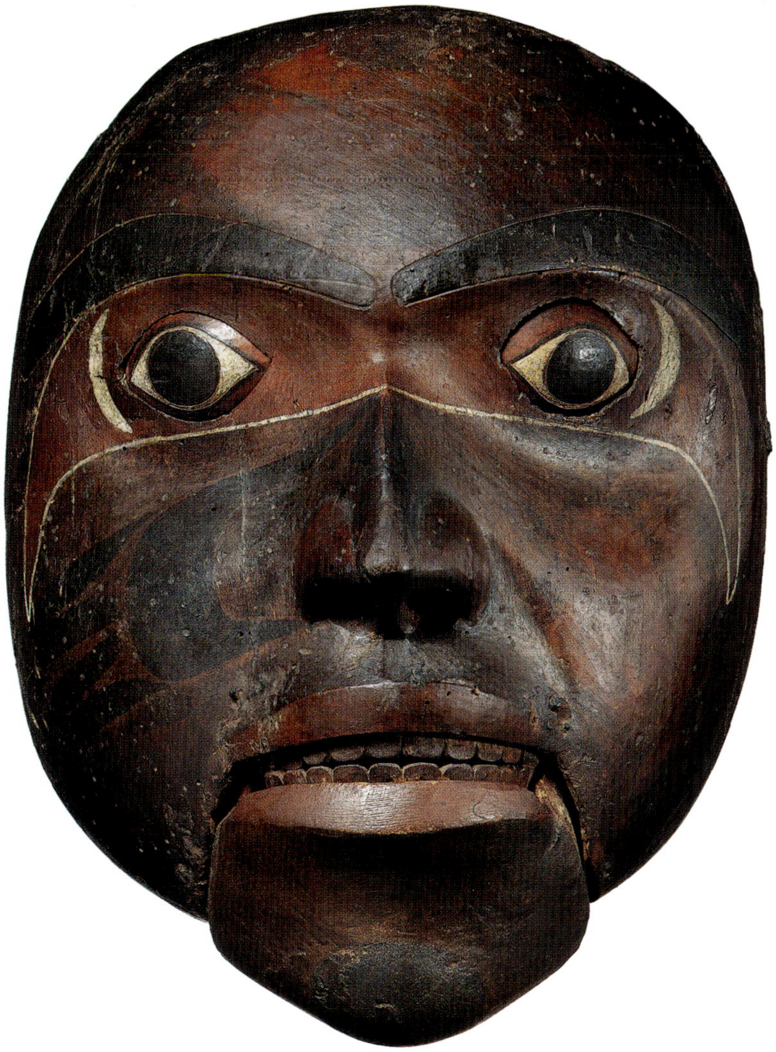

Mask with movable joints

Haida

Canada,
British Columbia
Late 19th century
Cedar wood, fibres, metal, dark green, red, black and white colours
51 x 25.3 x 15 cm
Donated by Aube and Oona Elléouët, former collection André Breton
Inv. 70.2003.9.2

Before the Haida Indians on the western coast of Canada were wiped out by epidemics, the mid 19th century marked the golden age of their art, following their encounter with the West and the opportunity to benefit from the metal tools obtained.
The masks created depict an ancestor or mythical hero, whose deeds were related through theatrical-style performances at initiatory winter festival ceremonial cycles. Such masks were passed around among the initiated and used over a period of several years.
The inside of this early 19th-century artefact contains tenons enabling the moving parts – the jaw and eyes – to be activated through an ingenious system of strings. Moon crescents painted on the temples and eyeballs appear when the eyelids are closed: the opening and closing of the eyes refers to the alternation of day and night. Like Yup'ik masks, British Columbian masks have also fascinated surrealists with their theatricality, extreme expressiveness, poetry, and – according to André Breton – their ability to embrace "one of the greatest human vestiges by achieving transformation not only of thought but also of action". MD-ED

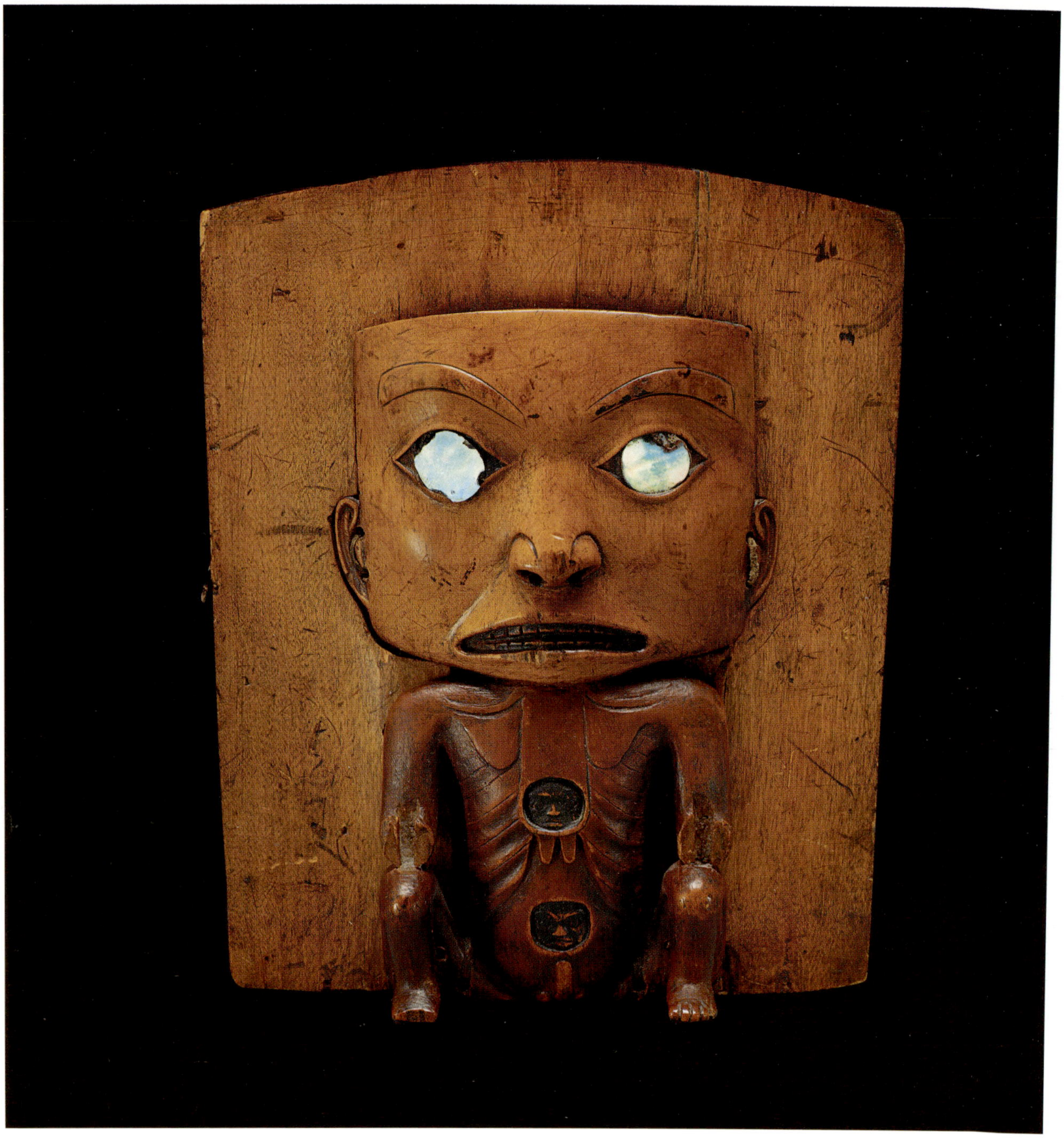

Forehead ornament for ceremonial headdress

Tsimshian

Canada,
British Columbia
19th century
Carved wood,
green mother-of-pearl
22 x 17.5 x 4.3 cm
Former collection
Claude Lévi-Strauss
Inv. 70.2002.31.1

The Tsimshian of British Columbia live by two systems, one civilian and the other religious, which correspond to the two seasons of the year. The first is expressed through potlatches*, and the second through initiation rites.

Potlatches are public events that usually took place in the summer for the purpose of wealth distribution. They were a kind of challenge, with some families going so far as to distribute all their assets in order to preserve or increase their prestige.

Everyone also had to belong to a secret society, under whose auspices winter festivals were held and during which initiation rites took place. A chief, wearing the type of adornment whose central piece can be seen here, presided over and led the dances. The full headdress was composed of feathers and such animal elements as ermine tails or seal whiskers.

This piece was made out of two different types of wood: most probably light maple for the base and face, and alder for the body. The sculpture represents the legendary hero Aitl. Mythical ancestors, in the form of human faces painted on the body, illustrate the legends of the brotherhood to which its former owner belonged. MD-ED

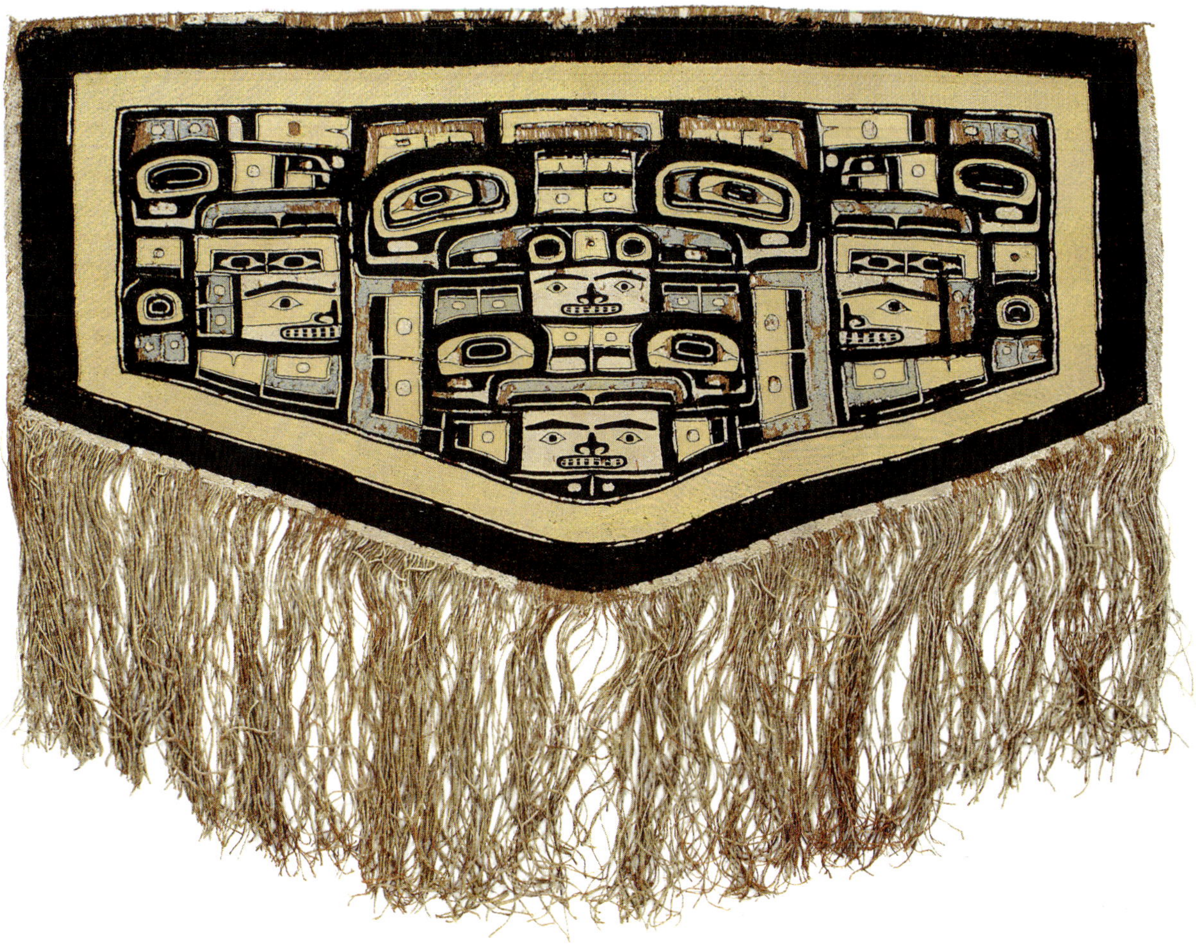

Ceremonial cape known as a "Chilkat blanket"

Tlingit

Canada, British Columbia
19th century
Goat's wool, cedar bark fibre
137.7 x 165.8 x 1 cm
Donated by the Smithsonian Institution, Washington
Inv. 71.1885.78.450

The Chilkat River flows through the north of the Tlingit region, in the southwest of Alaska, a region renowned in the 19th century for the remarkable quality of its textiles, particularly the great ceremonial capes known as "Chilkat blankets" produced there.
Chilkat blankets were a sign of wealth and were highly prized by local elders, who wore them during ceremonies. They could also be offered on the occasion of a potlatch. In some circumstances, they were placed on their owners' tombs as a token of respect, and left exposed to the elements until they were completely destroyed. It took six to twelve months to make one. They were woven from mountain goat wool by the women, who followed patterns designed by the men, the most frequently used colours being black, beige, yellow and blue. The most common main motif was a stylised heraldic animal, symbolising the clan to which the weaver's father or husband belonged, such iconographic motifs serving to evoke the clan's history and mythical origins. MD-ED

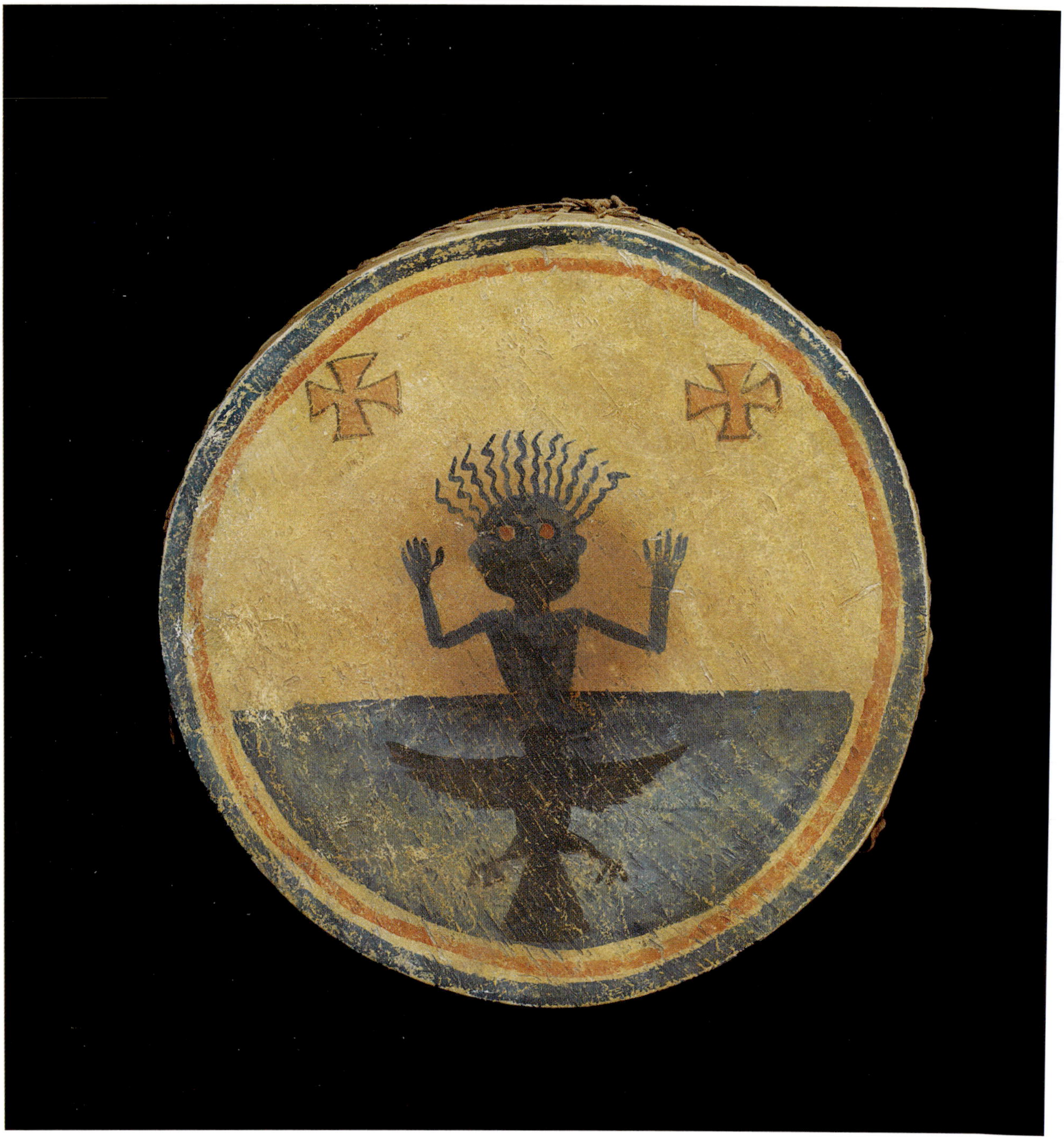

Frame drum

United States, Plains Region
20th century
Wood and painted hide
42 x 42 x 6.5 cm
Inv. 70.2002.18.2

The art of the Plains Indians is expressed in two forms: one, abstract, is of specifically female origin and associated with fertility; the other, figurative, is the work of men and may be read as a narrative, usually about feats of war.
Drums, like shields, reveal the artist's desire to imitate, and regularly depict birds (eagles or crows), buffaloes and deer.
The circular form evokes the notion of a link between past, present and future and, above all, of a passage from the chtonian* (under) world to the cosmic (upper) world, with its two reversed-arm stars. The central figure symbolises the rising sun, while the bird – a crow or nightjar* – beneath the solar star belongs to the realm of night.
This drum, whose theme and iconography make its origin uncertain, has affinities with the Pueblo* world, and may therefore be attributed to the west of the Great Plains of North America, where the Crow or, further south, the Comanche lived. ED

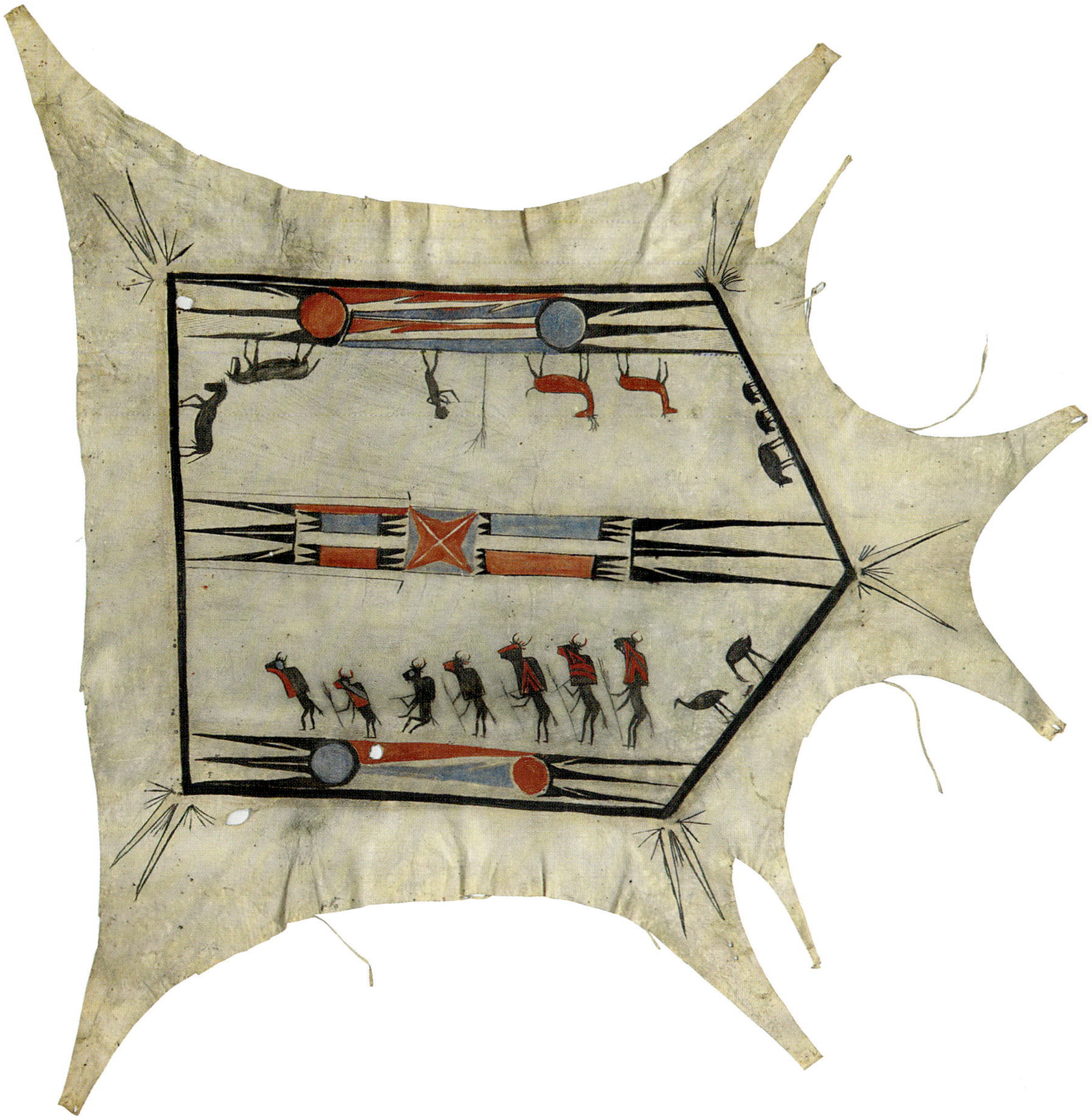

“Buffalo dance” coat

Quapaw

United States, Arkansas, Mississippi Valley
18th century
Painted deer hide
182.5 x 159 x 0.2 cm
Former collection the Marquis de Sérent,
Donated by the public library of Versailles
Inv. 71.1934.33.4

This mid 18th century painted hide comes from the Mississippi Valley and is attributed to the Quapaw Indians, who were living in present-day Arkansas when the Europeans arrived.

Its decoration features two matching figurative scenes – a “buffalo dance” and a deer hunt in which horses and men carrying rifles can be seen – which are framed by three strips comprising tricolour lanceolate motifs and circular or cross-shaped nodes. This iconographic style rapidly disappeared after the arrival of the Europeans.

While these hides give us some idea of the material and spiritual life of the Indians, their real significance remains a mystery. Objects of mediation and interbreeding, as evidenced by the presence of European weaponry, they were perhaps intended to be given to the representatives of the French colonial authority.

This piece comes from the natural history cabinet that the Marquis de Sérent set up at Versailles after 1783 upon request of the Count of Artois, Louis XVI’s brother, for his sons’ education. The cabinet was confiscated during the French Revolution and the artefacts it contained were put on display, along with others belonging to other noble émigrés, in a natural history museum created at Versailles, whose contents were absorbed by the collections at the musée de l’Homme in 1934. MD-ED

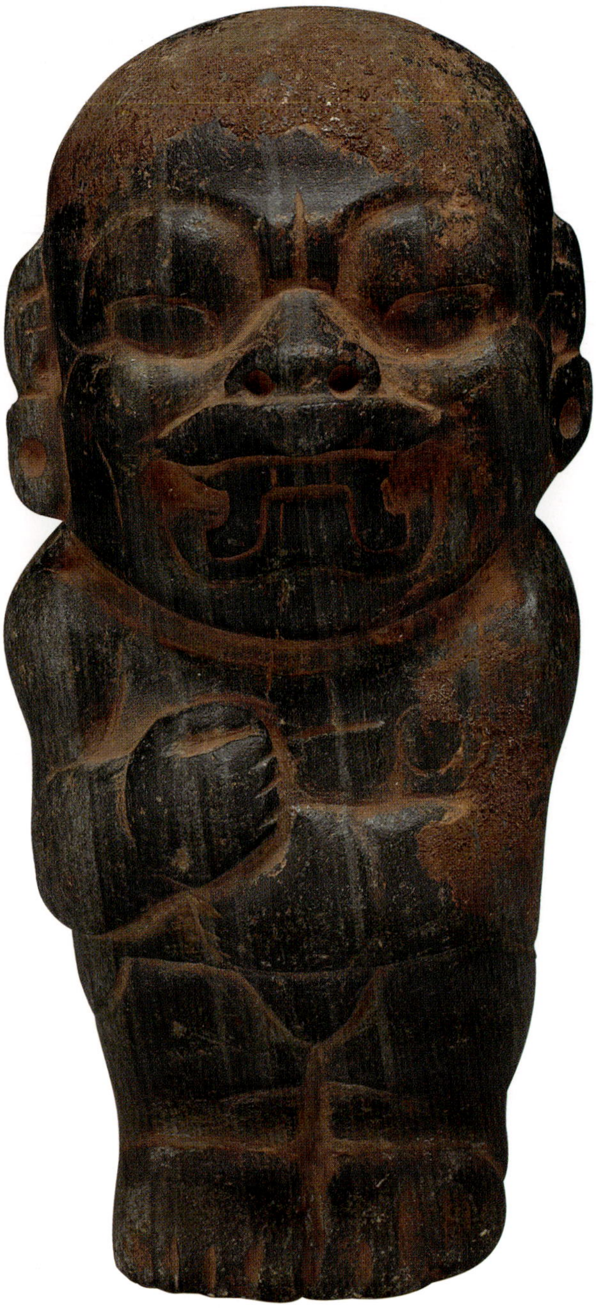

Anthropo-zoomorphic figure

Olmec style

Mexico, Oaxaca
900-600 BC
Green shale,
traces of cinnabar
12.9 x 5.6 x 5.7 cm
Donated by
the Société des amis du
musée ethnographique
du Trocadéro
Inv. 71.1931.33.39

The Olmec style, initially thought to be the artistic expression of a "mother culture" on the southern coast of the Golf of Mexico, was later identified in various other regions of Mesoamerica, from the centre of Mexico as far as Salvador. The widespread presence of this style, along with its recurring motifs, reflects an ideological system shared by a number of Mesoamerican peoples between 1200 and 600 BC. Although humans are the main theme depicted, Olmec art is also rich with animal or hybrid figures.

This figurine endows the human body with the attributes of a jaguar – its legs, mouth, incisors, muzzle and almond eyes – and wears the ear jewellery of a high-ranking individual. Interpretations of such hybrid beings are varied. According to the most recent, these compositions represent places of sacred geography, supernatural forces or their mythical counterparts. Countless iconographic examples link the jaguar with caves, the underground world, and fertility, which is renewed there. The green stone, coated in cinnabar*, could also allude to vegetal regeneration. FP

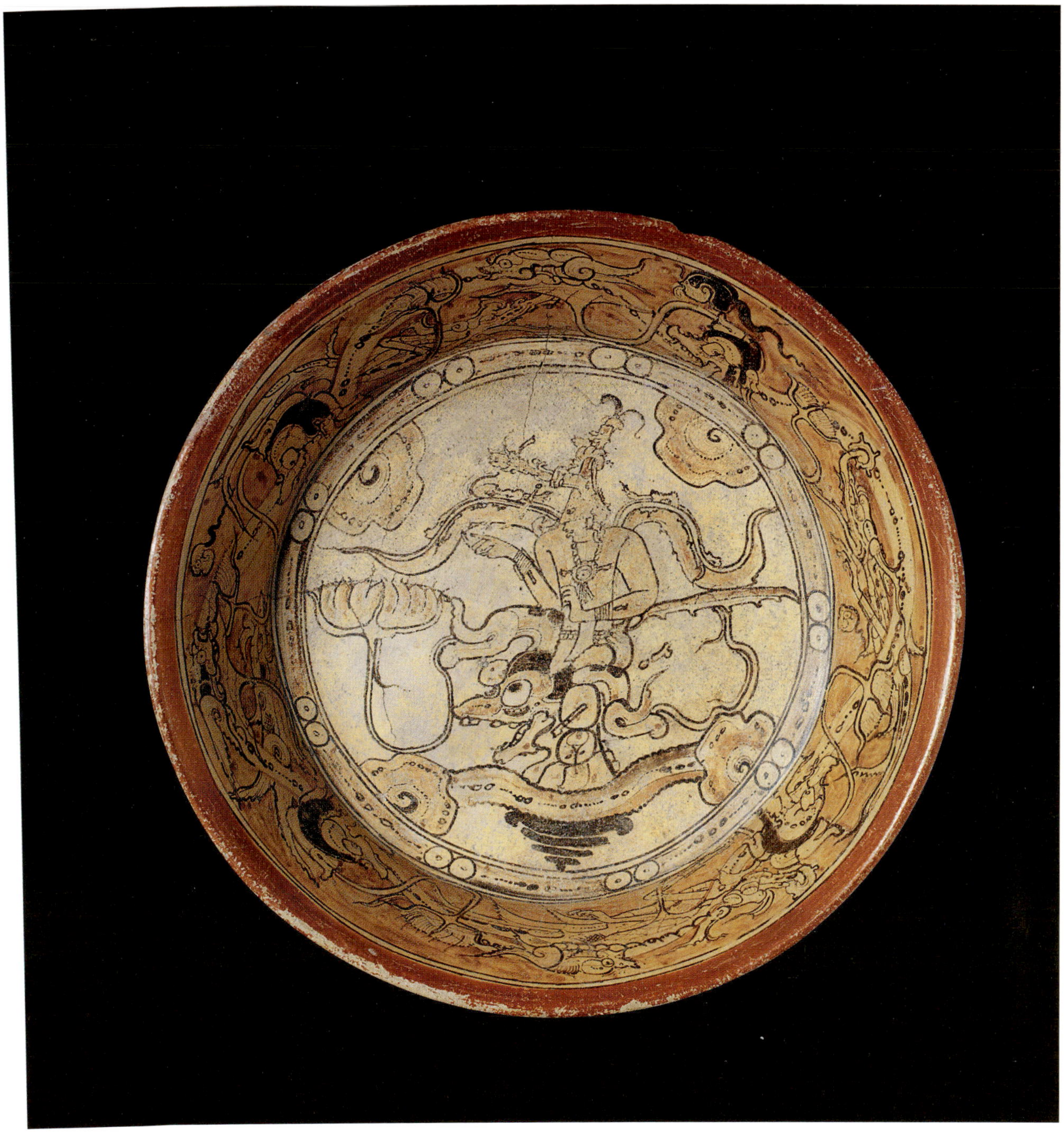

Multicoloured dish

Maya culture

Guatemala, Petén department, or Mexico
600-800
Ceramic
30.6 x 6 cm
Inv. 70.2001.36.1

Between the 4th and 3rd centuries BC, the Maya people settled in the southeast of Mexico and the north of Central America. Multicolour decoration of their pottery is apparent from the 1st century AD, a style that flourished during the Late Classic Period (600-800). Courtyard scenes and cosmological images with texts were commonly depicted.

The bottom inside of this dish is decorated with a recurrent theme: renaissance and fertility. A young man, personifying corn or representing eternal rebirth, comes back to life. He emerges from the emaciated head of a terrestrial monster, image of the earth, whose head is adorned with a water lily symbolising the surface of the waters which separate our world from the underground world. The scene is surrounded by four motifs indicating the cardinal points as well as the way to the world below (probably through a cave), the source of fertility.

The inside of the dish features an aquatic frieze presenting the snakelike form of the terrestrial monster. Its head, decorated with a water lily and repeated four times, is surrounded by a range of different creatures including fish, reminding us of the aquatic milieu from whence the young man is emerging. MD-FP

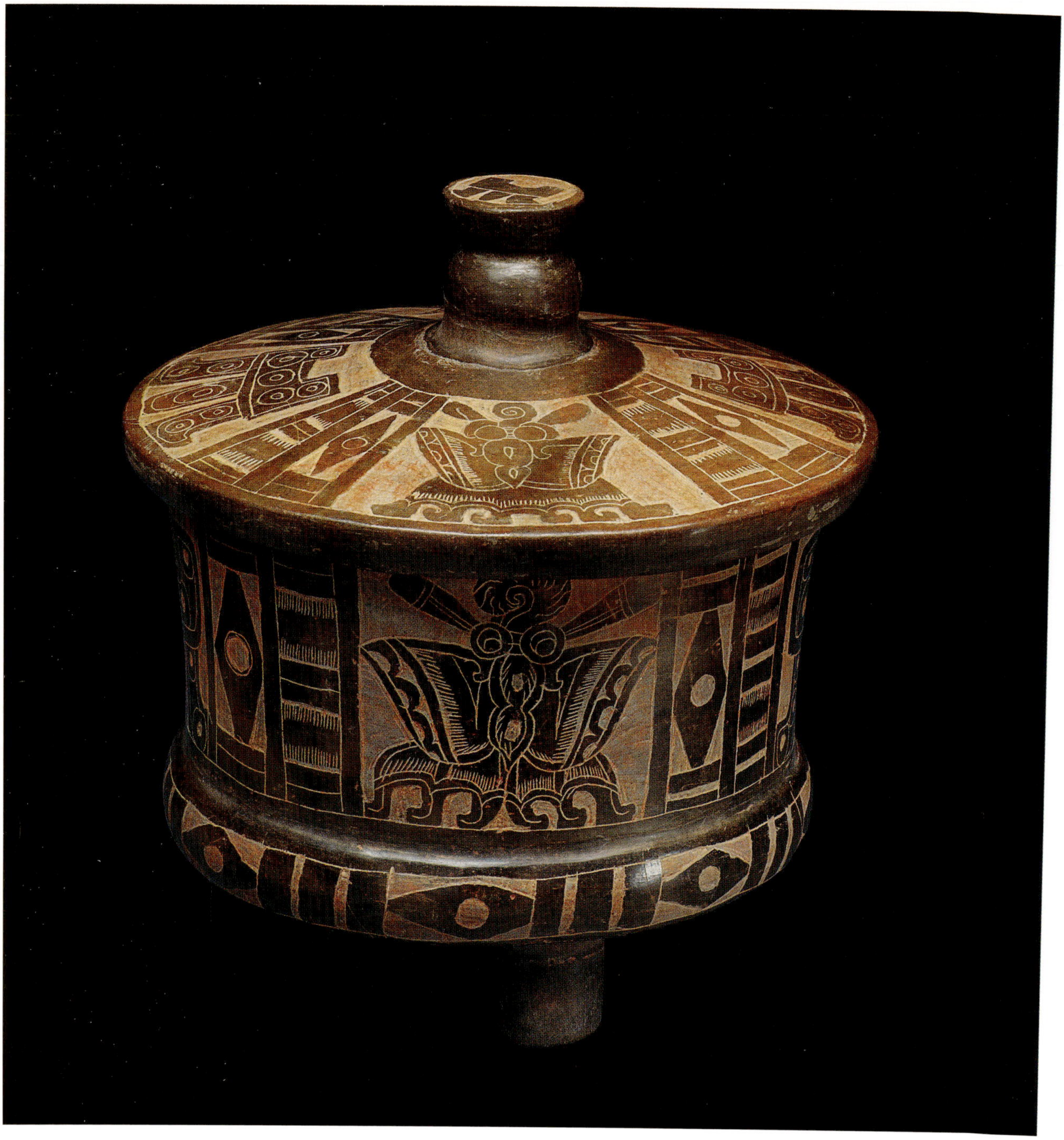

Tripodal vase

Teotihuacán culture

Mexico,
Mexico Basin
150-650
Ceramic
22.7 x 21.5 x 21.3 cm
Inv. 70.2000.5.1-2

Dominating the Mexico Basin for the first six centuries AD, Teotihuacán was the largest planned town in Mesoamerica, with 100,000 inhabitants from a variety of ethnic backgrounds. The associations of figures appearing in its sculpture, on wall paintings decorating palaces, on incense-burners and on pottery enable the gradual deciphering of the city's iconography, a task often facilitated by a number of recurring themes, appearing particularly in statuary and Aztec codices (books) up until the Spanish conquest.

This vase presents three alternating motifs: a butterfly, symbols of fire in the form of diamonds and segments, and a nasal ornament. In Teotihuacán, as in Aztec beliefs, butterflies were often linked with fire and represented the souls of warriors who died in combat or on the altar. Their nectar gathering also evoked vegetal regeneration. The third iconographic motif, a U-shaped bar lined with three feline fangs, symbolises by means of his nasal ornament the deity of water and the earth, ancestor of the Aztec god Tlaloc. FP

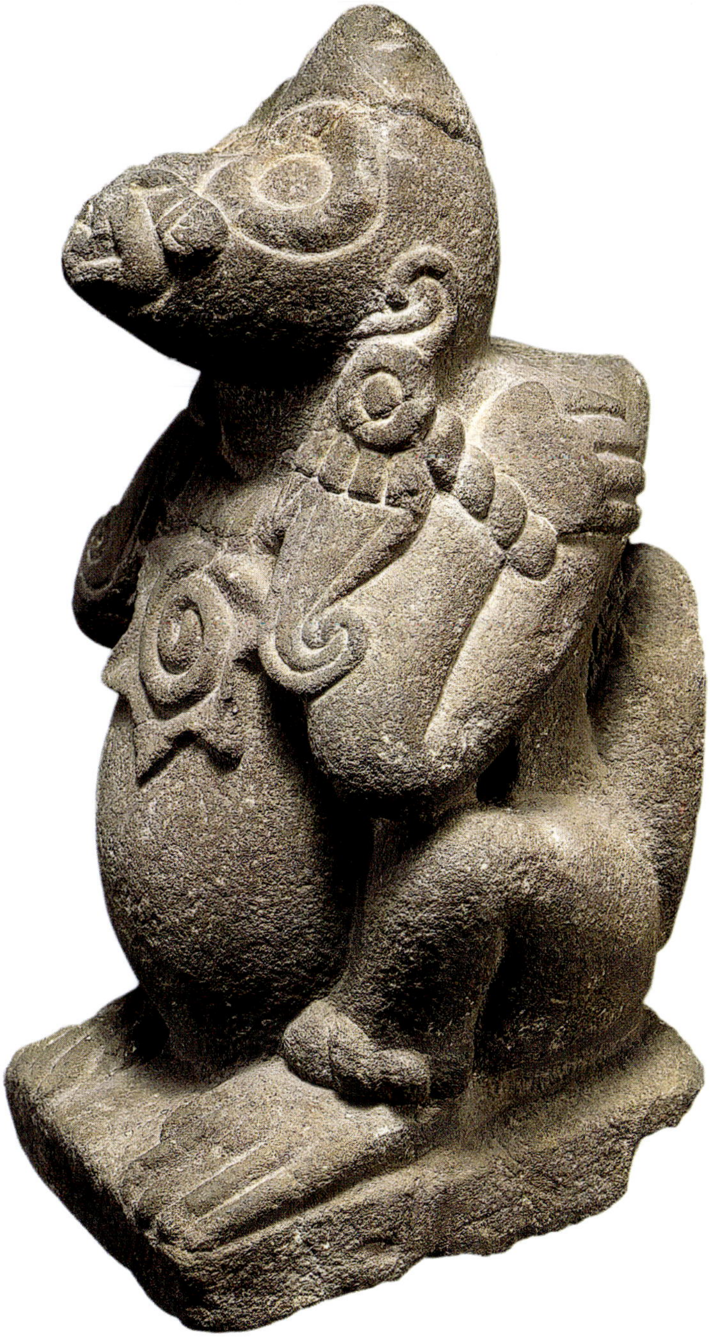

Ehécatl, god of wind

Aztec culture

Mexico,
Mexico Basin
1350-1521
Volcanic stone
44 x 25 x 24 cm
Donated by
Alphone Pinart
Inv. 71.1878.1.89

The Aztecs, or Mexica, settled in the Mexico Basin in the 12th or 13th century. Their civilisation reached its peak in the 14th century, and continued to flourish until 1521, when their empire fell to the Spanish conquerors. It is nevertheless through evidence from the colonial era, in Nahuatl as well as Latin and Spanish, that we have become familiar with the numerous multifaceted gods that made up the Aztec pantheon. Quetzalcóatl (plumed serpent) is one of the best known. Creator of humanity, inventor of the calendar and stealer of fire, he often appeared as the god of wind, Ehécatl, who blows the clouds to bring long-awaited summer rainfall.

Here, Ehécatl-Quetzalcóatl is represented in the form of a spider monkey, which was likened to air currents, spirals and whirlwinds because of its agility and restlessness. He wears his usual adornments: a pectoral composed of a shaped conch* shell, a tubular nose ornament with delicately carved tips, and spiral ear pendants. Nostrils flared, he blows skywards. MD-FP

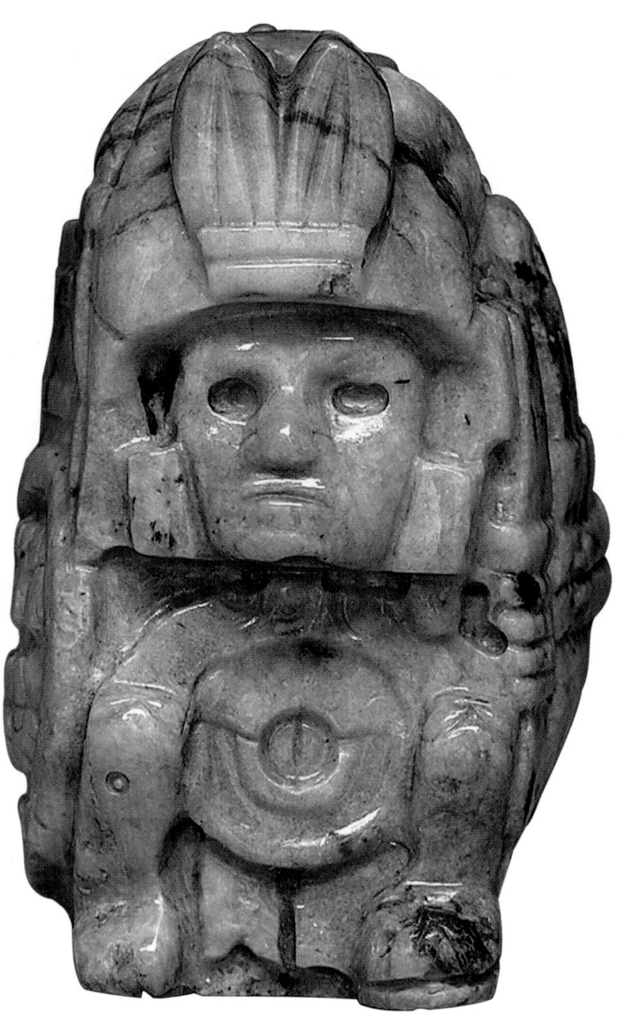

Huitzilopochtli, god of war

Aztec culture

Mexico
1350-1521
Jadeite
6.4 x 4 x 4.7 cm
Inv. 71.1930.100.43

Few representations of Huitzilopochtli, a major deity in the Aztec pantheon, remain, aside from those in codices or on bas-reliefs. This figurine is the only sculpture in the round to have reached us to date.

Legend has it that Huitzilopochtli, a protective god, drove the Aztecs from their place of origin, the mythical island of Azlán, to the lake of Texcoco. There, in 1325, they founded Mexico-Tenochtitlán, which became one of their empire's two capitals. God of war and the sun, Huitzilopochtli was also linked with the image of a young and courageous conqueror.

Here, the god is depicted seated, dressed in a cape of intertwined bones and skulls. He wears a headdress decorated with two heron feathers, two large ear pendants and two shell pendants, one on his chest and the other on his back. He holds a spear-thrower in his left hand, behind which a large sacrificial knife is visible. A circular shield hides his right hand and a snake's head replaces his left foot. This figurine was long considered to represent Tezcatlipoca, "smoking mirror", but the hummingbird which appears on his back undoubtedly identifies Huitzilopochtli, whose name means "the hummingbird on the left, or of the south". This bird represents the sun at its zenith. MD-FP

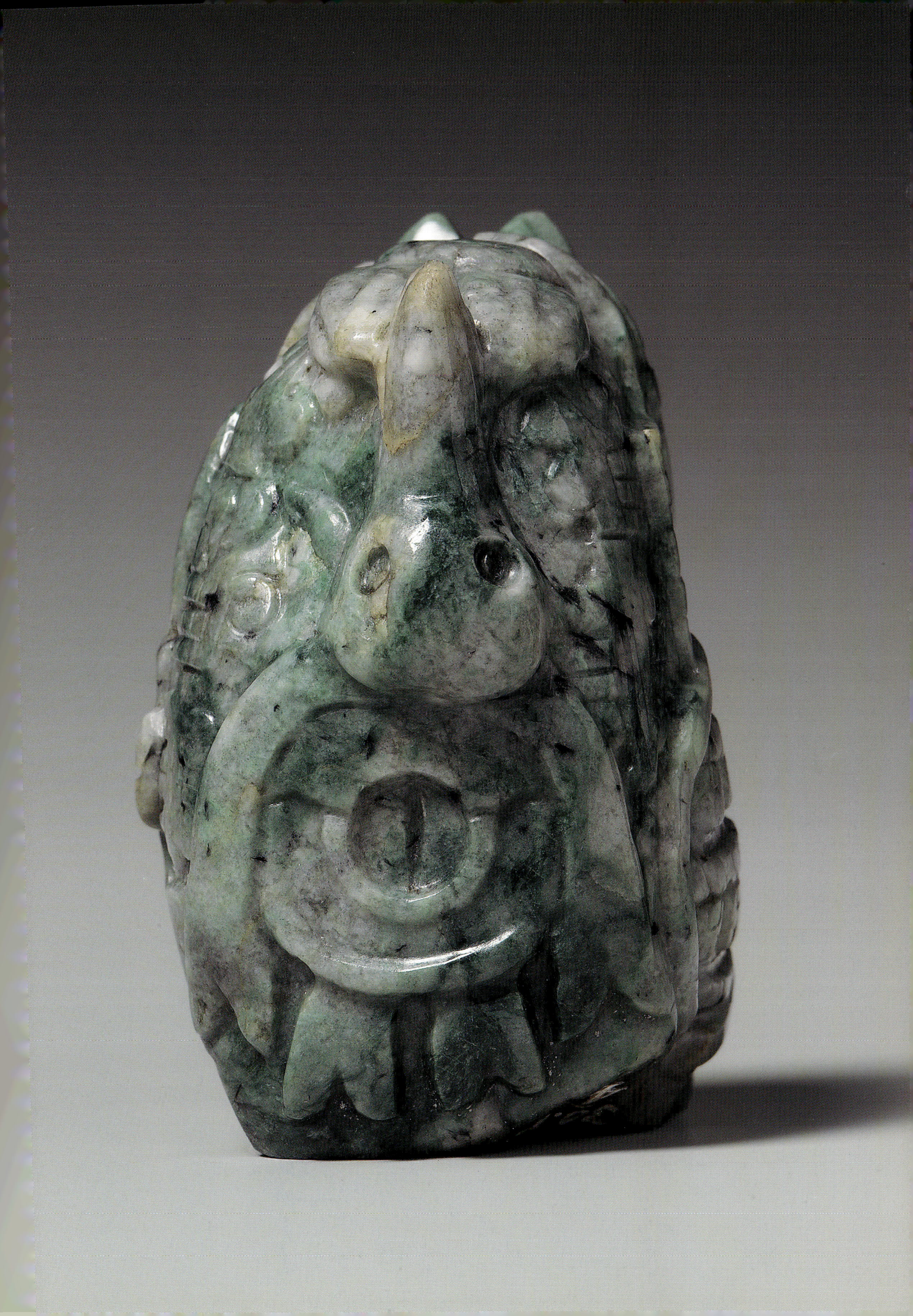

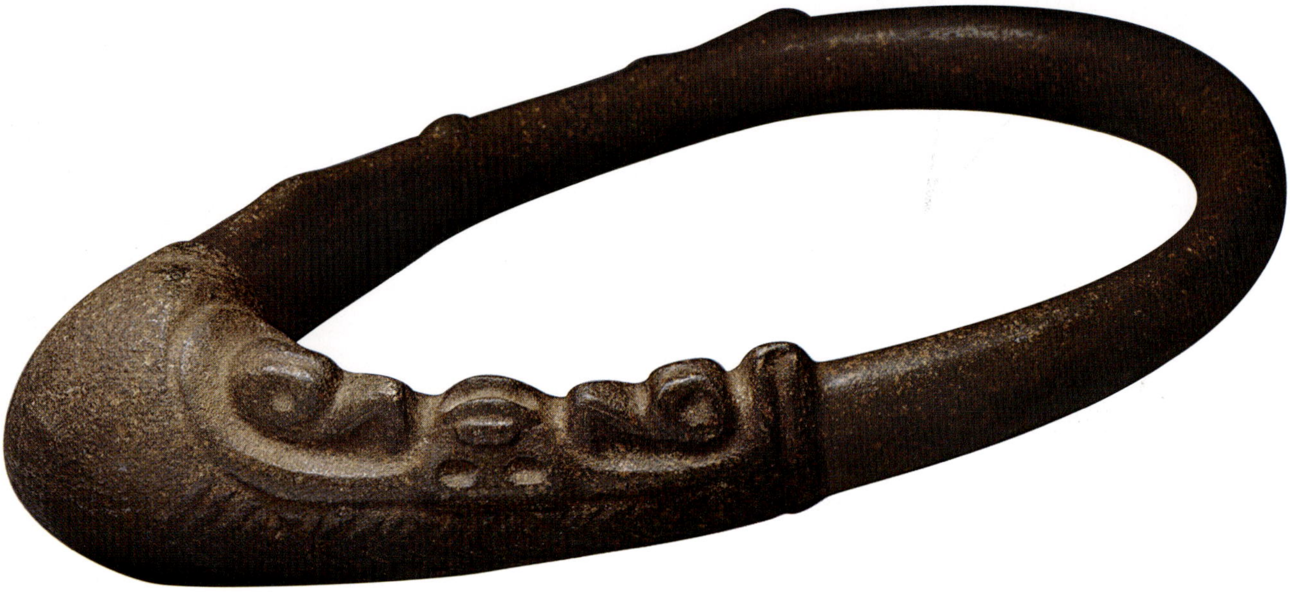

Necklace or yoke

Taino culture

Porto Rico
1200-1500
Stone
26,5 x 43,5 cm
Donated by
Dr Montane
Inv. 71.1891.49.1

When the Spanish arrived at the end of the 15th century, the Taino people of the Antilles lived in Porto Rico, Hispaniola, the east of Cuba, and the surrounding islands. Organised into chiefdoms under a cacique, these insular Amerindian societies played *batey*, a sacred ball game played with a rubber ball, of which we know little. Archaeological research has brought to light great ceremonial centres containing squares lined with engraved stones. A whole array of artefacts seems to be linked with the complex religious ceremonies held there, and during which the ball game was played, including carved stone rings, enigmatic pieces whose very names – necklace, yoke or belt – are still uncertain. According to some hypotheses, they could be reproductions of wooden or cotton belts worn as protection during the game. While much of the ring is smooth, one part of it features abstract decoration combined with figurative motifs, most probably a bat, and, under its wings, two bird heads. These symbols represent the *zemi*, spirits of Taino mythology and religion. AD

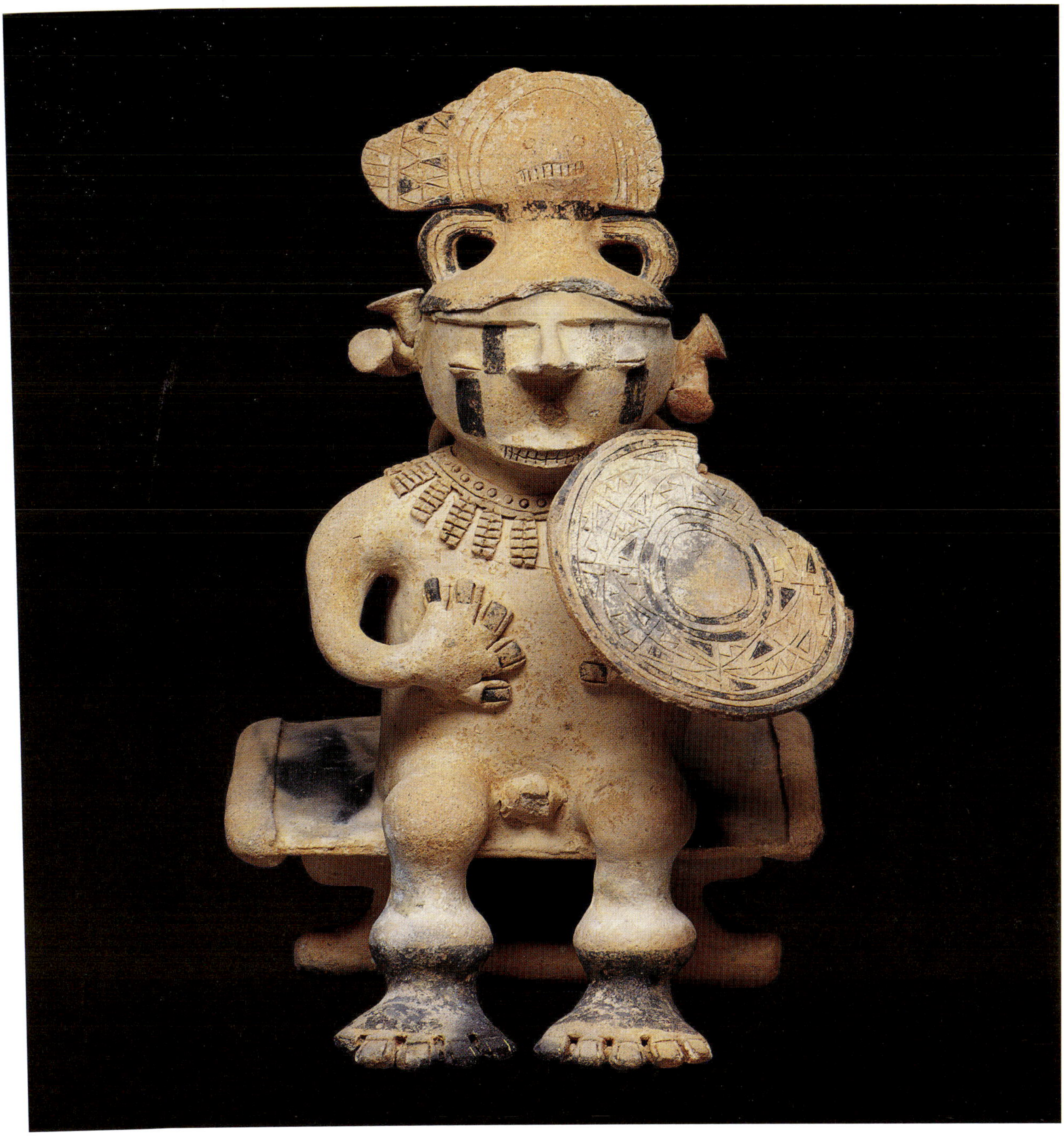

Statuette of a warrior sitting on a bench

Cauca culture

Columbia, Cauca department, Popayán region
1000-1600
Painted ceramic
24 x 36 x 22 cm
Legacy of Guillermo Valencia
Inv. 71.1947.31.1

The region of upper Cauca, in southwest Columbia, has yielded gold, silver and ceramic artefacts of a very particular style, produced somewhere between 1000 and 1600. Most of them came from clandestine and undocumented digs, and as a result, are difficult to date accurately.
Among the most exceptional of the ceramic artefacts is this votive statuette, of which only three models are known to exist worldwide. It depicts a warrior equipped with a shield, wearing a headdress, necklace and two large circular ear adornments, and decorated with facial paintings: warriors from this region decorated their bodies in this way to protect themselves from their enemies or to instil terror in them. Its calves are deliberately deformed, using tight straps to swell the muscles and produce a more impressive appearance.
Everything about the statuette is designed to enhance the warrior's imposing image. He is sitting on a bench, a sign of stability and wisdom. On his back is a fantastic animal with a long tail, perhaps symbolising the man's animal double, or some protective accompanying animal. PNR

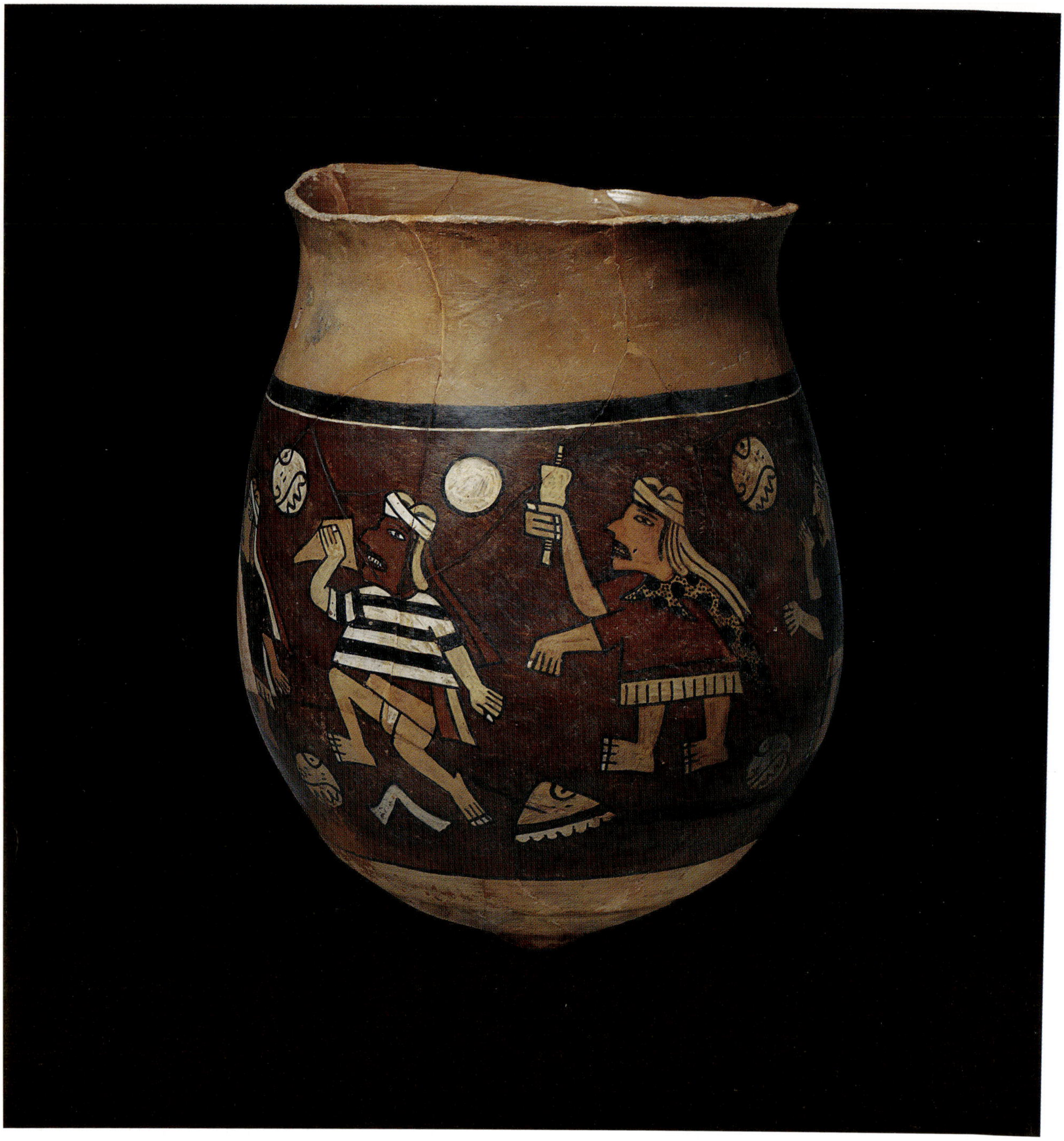

Drum body

Nasca culture

Peru,
Nasca region
200 BC-700 AD
Ceramic
63 x 47 x 47 cm
Donated by the Société des amis du musée de l'Homme
Inv. 71.1959.95.1

Ceramic artefacts were common in all Pre-Hispanic* Peruvian cultures. The Nasca people, inhabiting the valleys of the south coast of Peru between Pisco and Acari, combined a hugely diverse formal repertoire with a wide range of colours and highly varied iconographic motifs, both abstract and figurative.
This exceptionally large piece comes from the oldest phase of Nasca culture, characterised by its so-called "monumental" style, in which naturalist decoration stands out from a beige-brown or sometimes white background. The drum is decorated by a procession of dancers playing musical instruments, among which a rattle, panpipes and a wind instrument, probably a double flute, may be distinguished.
The ceramic was originally covered with a hide membrane that was struck with the bare hand, with a wooden stick, or possibly a section of human tibia. This round-based drum – an unusually large kettledrum to be exact – was most probably used during ritual ceremonies of a propitiatory character. MD

Ceremonial gauntlet
decorated with stylised birds and figures
Chimu-lambayeque culture

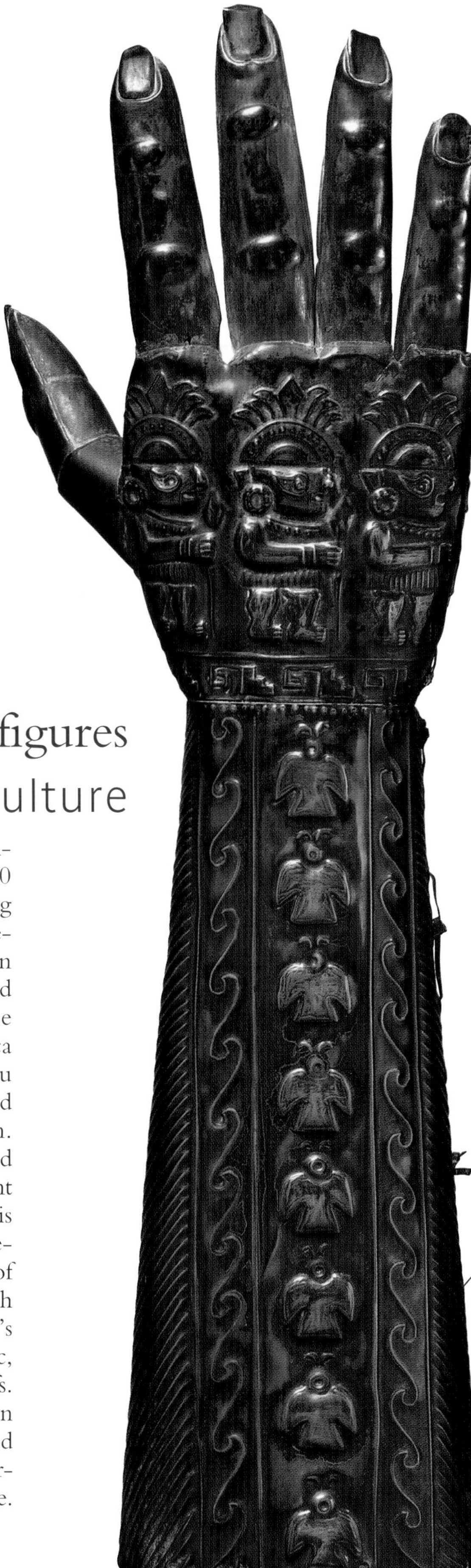

Peru, north coast
1100-1450
Silver
41.6 x 13 x 6.5 cm
Inv. 70.2002.7.1

When the north coast of Peru came to be dominated by the Chimor kingdom between 1100 and 1450, a fifteen-century-old metalworking tradition was already in place. Individual, three-dimensional human figures were depicted in particular, and such representations can be found on ceramics and in architecture from the Chavín* era (800-100 BC) and the Mochica period (100 BC-700 AD), while in the Chimu period, they were common on silver and gold artefacts. Forearm forms were common. Although this type of artefact is often referred to as a gauntlet, there is no evidence at present to confirm that this was what it was. This example seems to have had an essentially ceremonial function. Made from several sheets of silver, beaten, stamped and joined together with rivets, the gauntlet was designed to fit an adult's forearm. It is decorated all over with geometric, anthropomorphic and ornithomorphic motifs. The top of the hand is adorned with human figures, most probably representing armed warriors, wearing the plumed headdresses characteristic of the northern region of Lambayeque.
PNR

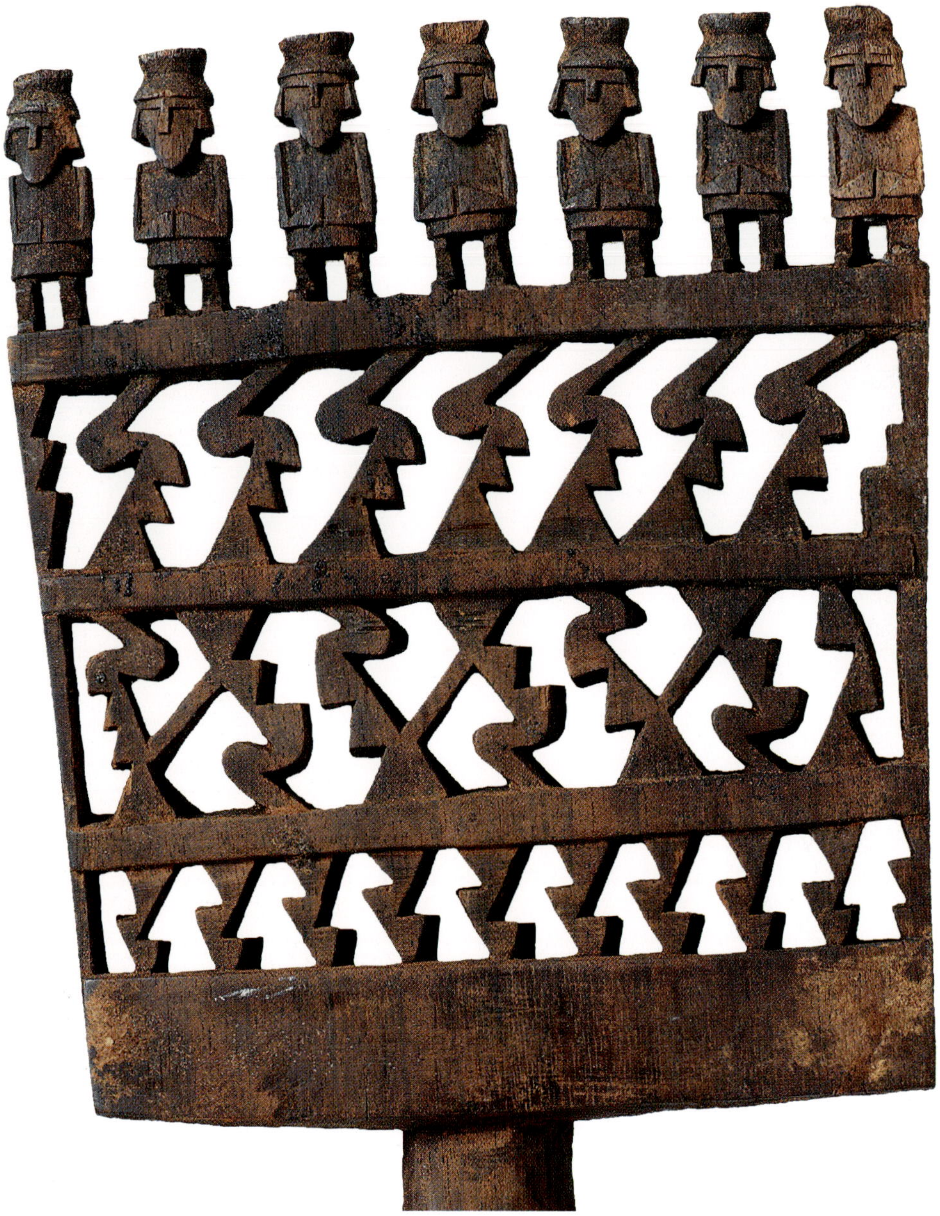

Ceremonial paddles

Ica-Chincha culture

Peru, south coast
1100-1532
Algarrobo wood
traces of multicolour decoration
229.5 x 23.2 x 5 cm
Inv. 70.2000.4.1 (detail)
218 x 21.5 x 4 cm
Inv. 70.2000.4.2

Before the Spanish conquest in 1532, the Chincha kingdom was one of the most prestigious in the Andes, and Peru's trade centre. Its most prosperous period lasted from 1200 to 1450, when it fell under Inca control. Located in the fertile valleys of the south coast of Peru, the kingdom had founded its economy on agricultural and maritime resources, and the expertise of merchant-sailors specialising in maritime trade.
Such long wooden blades with cylindrical handles, decorated with exquisite openwork and carved motifs, date back to this time of plenty. Similar in shape and size, they are decorated with rows of small human figures and friezes of birds, fish and geometric motifs. The upper tip of these two paddles, indented in the shape of a half-moon, would have been used as the handle.
The purpose of such artefacts is unknown. They could hardly have been designed for use, as there are no signs of wear and tear, and all specimens of known origin have been put in funerary contexts. Some may well have been ceremonial farming instruments, while others, representations of boat oars, were emblematic of the status of the merchant-sailors, who would have wished to take them to the great beyond. PNR

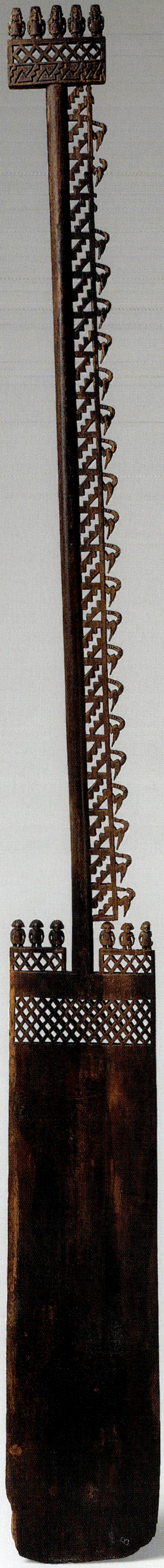

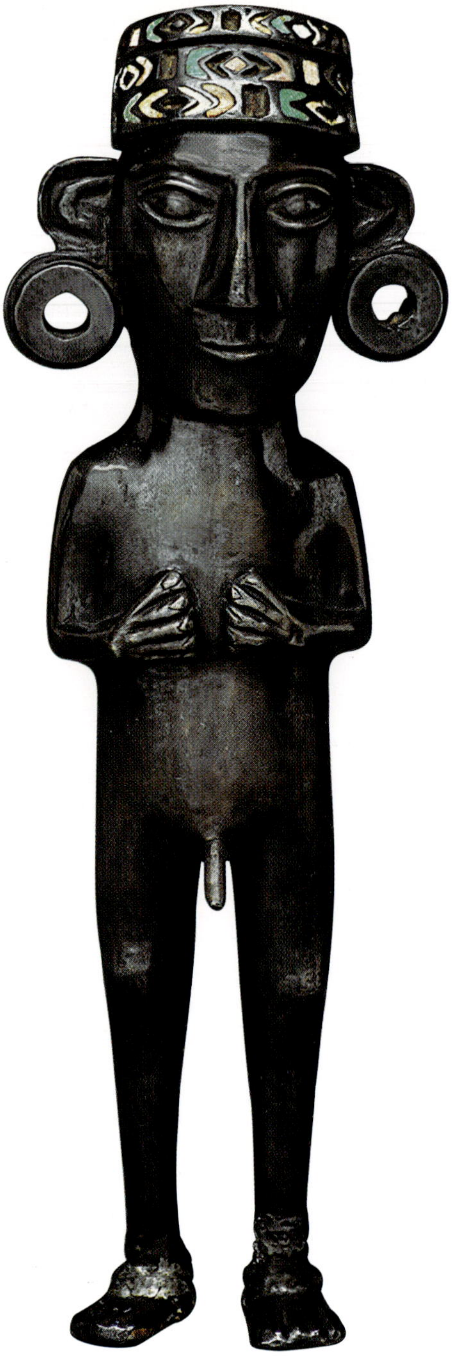

Male figurine

Inca culture

Peru, southern Andes
1450-1532
Silver, coloured paste inlays
20,1 x 6,4 x 4,5 cm
Former collection Auguste Le Moyne
Inv. 71.1887.114.90

The Inca Empire reached its peak between 1450 and 1532. During this period, Chimu silversmiths from the north coast of Peru, reputed as the most skilled of their time, were requisitioned by Inca authorities to work in State metallurgical workshops. Despite profuse production, few pieces of Inca silverware have reached us, as most were melted down by the conquistadors to be sent to Spain.

Production included small figurines fashioned from sheets of silver or gold, hammered and welded together, depicting people of either sexes or camelidae. They were placed as offerings in tombs and sanctuaries, and at sacred natural sites such as caves, springs, and mountaintops.

This male figure with a headband is wearing large circular ornaments in his pierced and stretched ear lobes, a deformation reserved for men of the Inca nobility as a sign of their status, and one that prompted the Spanish to give the nobles the nickname *orejones* ("men with big ears"). Originally, this type of statuette was probably adorned with miniature clothes in the fashion of the time – a coat, feather headdress and coca bag – few examples of which have come down to us. PNR

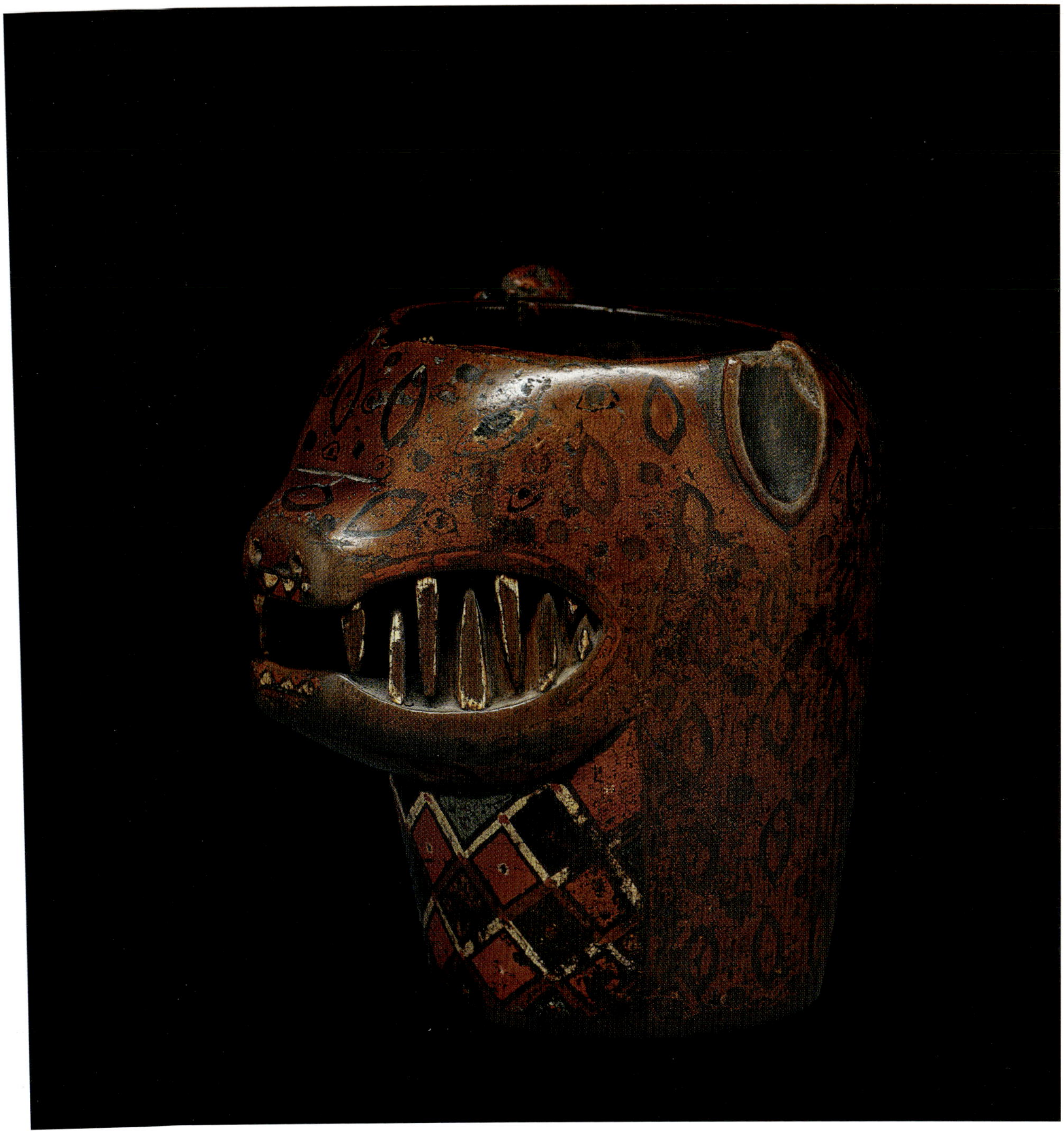

Ceremonial goblet or *kero*

Inca colonial era

Peru, Southern Andes, Cuzco region
18th century
Wood inlaid with coloured resins
22 x 15 x 21 cm
Donated by Mme la générale Mangin
Inv. 71.1933.128.1

In the 15th and early 16th centuries, the Incas expanded their empire over the Andes from their capital, Cuzco*, imposing artistic and cultural uniformity across an area covering more than 5,500 km, from Quito in Ecuador to the centre of Chile.

A *kero*, its Quechua* name, is a wooden cone-shaped goblet with a flat bottom, decorated using the champlevé* technique of hollowing out then painting in motifs with vibrantly coloured resins. This artefact, inspired by the ceramic goblets of the Tiwanaku culture (500-1150), assumed special importance in the Inca period when it was used for ritual libations of water and *chicha*, a corn-based fermented drink.

The production of *kero* continued into the colonial period up until the 18th century. Reserved for the nobility of Cuzco, they became displays of an iconography reflecting the resistance of the indigenous Inca world. The oldest pieces combine geometric and figurative motifs. More recent models, mostly made after the European invasion, took on the form of a human or animal head. Such is the case for this *kero*, in the shape of a feline head with protruding fangs and speckled skin. PNR

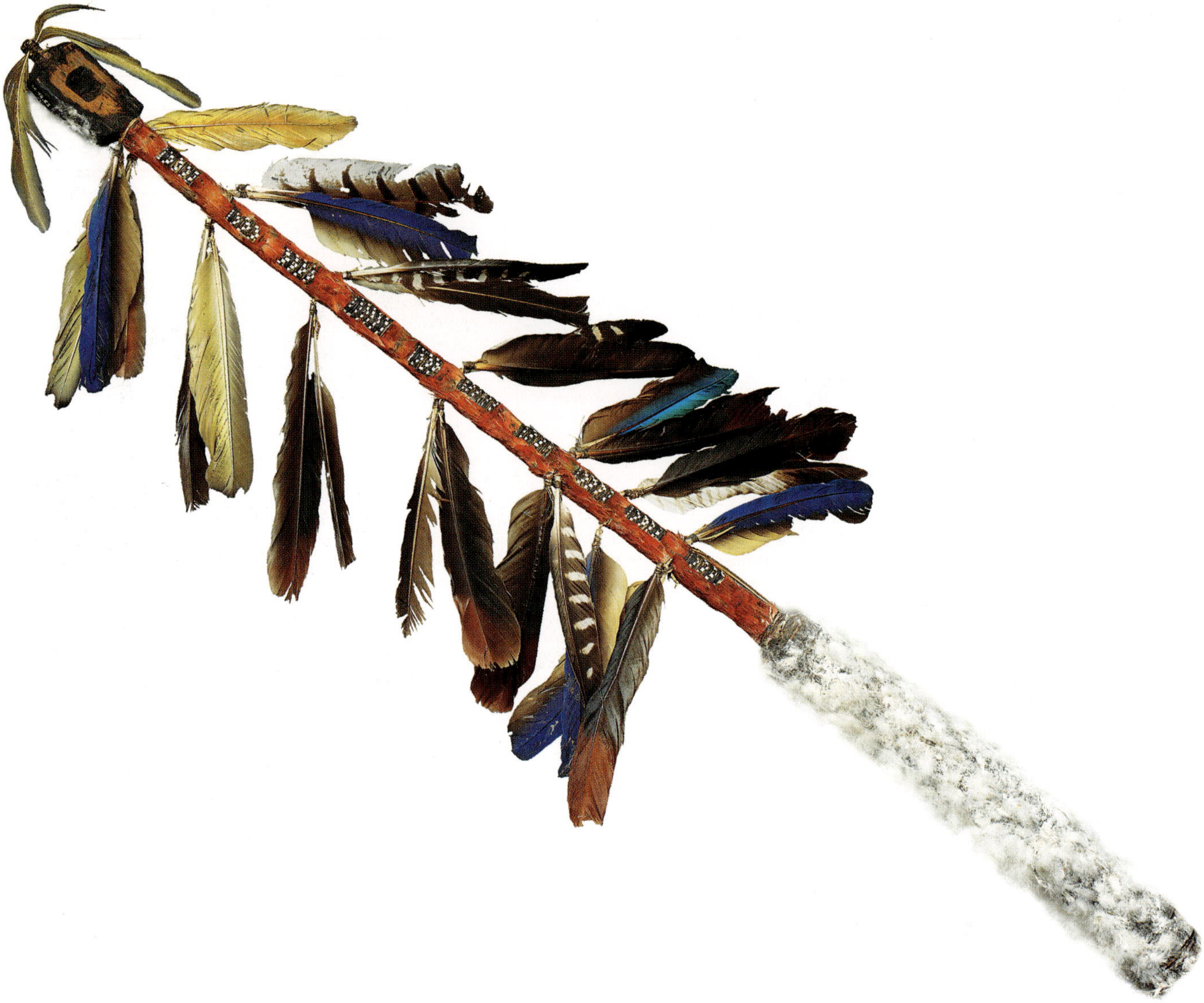

Lateral trumpet *ika*

Bororo

Brazil, State of Mato Grosso, rio Vermelho, Aldeia Kejara
19th century
Wood, feathers, porcupine quills
102 x 16.3 x 6.3 cm
Claude and Dina Lévi-Strauss Mission (collected in 1935-1936)
Inv. 71.1936.48.63

The complexity of the social organisation and wealth of mythology of the Bororo people, hunter-gatherers and horticulturists from Mato Grosso, have been a constant source of fascination for ethnologists. In 1935, Claude Lévi-Strauss spent some time in one of their villages and brought back a wide range of artefacts, including this musical instrument.

This wooden trumpet with a lateral opening is covered with down, porcupine quills and feathers from various species of birds, and its creation , a man's work, required ingenious and meticulous assembly and ligaturing.

The *ika* trumpet is linked to a mythological being whose voice it evokes. Like most musical instruments produced by this culture, it gives little variation of timbre or tone, but adapts to the melody of a song. It also accompanies dances, particularly during funerary rituals.

This exhibit alone summarises the importance sound held for the Amazonian Indians. It is also representative of feather art, stemming from a very strong tradition of identity in which each ethnic group distinguished itself through the use of material and colour. MD

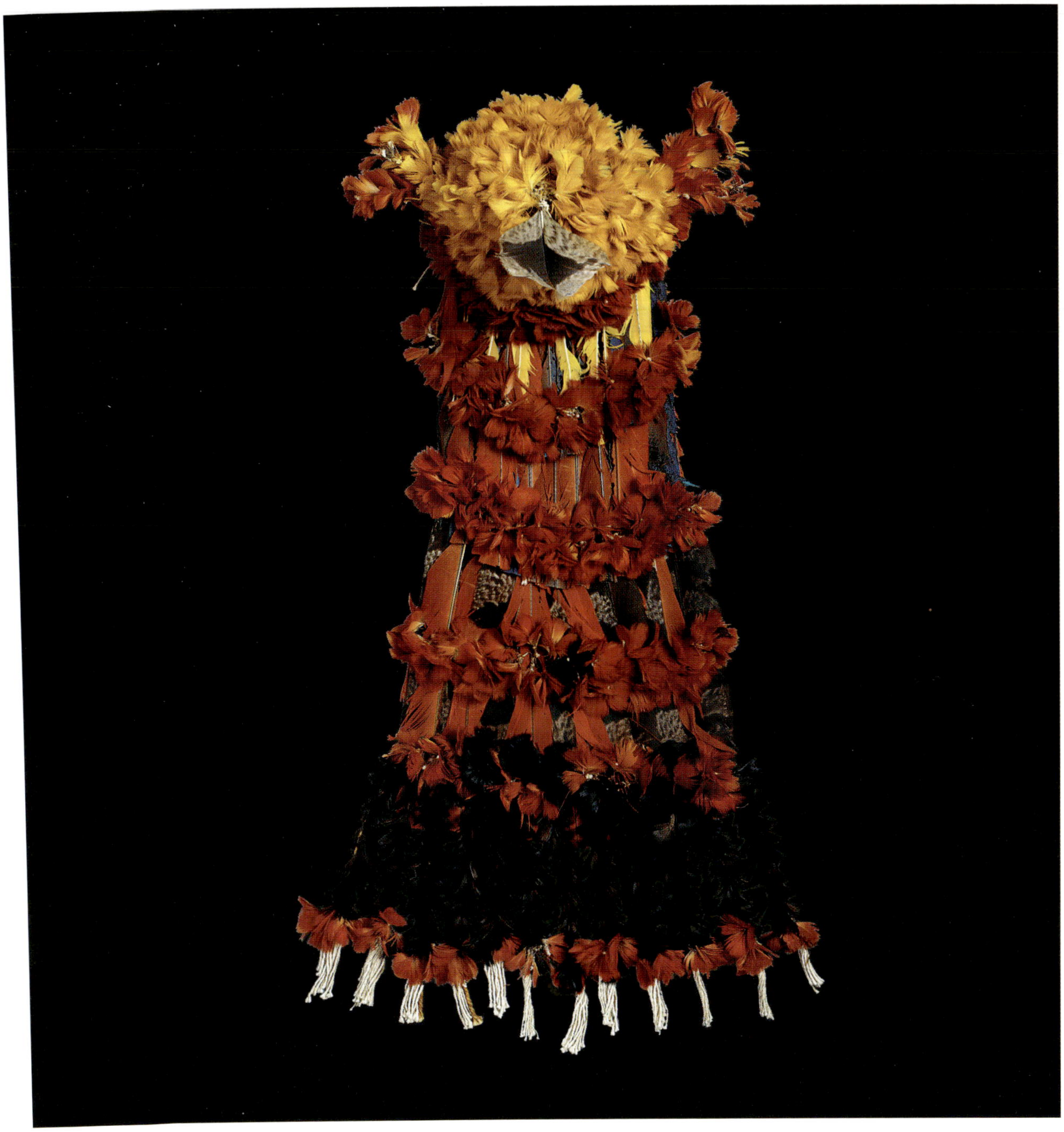

Headdress with neck cover

Munduruku

Brazil,
State of Para,
rio Tapajós
19th century
Feathers, cotton
75.5 x 12.8 x 32.5 cm
Inv. 71.1878.53.3

The Munduruku people, who speak Tupi, live in the middle Xingu region, in central Amazonia. Their existence was first noted by Europeans in 1768. Considered as fearsome warriors, they beheaded their enemies and turned their heads, mummified and adorned with feathers, cotton, resin and animal teeth, into ritual trophies. Three of these head-trophies are today on display in the musée du quai Branly collections.

The Munduruku were also remarkable crafts-people and past masters at feather art. This skilfully composed headdress is characteristic of Tupi feather art. It comprises a thick cotton bonnet covered with yellow feathers, and a neck cover made from tufts of small, mainly red feathers. Worn by men along with other accessories of the same colour – chains, armbands, bracelets, belts, leg adornments – on black body paintings of sophisticated design, such headdresses demonstrate the beauty and impact of the ceremonial attire worn by Amazonian peoples. ACT-AD

Areca nut Palm-tree fruit containing a nut which, rolled in lime-coated Betel leaf, is chewed in Asia and New Guinea.

Auto-da-fé Act of destroying by fire.

Bamana (or Banmana) Former name of the Bambara. This people lived mainly in Mali. They are renowned for their masks and powerful wooden sculptures, the oldest of which date back to the 14th century.

Beaming Preparation and mounting of warp during manufacture of a textile.

Behanzin (or Gbehanzin) King Behanzin is famous for having fiercely resisted French colonisation in Abomey. He succeeded his father, Glele, in 1889. His reign came to an end in 1894, when he was exiled.

Breadfruit tree Precious tree of the fig family, much appreciated in Tahiti for its fruit and for its bark, and from which clothing is made, using the famed tapa beaten bark cloth.

Captain James Cook (1728-1779) English sailor famed for his three great voyages in the South Seas. His shipboard journal is still required reading. He also brought back numerous artefacts, which are now dispersed in the collections of European museums.

Caryatid Architectural term for an upright female statue serving as a column.

Cassowary Bird inhabiting the tropical forests of Australia and New Guinea. It has supple brown plumage with hints of black, a brightly coloured neck, and a bony crest adorning the top of its head.

Champlevé Technique consisting of making hollows in a given material in order to obtain motifs in relief. The term is generally applied to enamelwork.

Chavín Great religious centre and one of the oldest civilisations in Peru (1500-2000 BC). Its technical and artistic production influenced a good many neighbouring cultures.

Chthonian Belonging to the earth or underground world.

Cinnabar Red mineral used as a colorant, and employed as a pigment under the name vermilion.

Conch Mollusc living in warm seas and harvested for its mother of pearl.

Congregation of Picpus Missionary society founded in the French city of Poitiers on Christmas Day 1800, and which introduced Catholicism to the Hawaiian Islands.

Core (wooden) Medium for a sculpture.

Cosmic tree In almost all traditions throughout the world, this giant tree forms the link between earth and sky, and is the source of life and of knowledge.

Cuzco Founded by the Incas in the 1st century AD, the city of Cuzco (its name means 'world navel' in the Quechua language) is now classed as World "Cultural Heritage" for the richness of its Inca and colonial architecture.

Dongsonian culture The Dongsonian civilisation, taking its name from Dong Son in North Vietnam, extended over South-East Asia until the 1st and 2nd century AD. It was in this era that the bronze drums to be found from China to Insulindia first appeared.

Enchantress In Nivkh myths, the embroideress is a magician. The term *nivkh*, used for "to embroider", also means to practise sorcery and cast evil spells.

End of mourning African ceremony following long periods of mourning. This is a time for the living to separate themselves definitively from the deceased, who can finally reach the land of the dead and the ancestors.

Enthronement Accession to the throne, to power.

Esparto Technique for fashioning artefacts from vegetable fibres.

Fon People inhabiting the former Kingdom of Dahomey, the present-day Republic of Benin. They were the first to practise African Voodoo, which was later introduced into the Caribbean Islands, Haiti in particular.

Grassland Western and north-western provinces of Cameroon.

Grebo This people emigrated from the southern Sahara in 1550 and settled in present-day Liberia. Grebo masks are highly stylised, and echoed the quest for modernism by early 20th century European artists.

Griaule Marcel (1898-1956) Pioneer of research in French territories in Africa, Mali in particular, he collected a large number of artefacts for the musée de l'Homme. His works on the Dogon are still required reading today.

Hafton House House built by James Hunter, a Glaswegian businessman, between 1816 and 1820.

Haussa People living to the southwest of Lake Chad, mainly in central Niger, northern Nigeria and the southern Sahara.

Headhunting Ritual custom practised on several continents, and particularly widespread in Oceania. It consisted of obtaining a "trophy head" during tribal wars, as an act of vengeance and desire for power, in order to achieve higher social status or, as regards young warriors, to achieve adult status. In Asia, it was a ritual act linked to the concept of fertility. In the north-east of India and Myanmar, Naga warriors took human heads to demonstrate their power and increase their fertility, extending it to the whole village by holding Merit Feasts*. The British put an end to the practice during the colonial period.

High warp Weaving technique in which warp yarns are stretched on a vertical loom.

In-the-round Sculpting technique enabling development of all three dimensions, and highlighting of hollows as well as reliefs.

Janus Roman god with two faces. More generally, the term signifies anyone who is "two-faced".

Mande Synonym of Mandingo. This people founded the Malian Empire, which flourished from the 12th to the 14th century and covered a vast group of African territories: Mali, Guinea, Senegal, Gambia, the Ivory Coast, Sierra Leone, and Liberia.

Matted Matt, as opposed to gloss.

Men's house Oceanian spirit and ancestor house. Men met within its walls to carry out rituals or make major decisions.

Merit Feast Collective ceremony at which a wealthy man puts on a feast for the whole community and makes codified offerings. A merit feast does not confer high status, but is a community's recognition of it. It legitimises an individual's wealth and emphasises that it springs not from his material possessions but from supernatural fertility.

Monoxylic In a single piece. A monoxylic artefact is fashioned from a single piece of material, with no assembly work needed.

Nasrid Name of the royal dynasty which ruled Grenada between the 13th and 15th centuries.

Nautilus Conch-shaped shell with a diameter of 20 to 25 cm. Its interior is in spiral form and is made up of small chambers separated by mother-of-pearl partitions.

Nephrite One of the two types of jade, the other being jadeite. Found in New Zealand and elsewhere.

Nightjar Reddish-brown, mainly nocturnal American passerine, with a gaping beak.

Parinarium nut Seed used to decorate Oceanian artefacts.

Potlatch Ceremonial exchange practised by the Indians of the North American north-west coast. These rituals, during which goods and food are distributed, celebrate an important event and consolidate the authority of the chief upon whose initiative the ceremony is held. In return, a "counter-gift" is expected from rival chiefs. Although banned by the government, potlatch has managed to survive into the present day by transforming its outward appearance.

Pre-Hispanic Pre-Columbian.

Prophylactic Preventing the appearance or spread of a disease.

Pueblo Sedentary peoples settled in the southwest of North America. They live in villages also called *pueblos*.

Quechua Official language of the Incas, still used today in Peru, as well as in other regions of the Andes from southern Colombia to northern Argentina.

Resist Procedure by which colorants are kept from penetrating certain areas of a piece of cloth or hank of yarn. In ikat, it is either the warp yarns or the weft yarns, or both together which are treated in this way. In batik, a wax resist is applied hot on to the fabric before dyeing, using a canting.

Skirts Each side of a horse's saddle, upon which the rider poses his inner thighs.

Slip Fine white clay used to polish and strengthen ceramic items.

Tellem People living in the Bandiagara Cliffs from the 11th to the 13th century, thus preceding the Dogon. They produced highly stylised wooden sculptures, often covered with sacrificial patina, which helped to preserve them in the caves where they were normally placed.

Tessera Small piece of stone, glass, or any other material generally used for creating a mosaic.

Theravâda Buddhism Since the early years of the first millennium, the peoples of "Indianised" South-East Asia have practised a variety of forms of Buddhism. Around the 14th century, societies in this region of the world adapted Theravâda ("the teachings of the elders"), which was considered the closest to the Buddha's original teachings.

Torah Name in Judaism for the first five books of the Old Testament (the Pentateuch), recording the 613 commandments revealed to Moses.

Tu Principal deity of the Mangareva Island pantheon, Tu is considered as the benefactor of mankind.

We Formerly known as the Guere, this people lives in the south-west of the Ivory Coast and in Liberia. Their masks represent terrifying entities with great magical powers. Their highly geometric forms are reminiscent of the Cubist aesthetic.

The collections area

The ramp, a long gentle slope, offers independent and easy access from the entrance hall to the collections area. The collections area is a vast open space exhibiting almost 3,500 works and divided up into four intercommunicating zones – Africa, Asia, Oceania and the Americas – linked by transversals that create points of exchange between civilisations.

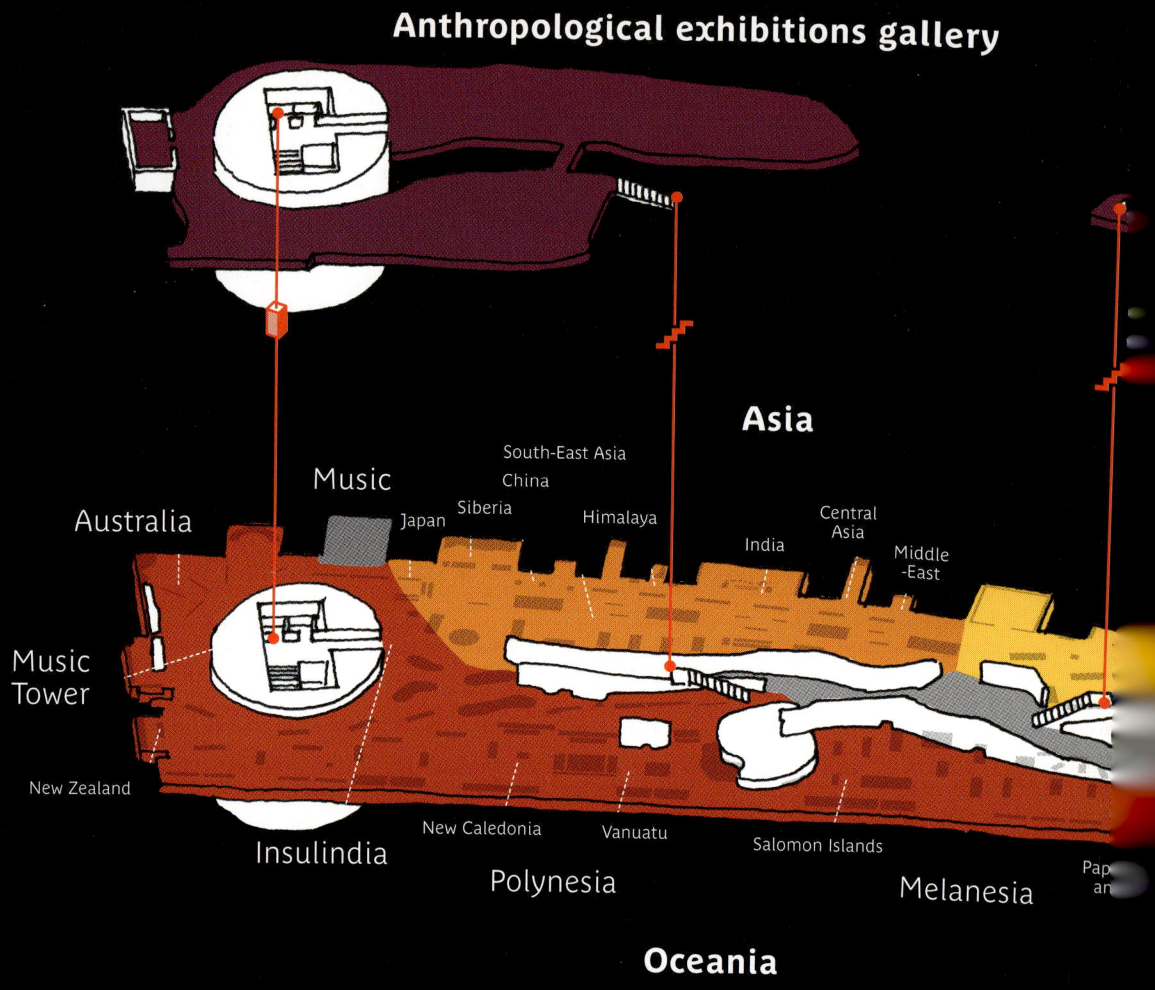

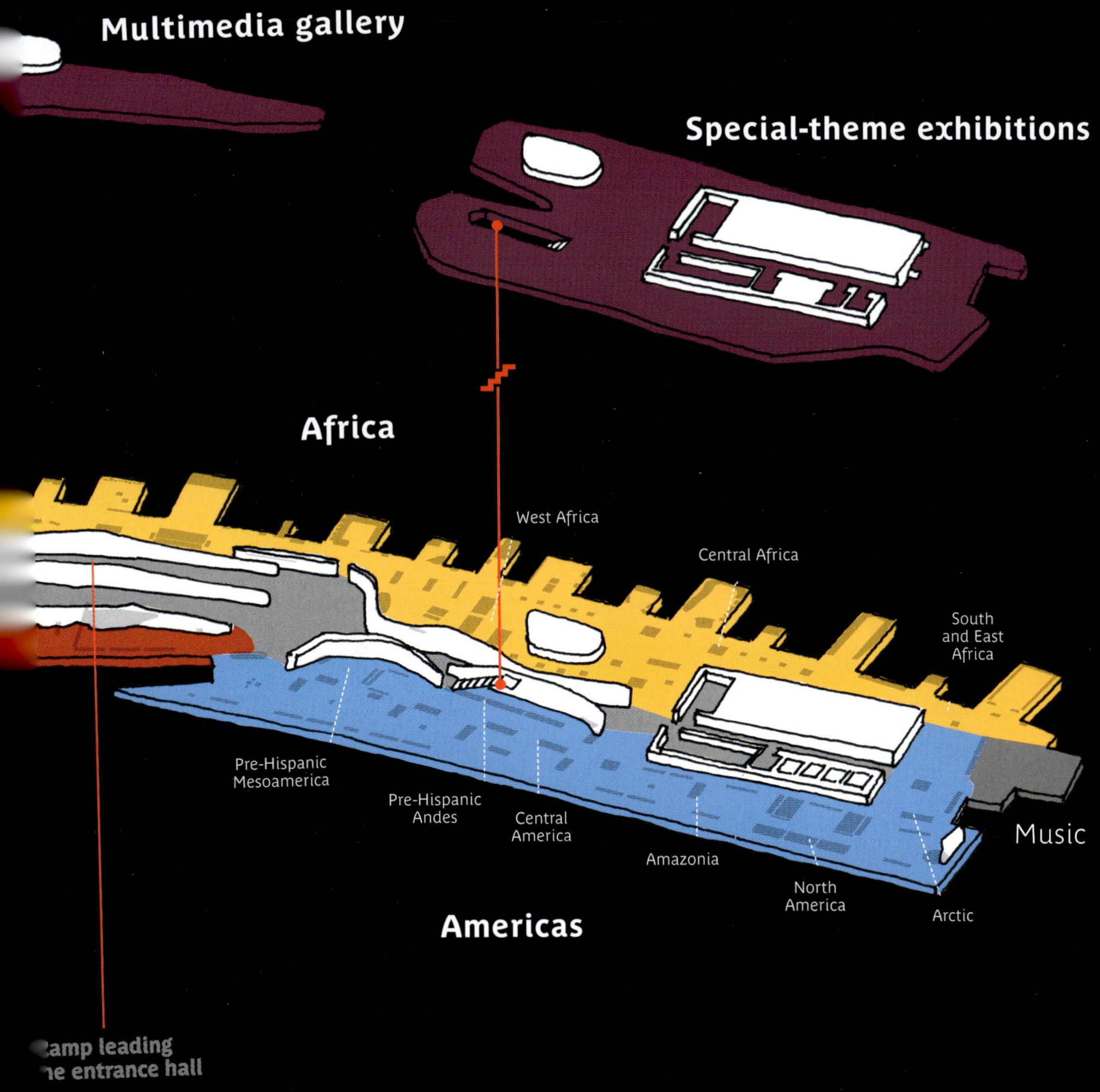

Multimedia gallery
Special-theme exhibitions
Africa
West Africa
Central Africa
South
and East
Africa
Pre-Hispanic
Mesoamerica
Pre-Hispanic
Andes
Central
America
Amazonia
North
America
Arctic
Music
Americas
amp leading
e entrance hall

Visiting the museum

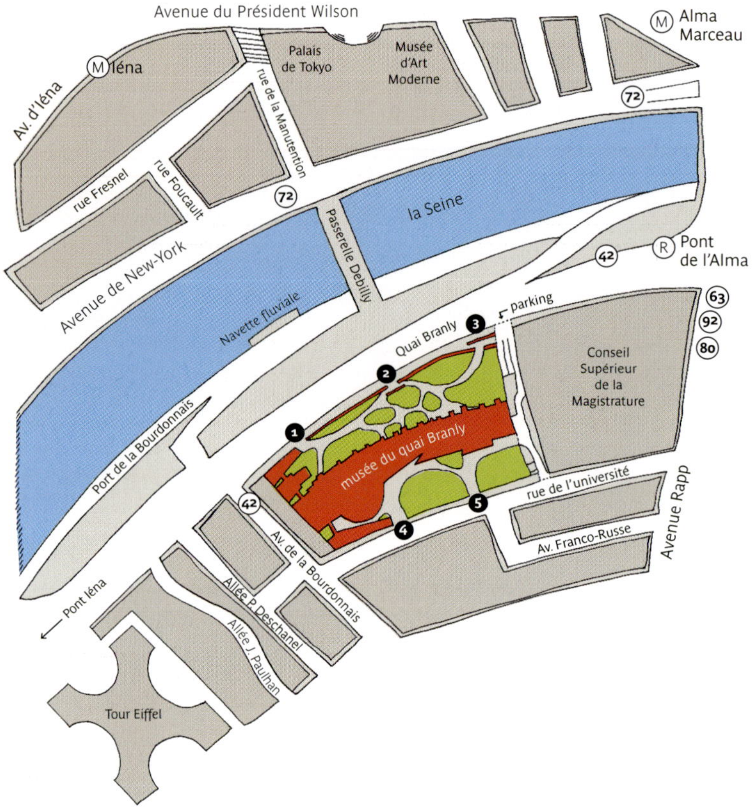

Opening hours
Tuesday to Sunday, from 10 am to 6:30 pm, special entry for groups from 9 am.
Thursday evenings until 10 pm.
Closed on Mondays.

Information
Telephone
+ 33 (0)1 56 61 70 70
Email contact@quaibranly.fr
Website www.quaibranly.fr

Reservations
Telephone
+ 33 (0)1 56 61 71 72
Email contact@quaibranly.fr
Fnac or Ticketnet sales points

By Métro
RER C
Pont de l'Alma

Line 6
Bir Hakeim

Line 9
Alma-Marceau
Iéna

By Bus
Line 42
Tour Eiffel

Lines 63, 80, 92
Bosquet-Rapp

Line 72
Musée d'Art moderne, Palais de Tokyo

River shuttle Batobus
Bateaux parisiens and Vedettes de Paris Tour
Tour Eiffel stop

Access on foot
The museum can be accessed from rue de l'Université or from quai Branly.

1. Branly entrance
51 quai Branly
2. Debilly entrance
37 quai Branly, across from the passerelle Debilly
3. Alma entrance
27 quai Branly
4. Université entrance
218 rue de l'Université
5. Bassins entrance
206 rue de l'Université

By car
Paying car park accessible from 25 quai Branly.
The pedestrian exit is on rue de l'Université, alongside the Garden.
520 spaces, 12 of which are reserved for persons with reduced mobility.

Before and after your visit: The museum website www.quaibranly.fr
The website is designed for the general public (in accordance with "Accessiweb" standards), and is both a learning tool and a forum for creativity and the exchanging of ideas:
- practical advice on planning your visit.
- current museum events, and the complete collections.
- a reference source, with updates on scientific developments in the field, as well as a directory with links to related websites.
- a platform for freely expressing one's ideas, open to the general public and to specialists: blogs, forums, and "cartes blanches".

Exploring the museum

Brochures and programmes
These give detailed information on musée du quai Branly programming, and are available at the information office.

Audioguide
The audioguide is designed for all types of visitors, and suggests an initial selection of items to be viewed, immersing the user in a world of "radiophonic mix" sound in harmony with the objects displayed. Different itineraries are available.
The audioguides can be rented at the booths in the garden, with pick-up in the reception hall.

Handicapped visitors
Special reception facilities in the reception hall
Visits and workshops are accessible to the hearing-impaired (videoguides and lectures in sign language), and are also adapted for the mentally-impaired. The museum puts a special emphasis on a multi-sensorial approach. The "Rivière", a unique and innovative design element, a full 200 metres in length, winds through the collections area, offering a totally tactile circuit accessible to all, with Braille texts, bas-reliefs, and multimedia screens.

The bookstore / shop
Located at 220 rue de l'Université, ground floor, the bookstore is France's leading sales point for works on tribal arts. Beneath its high ceilings, painted by Australian Aboriginal artists, a wide selection of books are on offer, along with postcards, posters, reviews, CDs and DVDs, and objects reflecting the cultures represented in the museum.
Tuesday to Sunday, from 10 am to 7 pm.
Thursday evenings until 10 pm.
Closed on Mondays.
Access for persons with reduced mobility.

Visits, workshops, and experiences
For a better understanding of the objects in the collections and the cultures they symbolize... The museum offers visitors a range of different ways of exploring and immersing oneself in the cultures represented.

"Discovery" visits and activities are designed to introduce the museum and acquaint visitors with the richness of the collections exhibited.

"Story-time" visits focus on oral traditions from across the world as a way of learning about its peoples.

"Question-time" visits enable visitors to exchange views with an expert before or after a visit to the museum.

"Explorations", transversal visits, enable visitors to cross geographical divides, and discover for themselves the visual and thematic resonance that unites the different objects.

"Day trips" are a truly unique experience: they allow visitors to reach a final destination through exposure: a journey through the museum collections, a living arts workshop (music, storytelling, dance, etc.), a discussion with an ethnologist, and an introductory lesson on the local dialect.

"Meetings" take place in the work-shops: the discovery of artistic practices (storytelling, music, dance, puppetry, etc.), or "performance-meetings" that present contemporary art forms in the context of the museum collections.

Major public and religious holidays provide opportunities for special events aimed at the public at large – special "Melting-pot" evenings, Cultural Heritage Days, and "Nuit Blanche" (Sleepless Night).

The mediatheque
The museum mediatheque is made up of four independent areas for visitors to enjoy:

The study and research mediatheque
25,000 works, plus approximately 100 periodicals.
5th floor, access from the Reception Hall by special lift.
Open to all, registration required.
180 seats, room equipped with a computer workstation adapted for the visually-impaired.
Tuesday to Saturday, from 10 am to 6:30 pm.
Thursday evenings until 9:30 pm.
Closed on Sundays and Mondays.
mediatheque@quaibranly.fr

Rare objects collections department
Rare and precious books.
5th floor, access from the Reception Hall by special lift.
Saturday, from 10 am to 6:30 pm by appointment only.
Thursday evenings until 9:30 pm.
Closed on Sundays and Mondays.
cabinetdesfondsprecieux@quaibranly.fr

The collection archives and documentation consultation room
3rd floor, access from the Reception Hall by special lift.
By appointment only.
Monday to Friday, from 9 am to 5:30 pm.
Closed on Saturdays and Sundays.

The Jacques Kerchache reading room
A documentary collection containing 5,000 works – 500 of which are specifically for children age seven and up – constantly updated and composed of exhibition catalogues, art books and atlases, informational and cultural reviews, and multimedia programs.
Ground floor, access via the reception hall.
Open to all visitors with a museum entry ticket or pass, 50 seats, room equipped with reading equipment for the visually-impaired
Tuesday to Sunday, from 10 am to 6:30 pm.
Thursday evenings until 9:30 pm.
Closed on Mondays.

The museum has received the generous support of

Major Patrons
- Pernod Ricard
- AXA
- Schneider Electric
- Caisse des Dépôts
- Fondation d'entreprise Gaz de France
- Fondation EDF
- Ixis - Corporate & Investment Bank - Groupe Caisse d'Épargne

Patrons
- Euro RSCG
- Sony France
- Sony Europa Foundation
- Issey Miyake
- Saint-Gobain
- JCDecaux
- Atos Consulting
- Martine and Bruno Roger
- Friends of the Australia Project, the Australian government, through the Australia Council for the arts and the Harold Mitchell Foundation; The French Foreign Ministry, through the permanent secretariat for the Pacific region; Martine and Bruno Roger; Veolia Environnement; AM Conseil.

Donors

Since 1997, the musée du quai Branly collections have been enriched by donations of works of art from

- Monsieur Benoît Aubenas
- Madame Patricia Aubenas
- Monsieur Rémy Audouin
- Axis Gallery, Inc.
- Monsieur Jean Paul Barbier-Mueller
- Madame Monique Barbier-Mueller
- Madame de Baillencourt
- Madame Marie-Claire Bataille-Benguigui
- Monsieur Georges Benguigui
- Madame Janine Claude Berge
- Madame Marie-Thérèse Berger
- Monsieur et Madame Jacques Blazy
- Madame Jacqueline Bocquet
- Monsieur et Madame Gérard Boëly
- Monsieur et Madame Samir Borro
- Monsieur et Madame Cayetana & Anthony JP Meyer
- Madame Mireille Clausse
- Madame Catherine Clément
- Father Michel Convers
- Monsieur Pierre Dartevelle
- Monsieur Sebastian Dass
- Madame Angelina Dass
- Madame Catherine Dass
- Mesdames Aube and Oona Elléouët
- Monsieur Asher Eskenazy
- Madame Claudine Foulon
- Monsieur Léonard Giannada
- Monsieur Hubert Goldet
- Monsieur Olivier Goldet
- Madame Véronique Guérin
- Madame Fernand Haïm
- Monsieur Georges Halphen
- Monsieur Udo Horstmann
- Monsieur Michel Huguenin
- Monsieur et Madame Jean-Charles Humbert
- Madame Hélène Joubert
- Monsieur Guy Joussemet
- Monsieur Jacques Kerchache
- Madame Anne Kerchache
- Monsieur et Madame Marcel Korolnik
- Monsieur Guy Ladrière
- Monsieur et Madame Pierre Langlois
- Chief Laukalbi (Tanna-Vanuatu tribe)
- Monsieur et Madame Jean Mansion
- Monsieur Daniel Marchesseau in memory of André Fourquet
- Monsieur Louis Jean-Pierre Mathieu
- Monsieur Pierre Messmer of the Institut de France
- Monsieur Alain de Monbrison
- Mr. Douglas Newton
- Monsieur Christophe Niemoller
- Madame Patricia Oyelola
- Monsieur Arthur Papadimitriou
- Monsieur Marc Petit
- Monsieur et Madame Pierre Pinson
- Radio France
- Madame Marie-Hélène Reichlen
- Mr. and Mr.s Jeffrey A. Rosen, American donators in honor of Martine Aublet and Bruno Roger
- Madame Rueff-Pigeat
- Monsieur Alain Schoffel
- Monsieur et Madame Guy Stresser Péan
- Madame Pierrette Tapie
- Monsieur et Madame Claude Vérité
- Monsieur de Vertenelle
- Monsieur Marcel Wislin
- Groupe AXA for the acquisition of a masterpiece of African art within the framework of France's law on patronage of the arts.

Société des Amis du musée du quai Branly

Since 2002, the Société des Amis du musée du quai Branly has provided support and fostered public interest in the museum as a place to discover and share knowledge about the cultures of the world.

amisdumusee@quaibranly.fr
www.amisquaibranly.fr

Contributors

Contributors, musée du quai Branly

Daria Cevoli, DC
Head of the Asia collections

Hana Chidiac, HC
Head of the Middle East collections

Françoise Cousin, FC
Head of the Textiles heritage and collections unit

Marine Degli, MD
Head of documentary studies

André Delpuech, AD
Head of the Americas heritage and collections unit

Emmanuel Désveaux, ED
Head of Research

Christine Hemmet, CH
Head of the Asia heritage and collections unit

Paz Nuñez-Regueiro, PNR
Head of the Americas collections

Philippe Peltier, PP
Head of the Oceania heritage and collections unit

Fabienne de Pierrebourg, FP
Head of the Americas collections

Anne-Christine Taylor, ACT
Director, Research and education department

Outside contributors

François-Ömer Akakça, FOA
Assistant Professor, Humboldt Univesität, Berlin

Mathieu Claveyrolas, MC
Ethnologist, Centre d'études de l'Inde (EHESS/CNRS)

Svetlana Jacquesson, SJ
PhD., Ethnology (INALCO/EHESS)

Jean-Luc Lambert, JLL
Professor, EHESS

Photography: collections
Patrick Gries
Bruno Descoings
Valérie Torre
Benoît Jeanneton
Vincent Chenet

Photography: building
Nicolas Borel
Ianna Andréadis

Editorial director
Clair Morizet

Editors
Muriel Rausch
Sophie Chambonnière

Translation
Tradutours

Copy editing
Valor

Photoengraving
MCP

Graphic design
Polymago
Juliette Weisbuch
Natalia Marrero

Printed in may 2006
by Imprimerie moderne de l'Est,
Baume-les-Dames